ZEW Economic Studies

Publication Series of the Centre for European Economic Research (ZEW), Mannheim, Germany

Christoph Spengel • Andreas Oestreicher

Common Corporate Tax Base in the EU

Impact on the Size of Tax Bases and Effective Tax Burdens

Physica-Verlag
A Springer Company

ZEW
Zentrum für Europäische
Wirtschaftsforschung GmbH

Series Editor
Prof. Dr. Dr. h.c. mult. Wolfgang Franz

Authors
Prof. Dr. Christoph Spengel
University of Mannheim
Centre for European Economic Research
Palace
68131 Mannheim
Germany
spengel@uni-mannheim.de

Prof. Dr. Andreas Oestreicher
University of Göttingen
Platz der Göttinger Sieben 3
37073 Göttingen
Germany
andreas.oestreicher@uni-goettingen.de

With the cooperation of: Christina Elschner, Timo Reister, Christof Ernst, Michael Grünewald and Katharina Finke

ISBN 978-3-7908-2755-2 e-ISBN 978-3-7908-2756-9
DOI 10.1007/978-3-7908-2756-9
Springer Heidelberg Dordrecht London New York

Library of Congress Control Number: 2011935223

Cover illustration: digitalstock

Printed on acid-free paper

Physica-Verlag is a brand of Springer-Verlag Berlin Heidelberg
Springer-Verlag is a part of Springer Science+Business Media (www.springer.com)

Preface

Our book presents a report which was prepared in 2007 and 2008 for the Taxation and Customs Union Directorate General of the European Commission, under contract no. TAXUD-2007 DE325.

The results are intended to serve the evaluation of the potential tax consequences arising from the introduction of a harmonised tax base for EU-resident companies, as contemplated by the European Commission. A harmonised tax base or common corporate tax base can help to eliminate the most important tax obstacles to cross-border EU-wide activities (compliance costs, denial of group wide consolidation of profits and losses, transfer pricing problems and double taxation caused by cross-border re-organisation and conflicting taxing rights) stemming from the great diversity of the Member States' tax systems.

A Common Corporate Tax Base (CCTB) as a policy option would replace the current 27 different tax codes for the calculation of taxable income across EU Member States with a single and common set of corresponding tax rules. The principle aim of the report is to provide an analysis of the consequences which an adoption of a CCTB would have on the size of the corporate tax bases and tax burden of EU companies located in each of the 27 Member States using the model of the "European Tax Analyzer". As the concept of the CCTB is narrower compared to the concept of a Common Consolidated Corporate Tax Base (CCCTB) which in addition takes into account consolidation, cross-border loss compensation and allocation of the tax bases to different Member States, the latter three elements of a CCCTB, are not addressed in this report.

On March 16th 2011, the European Commission published a proposal for a Council Directive on a Common Consolidated Corporate Tax Base (CCCTB). The findings of this report are included in the impact assessment to the proposal for the Council Directive. The permission to publish this report was granted in April 2011. Nevertheless, we explicitly state that the opinions expressed in this report are our own and do not represent the Commission's official position.

The report was carried out jointly by the ZEW, the University of Göttingen, and the University of Mannheim. Especially important roles were played by *Dr. Timo Reister*, *Christof Ernst*, *Katharina Finke* and *Michael Grünewald* who contributed to the project by supporting the quantitative parts and preparing the report.

Reinald Koch and *Jens Prassel* made further substantial contributions with respect to the statistical analyses and related elements of the work. In addition we gratefully acknowledge the excellent help and advice of *Dr. Christina Elschner.*

Mannheim and Göttingen, April 2011

Christoph Spengel and *Andreas Oestreicher*

Table of Contents

1 Introduction **1**

2 Methodology **3**
2.1 The European Tax Analyzer Model 3
2.2 Computation of the Effective Average Tax Burden 4
2.3 Tax Parameters Incorporated into the Model 6
2.4 Measurement of the Impact of Elements of a CCTB on the Size of the Tax Base 7
2.5 Model Firms and Data Base 15
2.5.1 Structure of the Model Firms and Economic Assumptions 15
2.5.2 Data Base and Applied Aggregation Methods 16

3 Future Value of the Tax Base and Effective Company Tax Burden **27**
3.1 Scenario of a Common Corporate Tax Base 27
3.2 Analysis of EU-Average Large Corporations 29
3.2.1 Benchmark Case Representing a Large Corporation 29
3.2.2 Sensitivity Analysis on Economic Model Assumptions 50
3.2.3 Sensitivity Analysis on Specific Sectors 58
3.2.4 Consideration of EU-15/EU-12 Average Large Corporation 66
3.3 Analysis of EU-Average Small and Medium-Sized Corporations 76
3.3.1 Benchmark Case Representing a Small and Medium-Sized Corporation 76
3.3.2 Sensitivity Analysis on Economic Model Assumptions 94
3.3.3 Sensitivity Analysis on Specific Sectors 102
3.3.4 Consideration of EU-15/EU-12 Average SMEs 107
3.3.5 Relationship Between Key Accounting Ratios and Overall Tax Base Effect 117
3.4 Consideration of Recent National Tax Reforms 119
3.5 Summary of Conclusions 124

Appendix **127**

List of Figures **169**

List of Tables **171**

References 175

Executive Summary

Introduction

EU companies face many obstacles in their cross-border activities as a result of the various corporate tax systems operated in different member states. These tax obstacles include high compliance costs, the lack of cross-border loss offset provisions and the risk of double taxation due to conflicting rights between tax jurisdictions. To address these problems, the European Commission envisages putting forward a proposal for a tax reform that would improve the efficiency and simplicity of corporate income tax systems across the EU. The most comprehensive approach would be a Common Consolidated Corporate Tax Base (CCCTB), encompassing all elements of cross-border consolidation and loss compensation. A less far reaching approach – the Common Corporate Tax Base (CCTB) – covers all other non consolidation and non loss-compensation related provisions defining the domestic tax bases of EU companies.

Purpose and Structure of the Report

This report assesses the impact of a CCTB on the size of the corporate tax bases of EU companies. The results of the report will help to evaluate the economic consequences of the introduction of a harmonised set of tax accounting rules for EU-based companies, as promoted by the European Commission and related Working Groups. The proposals for a CCTB covered in this report include the following elements: (A) depreciation on intangibles, machinery, buildings, furniture and fixture, (B) simplified valuation of inventories, (C) determination of production costs for stocks, (D) treatment of costs for R&D as part of production costs, (E) provisions for future pension payments, (F) provisions for legal obligations (e.g. warranty claims), (7) avoidance of double taxation regarding dividend income, and (G) loss relief. While all proposed elements of a CCTB could be applied separately or simultaneously (Option I), the idea of a CCTB is clearly based on a simultaneous application of all eight elements in all 27 member states.

The European Tax Analyzer was used to produce estimates on the impact that a CCTB would have on the size of corporate tax bases. The European Tax Analyzer uses a computer-based model-firm approach for the computation and comparison of international company tax burdens. The estimates on both corporate tax base sizes and effective average tax burdens are derived by simulating the growth of a corporation over a ten year period. The study looks first at the effects of a CCTB on two different model firms: (1) an average EU-27 large corporation and (2) an average EU-27 small and medium-sized corporation (SME). The analysis is based on tax regulations as they stood in the year 2006 and takes into account the CCTB options specified by the Commission's Steering Group. In a second step, the effects of alternate assumptions concerning economic data on the model companies are examined. To this end, various sensitivity analyses as well as computations for model companies from different economic sectors and geographical regions (EU-15/EU-12) are presented. Finally, in the last section, the effects of major tax reforms in five member states (Germany, France, Italy, the Netherlands and Spain) during 2006 and 2008 are explored.

Results for the Benchmark Case Scenarios

Our calculations show that with the introduction of a CCTB, the tax base of the EU-27 large model company would increase on average by 6.20% (see Table 1).

Table 1: Changes in the value of the tax base in case of a CCTB (large company)

	National GAAP		**CCTB Options (all)**			
	Future Value Tax Base in € Millions	Rank	Future Value Tax Base in € Millions	Rank	Deviation in %	Rank
AT	81.19	5	86.02	5	5.9	0
BE	78.55	4	80.93	4	3.0	0
BG	94.64	14	107.00	27	13.1	-13
CY	104.98	27	97.97	13	-6.7	14
CZ	95.97	21	105.51	24	9.9	-3
DE	74.05	3	77.58	3	4.8	0
DK	91.36	8	94.81	8	3.8	0
EE	103.22	26	105.90	26	2.6	0
ES	85.05	6	88.98	6	4.6	0
FI	95.06	17	104.03	18	9.4	-1
FR	55.43	2	60.86	2	9.8	0
GR	95.90	20	104.65	21	9.1	-1
HU	41.70	1	46.82	1	12.3	0
IE	101.06	25	99.50	14	-1.5	11
IT	94.72	16	103.01	17	8.8	-1
LT	93.70	12	104.08	19	11.1	-7
LU	93.42	9	96.92	10	3.7	-1
LV	93.84	13	104.44	20	11.3	-7
MT	98.18	24	101.95	16	3.8	8
NL	95.66	19	97.80	12	2.2	7
PL	97.46	23	104.95	23	7.7	0
PT	94.67	15	104.67	22	10.6	-7
RO	95.16	18	99.86	15	4.9	3
SE	93.60	11	97.69	11	4.4	0
SK	96.26	22	105.69	25	9.8	-3
SL	89.26	7	96.91	9	8.6	-2
UK	93.45	10	93.67	7	0.2	3
Ø	89.91		95.27		6.20	

On a country-by-country basis, the change in the tax base varies between 13.1% in Bulgaria and -6.7% in Cyprus. Countries affected most include Hungary, Latvia, Lithuania and Portugal. Aside from Cyprus, Ireland is the only country that registers a decline in the tax base (-1.5%).

Of all eight CCTB options, common depreciation rules have the greatest impact on the size of the tax base. Rules concerning future warranty liabilities rank second in significance. A relatively minor impact, by contrast, is exerted by common rules for the determination of production costs, the treatment of R&D-related costs as production costs and the proposed provisions for offsetting losses.

In order to gauge the effects of a CCTB on companies of different sizes, a model SME is also included in the analysis. In this case, as well, our calculations show that the proposed CCTB would increase the size of the tax base in almost all member states (see Table 2). Compared to the large model company, the EU-wide increase for the SME is slightly lower at 5.57%. Yet the considerable variation between member states remains. Hungary witnesses the largest increase (15.4%), and Cyprus the largest decline (-6.9%). In this case as well, depreciation rules have the greatest positive impact on the size of the tax base.

Table 2: Changes in the value of the tax base in case of a CCTB (SME)

	National GAAP		**CCTB Options (all)**			
	Future Value Tax Base in € Millions	Rank	Future Value Tax Base in € Millions	Rank	Deviation in %	Rank
AT	2.87	4	2.99	4	4.3	0
BE	2.94	5	2.99	4	1.5	1
BG	3.43	19	3.83	27	11.8	-8
CY	3.74	27	3.49	13	-6.9	14
CZ	3.45	21	3.78	25	9.5	-4
DE	2.68	3	2.76	3	2.9	0
DK	3.29	8	3.36	7	2.4	1
EE	3.60	26	3.67	17	1.8	9
ES	3.07	6	3.15	6	2.6	0
FI	3.42	18	3.73	19	9.2	-1
FR	2.36	2	2.48	2	5.3	0
GR	3.41	15	3.76	23	10.3	-8
HU	1.08	1	1.25	1	15.4	0
IE	3.54	25	3.52	14	-0.8	11
IT	3.39	13	3.69	18	8.8	-5
LT	3.38	12	3.74	20	10.5	-8
LU	3.35	9	3.43	9	2.3	0
LV	3.40	14	3.75	21	10.4	-7
MT	3.46	22	3.65	16	5.4	6
NL	3.41	15	3.46	12	1.3	3
PL	3.46	22	3.77	24	8.8	-2
PT	3.41	15	3.75	21	9.9	-6
RO	3.44	20	3.53	15	2.5	5
SE	3.36	10	3.45	11	2.7	-1
SK	3.46	22	3.79	26	9.5	-4
SL	3.17	7	3.44	10	8.3	-3
UK	3.36	10	3.38	8	0.7	2
Ø	3.22		3.39		5.57	

The radar chart presented in Figure 1 illustrates the impact of each individual CCTB option on the value of the tax base for the EU-27 large company and SME. The impact is measured as the proportion of the increase resulting from each single option against the overall increase from all options combined. It demonstrates that the influence of the isolated options is similar for the large company and the SME. In both cases depreciation has the strongest impact on the increase in the tax base. Provisions for warranty claims and the avoidance of double taxation have a notable influence as well, and in isolation lead to a decrease in the tax base. The isolated variation of the other options exerts only minor influence and is similar for the large company and the SME.

Figure 1: Proportion of EU-27 average overall increase of the value of the tax base for each option

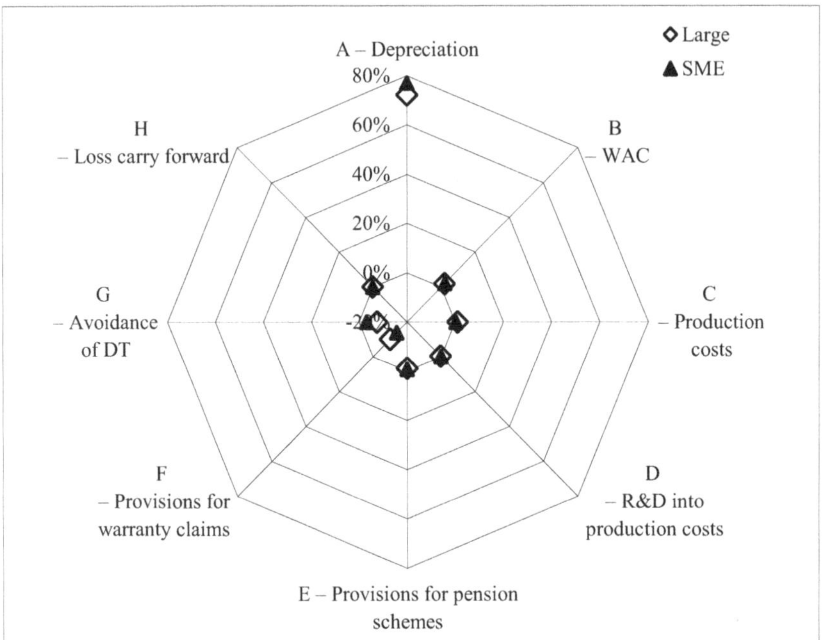

Sensitivity Analyses

The above findings are relevant for model companies that represent the EU average companies. Alternately structured firms with different financial ratios were also investigated in the study. Sensitivity analyses were conducted to gauge the impact of a CCTB under varying economic data assumptions and on model firms from different industries and regions.

To see how changes in economic model assumptions influence the effects of the proposed CCTB, sensitivity analyses on the firms' capital intensity, profitability, labour intensity and inventory intensity were carried out. Our calculations show that the direction of impact exerted by alternate economic assumptions is the same under both the national GAAP and the CCTB accounting systems. An increase in capital intensity and labour intensity reduces the value of the tax base. By contrast, greater profitability and inventory intensity increase the size tax base. Looking at the magnitude of the deviation between accounting systems under alternate data assumptions, we find that higher capital intensity results in an increasing deviation. The deviation between the accounting systems decreases, however, with higher profitability, labour intensity and inventory intensity. The results of the sensitivity analysis are confirmed by a multiple regression analysis, which reveals that changing profitability and capital intensity have a significant impact on the value of the tax base.

Sector Specific Analyses

To enlarge the spectrum of analysis, additional calculations were conducted for sector-specific companies. These sectors are: construction, commerce, energy manufacturing, service/trade transport. The sector analysis can be understood as an analysis considering a simultaneous variation of the financial rations from the benchmark case. Composite model companies were assembled for each sector using data from all 27 member states. Table 3 displays the average increase in the size of the tax base induced by the introduction of a CCTB.

Table 3: Value of the tax base under national GAAP and increase in % with the introduction of a CCTB (sector averages)

	Average future value of the tax base under national GAAP (in € millions)	**Average increase of the future value of the base with a CCTB (%)**
Large Company		
EU-27 (benchmark)	89.91	6.20
Commerce	84.26	4.73
Construction	56.00	4.46
Energy	228.76	12.34
Manufacturing	119.69	7.21
Service	47.45	9.44
Transport	21.77	51.72
Small Company		
EU-27 (benchmark)	3.22	5.57
Commerce	4.82	1.99
Construction	2.19	4.70
Energy	4.73	32.71
Manufacturing	3.41	5.98
Service	1.75	3.31
Transport	3.08	11.49

The main findings for the sector-specific sensitivity analyses can be summarised as follows. With the introduction of a CCTB, the value of the tax base would increase for all sector-specific EU-27 model companies. There is a considerable variation between sectors, however. The increase for the large companies varies between 4.46% (construction) and 51.72% (transport). For the SME companies there is again considerable but – compared to the large sector-specific model companies – less variation between sectors. Here the increases vary between 1.99% (commerce) and 32.71% (energy). Aside from commerce and construction (in the case of the large model company), and commerce, construction and service (in the case of the model SME), the increase in the tax base is always higher for the sector-specific companies than in the relevant benchmark case, which is composed of data from all sectors.

As was the case for the benchmark companies, alternate depreciation rules have the largest impact of all CCTB options on the value of the tax base. For this reason, varying levels of capital intensity among the sector-specific companies is a key factor in accounting for the observed changes in the tax base values. High capital intensity is, for example, decisive in the large increases witnessed for the energy-sector SME and the transport-sector large company. Another important factor is profitability.

The countries most affected by the introduction of a CCTB are again Bulgaria, Hungary, Lithuania, Latvia and Portugal. But also France (service), Greece (manufacturing), Slovakia (energy) show a considerable increase in the value of the tax base. Ireland and particularly Cyprus show declining tax base values for most sector-specific companies.

EU-15 and EU-12 Companies

An additional analysis was conducted of model firms representing an average large company and SME from the EU-15 and EU-12 regions. EU-15 denotes the original 15 EU member states and EU-12 the accession countries which joined the EU in 2004 and 2007.

Table 4: Value of the tax base under national GAAP and deviation in case of a CCTB

	Average future value of the tax base under national GAAP (in € millions)	Average increase in the future value of the base with a CCTB (%)
Large Company		
EU-27 (benchmark)	89.91	6.20
EU-15	115.72	3.95
EU-12	31.57	7.30
Small Company		
EU-27 (benchmark)	3.22	5.57
EU-15	4.02	3.14
EU-12	2.48	6.34

As was the case in the sector analysis, the model companies differ in their balance sheet structure and financial ratios. Both company models are applied to the respective subgroup of countries. The results displayed in Table 4 show increases of the values of the tax bases for all regional company models.

While the increase in the future value of the tax base in the EU-12 accession countries exceeds the EU-27 average increase whereas the increase of the future value of the tax base in the original EU-15 countries ranges below the EU-27 average. This finding holds true for the large company as well as for the small and medium-sized company.

Impact of Recent Tax Reforms in Certain Member States

Finally, consideration was given to major tax reforms in five countries (France, Germany, Italy, the Netherlands and Spain) which became effective in 2007 and 2008. The tax reforms resulted in a broadening of the tax bases under national GAAP. Therefore, after the tax reforms became effective in these countries, the increases of the values of the tax base in the event of the proposed CCTB are smaller for both the EU-27 large and the EU-27 SME company. Respect given to the EU-27 average, the increases of the values of the tax base amount to 5.86% in case of the EU-27 large company (compared to 6.20% in the benchmark case) and to 5.30% in case of the EU-27 SME company (compared to 5.57% in the benchmark case).

Conclusions

According to our analysis, the introduction of a CCTB would have a considerable impact on the tax base values in all EU member states. An enlargement of the tax base would be witnessed in all countries aside from Cyprus and Ireland.

The results show considerable variation between companies depending on their size, economic sector and financial characteristics. In this connection, assumptions regarding capital intensity and profitability have the most significant impact on estimates of the tax base changes which would result from a CCTB.

Each individual CCTB option has varying effects on the value of the tax base. CCTB rule modifications concerning depreciation have by far the strongest impact on future tax base values.

The countries which would be affected most by a CCTB are Bulgaria, Hungary, Latvia, Lithuania and Portugal. Sensitivity analyses show that Greece, France and Slovakia would also be significantly impacted. The introduction of a CCTB as considered here has a considerable impact on the values of the tax base in the EU member states. Except for Cyprus and Ireland, the values of the tax base would increase in all countries.

There is considerable variation among sectors and the size of companies. In this context, capital intensity and profitability turn out to be the most relevant factors out of the economic assumptions in the event of a CCTB.

The considered options for a CCTB show different impacts on the value of the tax base. The option with the strongest impact on the tax base is the rule concerning depreciation.

Countries affected most by the introduction of a CCTB are Bulgaria, Hungary, Latvia, Lithuania and Portugal. Sensitivity analyses reveal Greece, France and Slovakia as countries with strong impact as well.

1 Introduction

The aim of this report is to help evaluate the economic consequences of introducing a harmonized tax base for EU companies, as proposed by the European Commission. A harmonised tax base would help to eliminate the most important tax obstacles to EU-wide cross-border activities, including compliance costs, denial of group-wide consolidation of profits and losses, transfer pricing problems, double taxation caused by cross-border reorganisations and conflicting taxing rights. These obstacles are a product of the large discrepancies between the tax systems of each EU member state.

A Common Corporate Tax Base as a policy option would replace the current 27 tax codes for the calculation of taxable income across EU member states with a single and common set of tax rules. The principle aim of this report is to provide an analysis of the consequences that an adoption of a Common Corporate Tax Base (CCTB) would have on the size of the corporate tax bases of EU companies located in each of the 27 member states, using the model of the "European Tax Analyzer". The proposed CCTB is narrower in scope than the proposals for a Common Consolidated Corporate Tax Base (CCCTB), which includes provisions for consolidation, cross-border loss compensation and the allocation of tax bases to different member states. Consequently, these elements of the CCTB are not addressed by the present study.

In specific terms, our study evaluates the change in the size of EU companies' tax bases – and, therefore, in their effective tax burdens – associated with a transition from national corporate tax systems to a CCTB, i.e. the EU-wide harmonisation of corporate tax bases with the omission of the consolidation and cross-border loss provisions found in the more expansive CCTB proposal. In order to achieve reliable results, the quantitative analysis is based on two model companies: (1) an average EU-27 large company, and (2) an average EU-27 small to medium-sized company (SME). Furthermore, we not only analyse the cumulative effects of common tax accounting rules on the tax base and on effective tax burdens, but also isolated effects of the different elements of a CCTB.

The aim of the quantitative analysis is to measure the corporate tax base, as defined by current national tax provisions (benchmark case) for different types of "EU companies" in each member state and to compare the results with the tax base yielded with the application of alternative options for a CCTB. The benchmark case takes into account the EU member states' tax provisions as the law stood for the fiscal year 2006. Since the focus of this report is on the corporate tax base and the resulting effective corporate tax burdens, the analysis is limited to corporations (i.e. transparent entities are not taken into account) and to taxes borne at the corporate level (i.e. personal taxes of shareholders are not taken into account).

In order to estimate the quantitative effects of alternative CCTB options on the size of EU company tax bases by computing tax bases and effective company tax burdens, it was first necessary to collect and verify the relevant tax variables as defined by national tax provisions for the fiscal year 2006 in each of the 27 EU member states. Furthermore, alternative options for a CCTB underlying this report were defined in co-operation with the Commission's Steering Group in January 2008.

On this basis, verified data and alternative CCTB options were implemented into the model of the European Tax Analyzer. Furthermore, company data for the different types of EU companies were extracted from databases containing balance sheet and profit-and-loss statement data; these data were also implemented into the European Tax Analyzer. With these steps the requisite data pool for the quantitative analysis was thus obtained.

The report is divided into two broad sections. Section 2 introduces the European Tax Analyzer and the underlying methodological concept for the computation of tax bases and effective company tax burdens. As the European Tax Analyzer model was previously approved by the European Commission in an earlier report conducted on behalf of by the Commission (see Jacobs & Spengel, 2002), the description only highlights the main underlying assumptions and recent modifications and improvements to the model. In addition, it contains a detailed description of how company data for different types of EU companies were derived from the AMADEUS database and aggregated to data for a model firm. Section 3 then computes and analyses the effects on tax bases and effective tax burdens resulting from the adoption of a CCTB in the 27 EU member states. Section 3 is divided into three parts. In the first part, this report applies the proposed options for a CCTB for both an average EU-27 large and an average EU-27 small and medium-sized corporation. The analysis is based on tax rules as they stood in the year 2006 and takes into account the CCTB options specified by the Commission's Steering Group. In the second part, the report examines how the results are affected by alternative assumptions on the economic data of the model companies. Various sensitivity analyses as well as computations for model companies belonging to different economic sectors and geographical regions (EU-15/EU-12) are carried out. Finally, in the third part, the effects of major tax reforms in five member states (Germany, France, Italy, the Netherlands and Spain) during 2006 and 2008 are examined.

2 Methodology

2.1 The European Tax Analyzer Model

The European Tax Analyzer is a computer program for a model firm that calculates and compares effective average tax burdens for companies located in different jurisdictions.[1] The current version covers the tax systems of 27 member states. Since the standard model firm is designed as a corporation, the effective average tax burden can be calculated at the level of the corporation as well as at the level of the shareholders. This study will exclusively consider the effective average tax burden at the corporate level. The effective average tax burden is derived by simulating the development of a corporation over a ten year period. For the computation of the effective average tax burden the model uses the economic data of the corporation and tax data as inputs.

The European Tax Analyzer Model was approved in an earlier study for the European Commission (see Jacobs & Spengel, 2002). The following description therefore highlights only the basic assumptions and the most recent amendments to this approach. The European Tax Analyzer calculates and compares effective average tax burdens for companies over a period of ten years. The development of the corporation is based on the initial capital stock and estimates for its future development (corporate planning).

Initial capital stock: The capital stock includes the firm's total assets and liabilities which are either new or have already existed before. The assets consist of real estate, office and factory buildings, plant and machinery, office equipment, intangibles (patents and royalties), financial assets, shares in other corporations (both domestic and foreign), inventories, trade debtors, cash funds and deposits. The liabilities include new equity capital, long-term and short-term debt, and trade creditors.

Development of capital stock: Corporate planning furnishes data about the expected development of the capital stock over the simulation period of ten years. Estimates are based on periodical assumptions for production and sales, acquisition of goods, staff expenditure (e.g. number of employees, wage per employee and pension costs), other receipts and expenses (e.g. expenses for

---

[1] For detailed descriptions of the model see Spengel, 1995; Jacobs and Spengel, 1996; Meyer, 1996; Stetter, 2005; Gutekunst, 2005; Hermann, 2006.

R&D), investment, distribution and costs of financing. Goods are assumed to be either stocked or sold on the market in the same period as they are produced. Therefore, multi-period production is possible. Additional assumptions are made for material and labour with regard to production costs. It is further assumed that depreciable assets (i.e. buildings, plant and machinery, office equipment and intangibles) are run down at the end of their expected economic life. Reinvestments in new assets are made at that point based on the historical costs of the deposited assets adjusted for inflation. The model's assumptions regarding investment make sure that the initial capital stock at least remains constant. In addition to differing rates of price increases, other macro-economic data considered are credit and debit interest rates, exchange rates for the given countries and the costs of energy and electricity.

Corporate finance: The initial capital stock contains new equity as well as both long and short term debt capital. Since the corporate plans, *inter alia*, make assumptions about the distribution policy, the company can be financed by retained earnings (e.g. the distribution rate is below 100%) in addition to new equity and debt financing. If the national tax codes allow for internal book reserves (e.g. book reserves for bad debts), the money put into these reserves can also serve as a source of internal financing.

For the sake of comparability, it is assumed that the model firm always shows identical data before any taxation. Due to this necessary assumption any differences between pre- and post-tax data in the model can be solely attributed to the applied national taxation rules.

2.2 Computation of the Effective Average Tax Burden

The measures for tax base and for tax burden are expressed in currency units. The effective tax burden is the difference between the pre-tax and post-tax value of the firm at the end of the simulation period (i.e. period 10). The value of the firm is represented by the equity, which includes the capital stock and the cumulative net income of each of the ten periods. At the end of period 10, the tax value of assets and liabilities may differ from their fair value, depending on the tax rules which are to be applied. These hidden reserves and liabilities are added to the taxable income in period 10 and are taxed accordingly. As a consequence, only the effects of different tax accounting rules on the liquidity are taken into account. Remaining loss carry forwards at the end of the simulation are dissolved liquidity-related whereas a devaluation of 50 per cent is made if there are no restrictions for the use of loss carry forwards and a devaluation of 75 per cent if there are any restrictions. The computation of the absolute effective average tax burden requires two steps.

In the *first step*, the pre-tax value of the firm at the end of the simulation period is calculated. The pre-tax value of the firm is derived from the estimated cash flows and the value of the net assets at the end of the simulation period. The cash flows are derived from estimates for the cash receipts (sales and other receipts, gains upon the disposal of assets, interest and dividend income) and expenses (wages and pension payments, expenses for material, energy consumption and other expenses, new investment, interest expenses and distributed profits) covered by the corporate planning model. The cash flow (= liquidity) is calculated in each period. Thereby it is assumed that any given amount of surplus cash flow at the end of a single period can be invested at a given interest rate and any given deficit can be covered by borrowing money at a given debit rate (balancing investment or credit). The interest receipts or expenses plus the amount of the underlying balancing investments or credits are considered for the calculation of the cash flow in the following period. The value of the net assets at the end of the simulation period is computed by deducting the liabilities of the corporation from the assets. Both the assets and the liabilities are valued at calibrated parameters that are the same in each country. For assets we use replacement prices and for liabilities nominal values.

	Pre-tax cash flow at the end of the simulation period
+	Value of the net assets at the end of the simulation period (= assets in the capital stock at replacement prices
–	Liabilities in the capital stock at nominal values)
=	Pre-tax value of the firm at the end of the simulation period

In the *second step,* we calculate the post-tax value of the firm at the end of the simulation period. The determination of the post-tax value of the firm only has cash flow effects and no impact on the value of the net assets. The post-tax cash flow is derived in each period by deducting the tax liabilities from the pre-tax cash flow. In order to calculate the absolute amount of tax liabilities, receipts and expenses are entered into the tax balance sheet and/or into the tax profit and loss account following national taxation rules (e.g. regarding the computation of depreciation allowances). After having applied the national tax rates, we allow for other relevant components such as loss carryovers and tax credits in order to come to the amount of tax liabilities. The reduction of the cash flow due to tax payments (liabilities) also has an impact on the balance of investment and credit and the connected interest receipts or payments. By taking into account these tax-induced effects on the interest income or expense of each period, the deferral of tax payments is integrated into the model. Hidden reserves and liabilities are only relevant for taxation matters at the very end of the simulation.

	Pre-tax cash flow at the end of the simulation period
–	Tax liabilities in each period
=	Post-tax cash flow at the end of the simulation period
+	Value of net assets at the end of the simulation period (= assets in capital stock at replacement prices
–	Liabilities in capital stock at nominal values)
– / +	Tax liabilities on hidden reserves / tax refunds on hidden liabilities
=	Post-tax value of the firm at the end of the simulation period
	Pre-tax value of the firm at the end of the simulation period
–	Post-tax value of the firm at the end of the simulation period
=	Effective average tax burden

In contrast to models which compute tax burdens solely based on pre-tax returns (yields),[2] calculations based on cash receipts and cash expenses regarding balancing investments allow for the entire computation of all tax bases at any time during the period of simulation (because all relevant income and assets have been entered into the tax base). As a consequence, the model can include complicated tax provisions such as progressive tax rates, tax credits (e.g. for foreign taxes) with upper ceilings, and loss carryovers without any difficulty.

2.3 Tax Parameters Incorporated into the Model

The tax base and the effective average tax burden are calculated for the EU-27 member states. In order to calculate the tax liability in each country, the European Tax Analyzer takes into account all taxes that may be influenced by the investments and financing at the level of the corporation (see Table 5).

Table 5: Considered Taxes

	Real Estate Tax	Payroll Tax	Trade Tax on Income/ Value Added	Trade Tax on Capital	Net Wealth Tax	Corporate Tax (incl. Surcharges)
AT	√	√				√
BE	√					√
BG	√					√
CY	√	√				√
CZ	√					√
DE	√		√			√
DK	√					√
EE	√					√
ES	√			√		√
FI	√					√
FR	√	√		√		√
GR	√					√
HU	√		√			√
IE	√					√
IT	√		√			√
LT	√					√
LU	√		√		√	√
LV	√					√
MT						√
NL	√					√
PL	√					√
PT	√					√
RO	√					√
SE	√					√
SK	√					√
SL		√				√
UK	√					√

2 See Schreiber, Spengel and Lammersen, 2002.

A detailed description of the tax parameters is not given here. They are instead explained in detail in section 3.2, where the tax burdens of different countries are compared with each other.

When calculating the tax bases, the most relevant assets and liabilities and the effects of the corporate planning are considered. Furthermore, the tax module allows the selection of several accounting options (tax electives) by which a company can influence its taxable profits. The following elements are considered for profit computation:

1. Depreciation (methods and tax periods for all considered assets, extraordinary depreciation)
2. Inventory (stock) valuation (production costs, FIFO, LIFO and the average costs method, inflation reserves)
3. Research and development costs (immediate expensing or capitalisation)
4. Taxation of capital gains (roll-over relief, inflation adjustment, special tax rates)
5. Employee pension schemes (deductibility of pension costs, contributions to pension funds, book reserves)
6. Provisions for bad debts
7. Guarantee accruals
8. Elimination and mitigation of double taxation on foreign source income (exemption, foreign tax credit, deduction of foreign taxes)
9. Loss relief

Finally, with regard to tax rates, the calculations consider statutory linear as well as progressive tax rate structures. In the case of progressive rates – relevant for special provisions for SMEs in some countries – the tax rates enter into the model as functions of the relevant income or net assets (non-profit taxes) according to tax laws.

2.4 Measurement of the Impact of Elements of a CCTB on the Size of the Tax Base

The major aim of the study is to measure the impact of a CCTB on the size of the tax bases in the EU member states. In the following section, the measurements used to quantify this impact are introduced. A simplifying example for a change from national tax accounting (GAAP) to a CCTB is considered in a 4-period setting. The national GAAP is represented by accelerated depreciation whereas the CCTB would prescribe straight line depreciation.

The impact on the size of the tax base in per cent can be written as follows:

$$Impact\,on\,tax\,base\;(in\;\%) = \frac{Tax\,Base(CCTB) - Tax\,Base\;(Nat.GAAP)}{Tax\,Base\;(Nat.GAAP)}.$$

There are basically two possible measures to account for the *size of the tax base*. First, one could take the accumulated sum of tax bases over the considered 4 periods. Expressed as a formula, it can be written as:

$$Sum\,of\,Tax\,Base = \sum_{t=1}^{4} Tax\,Base_t\ .$$

Second, one could consider the future value of the tax bases over the considered 4 periods. The *future value* is one of the most commonly used financial measures to assess and evaluate economic problems which have time as a dimension. The definition of the future value is derived as follows: The future value of the tax base is the sum of all periodical tax bases in period 4 (the last period) valuated with the nominal interest rate *i*. Expressed as formula it can be written as:

$$Future\,Value = \sum_{t=1}^{4} Tax\,Base_t * (1+i)^{T-t}\ .$$

To clarify: in contrast to the described future value the so called *present value* would consider the discounted sum of the tax bases at the beginning of period 1. In the following, in accordance with the design of the European Tax Analyzer, the impact of a change in tax accounting rules from national GAAP to a CCTB is measured in the last period and therefore the future value is used.[3]

The difference between the sum of tax bases and the future value of the tax base is the precise valuation of timing effects. These effects arise, for example, if a tax base in earlier periods is higher than in later periods.

The following example illustrates these findings. For the sake of clarity, the underlying assumptions are simplified here.[4] An identical investment with the two different depreciation rules mentioned above (national GAAP: accelerated depreciation with first-year allowance; CCTB: straight line depreciation) is considered here. The investment consists of the acquisition of machinery which generates declining income receipts (€1100, €800, €600, €400) over the useful life of 4 periods. The acquisition costs of machinery shall amount to €1000 and are depreciable in total. In this example we assume an interest rate of 10% for cash flow available for investment (liquidity) in order to gain distinct results. The future value of the tax base is obtained by valuating the tax base of each period with an interest rate of 10%.

In the first example, the corporate income tax rate is 0% (i.e. no tax is levied). Thus, to illustrate the influence of the temporal distribution of the tax base, we oppose national GAAP (accelerated depreciation, see Table 6) to a CCTB option (straight line depreciation, see Table 7). The visualization of financial implications reveals for the calculus in the absence of tax an unequal distribution of the periodical tax bases, due to the different methods of depreciation. In the absence of taxation, the liquidity is not affected by different depreciation regimes as depreciation itself does not affect cash flows.

---

[3] Present values are provided in Appendix 6.

[4] The calculations in section III are then based on a 10-period approach using the European Tax Analyzer Model. Moreover, the calculations take into account the existing national tax accounting rules and the CCTB options agreed upon with the Commission.

Table 6: National GAAP, accelerated depreciation (case without tax; in €)

Period	**0**	**1**	**2**	**3**	**4**
Capital expenditure on depreciable asset	-1,000				
Receipts		1,100	800	600	400
Interest receipts		0	110	201	281
Depreciation		1,000	0	0	0
Tax base (corporate income tax)		100	910	801	681
Sum of tax base over time					2,492*
Future value of the tax base					2,796**
Tax payment		0	0	0	0
Cash flow available for investment after taxation		1,100	910	801	681
Future value of the investment		1,100	2,010	2,811	3,492

* 2,492 = 100 + 910 + 801 + 681 | **2,796 = 100 * 1.331 + 910 * 1.21 + 801 * 1.1 + 681 (with $1.331 = 1.1^3/1.21 = 1.1^2/1.1 = 1.1^1$)

Table 7: CCTB option, straight line depreciation (case without tax; in €)

Period	**0**	**1**	**2**	**3**	**4**
Capital expenditure on depreciable asset	-1,000				
Receipts		1,100	800	600	400
Interest receipts		0	110	201	281
Depreciation		250	250	250	250
Tax base		850	660	551	431
Sum of tax base over time					2,492
Future value of the tax base					2,967
Cash flow available for investment		1,100	910	801	681
Future value of the investment		1,100	2,010	2,811	3,492

Therefore, cash flows available for investment and interest receipts earned on the cumulative income of the previous period are the same in both cases. In addition, when calculating without tax, both depreciation regimes lead to the same sum of tax base over time (= €2,492). The future value of the tax base, in contrast, differs due to the depreciation methods considered (national GAAP: €2,796 vs CCTB: €2,967). This difference only fails to have financial consequences in a case with a tax rate of 0%. As such a case cannot be observed within the EU-27 member states, a corporate tax rate of 25% is introduced in the next example.

If corporate income tax is levied, the amount of depreciation and therefore the size of the tax base in each period affect tax payments and, thus, liquidity. As a first result, the comparison of the case with and without tax (Tables 6–9) indicates that the sum of tax base and the future value of the tax bases change (e.g. national

GAAP, 0% corporate tax rate: €2,492/€2,796 vs 25% corporate tax rate: €2,417/€2,718).

Focusing now on a comparison of Table 8 and Table 9 in period 1, the tax base and the corresponding tax payments are lower under national GAAP than the CCTB option. A lower cash outflow of tax payments under national GAAP is associated with higher liquidity available for investments.

Table 8: National GAAP, accelerated depreciation (case with 25% income tax; in €)

Period	**0**	**1**	**2**	**3**	**4**
Capital expenditure on depreciable asset	-1,000				
Receipts		1,100	800	600	400
Interest receipts		0	108	176	234
Depreciation		1,000	0	0	0
Tax base		100	908	776	634
Sum of tax base over time					2,417
Future value of the tax base					2,718
Tax payment		25	227	194	158
Cash flow available for investment		1,075	681	582	475
Future value of the investment		1,075	1,756	2,337	2,813

Table 9: CCTB option, straight line depreciation (case with 25% income tax; in €)

Period	**0**	**1**	**2**	**3**	**4**
Capital expenditure on depreciable asset	-1,000				
Receipts		1,100	800	600	400
Interest receipts		0	89	162	225
Depreciation		250	250	250	250
Tax base		850	639	512	375
Sum of tax base over time					2,375
Future value of the tax base					2,842
Tax payment		213	160	128	94
Cash flow available for investment		888	729	634	531
Future value of the investment		888	1,617	2,250	2,782

Consequently, the resulting tax deferral gives rise to an increase in interest receipts in consecutive periods. This results in a higher sum of tax base over time (national GAAP: €2,417 vs CCTB option: €2,375). Therefore, one could conclude that the introduction of the CCTB option would reduce the size of the tax base and thus would indicate an advantage for investments. But this conclusion turns out to be misleading: In fact the future value of the tax base is lower under national GAAP (= €2,718 vs €2,842) as the investment is depreciated earlier and the resulting timing effects are captured in the future value. Therefore, the CCTB option turns out to be disadvantageous from an investment perspective. This clearly shows that the sum of tax base over time is not an appropriate measure for capturing the size of the tax base.

The impact of different CCTB options on the size of the tax base in this study is therefore measured as:

$$Impact\,on\,tax\,base\ (in\ \%) = \frac{Future\,Value_{Tax\ Base,CCTB} - Future\,Value_{Tax\ Base,Nat.GAAP}}{Future\,Value_{Tax\ Base,\ Nat.GAAP}}.$$

Next, the relation between the future value of the tax base (i.e. impact on the size of the tax base) and the effective average tax burden is considered. The effective average tax burden is based on the future value of an investment instead of the future value of the corporate tax base (for a detailed description, see section 2.2 above). It is defined as the difference between the future value of the investment before (pre-tax) and after tax (post-tax). The effective tax burden is a more comprehensive measure as it also accounts for elements not included in the corporate income tax base, such as non-deductible taxes and other non-deductible elements.

The impact in per cent of different elements of a CCTB on the tax burden can be written as follows:

$$Impact\,on\,tax\,burden\ (in\ \%) =$$

$$\frac{\left(Future\,Value_{Invest.,Pre\ tax} - Future\,Value_{Invest.,CCTB}\right) - \left(Future\,Value_{Invest.,Pre\ tax} - Future\,Value_{Invest.,Nat.GAAP}\right)}{Future\,Value_{Invest.,Pre\ tax} - Future\,Value_{Invest,\ Nat.GAAP}}$$

As the effective tax burden is based on the future value of the investment, tax-induced timing effects through tax payments and resulting liquidity effects through interest income are taken into account.

When the modeled impact on the future value of the tax base is compared to the impact on the effective tax burden, it becomes clear that the direction of change is the same. In the example with a 25% corporate tax, both measures indicate an increase of 4.56% of either the tax base or the effective tax burden (see Table 6). That means, no matter which measurement is used, the impact is generally exactly the same. The respective values in Table 10 are taken from the tables above (period 4).

Since several countries do not only levy corporate income taxes but also non-profit taxes like real estate tax or other taxes on capital, the following example assesses the impact of non-profit taxes on both the future value of the tax base and the effective tax burden.

In this third example, a capital tax on real estate of 5% in addition to a corporate income tax of 25% are considered. Real estate is valued at €2,000 and, thus, the tax amounts to €100. The real estate tax shall be deductible for the purpose of the corporate income tax. All other assumptions are left unchanged.

Table 10: Comparison of impact assessed with effective tax burden and impact assessed with future value of the tax base (case with 25% income tax; post-tax)

Effective Tax Burden					
	Pre-tax value (in €)	Post-tax value (in €)	Effective tax burden (in €)	Delta effective tax burden (in €)	in %
Immediate full depreciation	3,492	2,813	680		
Straight line depreciation	3,492	2,782	711	31	4.56
Future Value of the Tax Base					
	Post-tax value (in €)	Effective deviation of future value (in €)			
Immediate full depreciation	2,718				
Straight line depreciation	2,842	124			4.56

Table 11: National GAAP, accelerated depreciation (case with 25% income tax and 5% real estate tax; post-tax including capital tax; in €)

Period	**0**	**1**	**2**	**3**	**4**
Capital expenditure on depreciable asset	-1,000				
Receipts		1,100	800	600	400
Interest receipts		0	100	160	210
Depreciation		1,000	0	0	0
Capital tax		100	100	100	100
Tax base (corporate income tax)		0	800	660	510
Tax base over time					1,970
Future value of the tax base					2,204
Income tax payment		0	200	165	127
Capital tax payment		100	100	100	100
Cash flow available for investment after taxation		1,000	600	495	382
Future value of the investment		1,000	1,600	2,095	2,477

Table 11 shows the results for national GAAP (accelerated depreciation) and Table 12 shows the results for the CCTB option (straight line depreciation). It is now possible to calculate the indicated impacts based on the respective measures future value of the tax base and effective tax burden (see Table 13). The respective values in Table 13 are taken from the tables above (period 4).

Table 12: CCTB option, straight line depreciation (case with 25% income tax and 5% real estate tax; post-tax including capital tax; in €)

Period	**0**	**1**	**2**	**3**	**4**
Capital expenditure on depreciable asset	-1,000				
Receipts		1,100	800	600	400
Interest receipts		0	81	146	201
Depreciation		250	250	250	250
Capital tax		100	100	100	100
Tax base		750	531	396	251
Tax base over time					1,928
Future value of the tax base					2,328
Income tax payment		188	133	99	63
Capital tax payment		100	100	100	100
Cash flow available for investment		813	648	547	438
Future value of the investment		813	1,461	2,008	2,446

Table 13: Comparison of impact assessed with effective tax burden and impact assessed with future value of the tax base (case with 25% income tax and 5% capital tax on real estate; post-tax)

Effective Tax Burden (Case with Capital Tax)

	Pre-tax value (in €)	Post-tax value (in €)	Effective tax burden (in €)	Delta effective tax burden (in €)	in %
Immediate full depreciation	3,492	2,477	1,015		
Straight line depreciation	3,492	2,446	1,046	31	3.06

Future Value of the Tax Base (Case with Capital Tax)

	Post-tax value (in €)	Effective deviation of future value (in €)	in %
Immediate full depreciation	2,204		
Straight line depreciation	2,328	124	5.63

Table 10 (case without capital tax) and Table 13 (case with 5% capital tax) reveal the following: In a setting without capital tax and a proportional corporate income tax, the impact of different rules for tax accounting on the effective tax burden and the future value of the tax base is the same. Both show an increase of 4.56%. With a capital tax, by contrast, a change from accelerated to straight line depreciation increases the effective tax burden by only 3.06%, whereas the future value of the tax base rises 5.63%. This different indication of the impact is due to a base effect. The absolute change in the effective tax burden (€31) and in the future value of the tax base (€124) is the same in both with and without capital tax (see Table 10 and Table 13). Yet the bases to calculate the change in per cent are affected differently by the introduction of a capital tax into the analysis. The tax base declines (from €2,718 to €2,204), since the capital tax is deductible as a business expense in each period. The effective tax burden, however, increases (from €680 to €1,015) since the capital tax is part of the tax burden and thus increases the tax due on the investment.

As a result for our analysis, thus, it can be expected that countries which have an important share of non-profit taxes, will show a lower impact of a tax base broadening regulation (like the switch from accelerated to straight line depreciation) when the impact is calculated using the measure effective tax burden; but it will show a stronger impact when the impact is calculated using the measure future value of the tax base, compared to a country which has only corporate income tax. The direction of the impact in both cases is, however, the same (positive in our example).

The above findings are summarised as follows:

First, the sum of tax base over time is not an appropriate measure for analysing the effects of changes in tax accounting rules as it disregards the timing effects of taxation.

Second, measuring in terms of the effective tax burden and future value of the tax base capture comprehensively the effects of the considered CCTB options. Consequently, it is appropriate to use these measures in the analysis. It has to be kept in mind that all elements of a CCTB except loss carry forward and participation exemption for dividends will have timing effects.

Third, both indicators – the impact based on the future value of the tax base and the impact based on the effective tax burden – show a very similar change due to changes in tax accounting rules, if there is only corporate income tax with a proportional tax rate. When non-profit taxes are considered in addition, the indicated impact in per cent, when measured in terms of the effective tax burden, is different than the impact in per cent measured in terms of the future value of the tax base.

Therefore, in addition to the effective tax burden, the study will evaluate the impact of a CCTB on the size of the tax bases by measuring the change in the future value of the tax base as follows:

$$Impact\,on\,tax\,base\ (in\ \%) = \frac{Future\,Value_{Tax\ Base,\,CCTB} - Future\,Value_{Tax\ Base,\,Nat.GAAP}}{Future\,Value_{Tax\ Base,\ Nat.GAAP}}.$$

2.5 Model Firms and Data Base

2.5.1 Structure of the Model Firms and Economic Assumptions

Various assumptions have to be made in order to define and describe the model firms analysed in this report, in addition to the economic conditions which are assumed to prevail. These assumptions are presented in the following section.

In this study two model firms – one large company and one SME – are implemented into the model. These firms represent EU-27 average companies. As such, country and industry-specific effects on pre-tax data are ignored, meaning that balance sheet, profit and loss accounting and corporate planning are not dependent on country-specific taxation rules. The data determining the implemented model firms were mainly taken from the AMADEUS database (see section 2.5.2).

Table 14: Balance sheets of the implemented EU-27 model firms (period 6, in €)

Assets	SME	Large	Liabilities	SME	Large
I. Fixed assets	1,273,098	49,641,583	I. Shareholder funds	1,254,419	43,415,131
1. Intangible fixed assets	74,800	2,875,872	1. Capital	420,924	18,207,742
2. Tangible fixed assets	1,085,961	37,793,443	2. Other shareholder funds	833,495	25,207,389
3. Other fixed assets	112,337	8,972,268	II. Non-current liabilities	747,802	27,433,693
			1. Long-term debt	469,217	21,248,099
			2. Other non-current liabilities	278,585	6,185,594
II. Current assets	2,985,322	76,792,466	III. Current liabilities	2,256,199	55,585,225
1. Stocks	877,820	22,936,037	1. Loans	469,217	21,248,099
2. Debtors	1,433,559	15,945,781	2. Creditors	935,447	10,070,619
3. Other current assets	673,943	37,910,648	3. Other current liabilities	851,535	24,266,507
Total	4,258,420	126,434,049	Total	4,258,420	126,434,049

Table 14 shows the balance sheets of the model firms at the end of year 6 (the mid-point of the 10 year comparison). The balance sheets depict the different types of assets (investments) and their sources of financing. Table 14 also highlights the relative weight of these investments and the sources of finance.

The balance sheets of the model firms and their sales figures as well as the amount and structure of expenses at the end of year 6 give the model firms a unique set of characteristics, as expressed by the common financial ratios in Table 15.

Table 15: Financial ratios of the implemented EU-27 model firms (period 6)

	Average EU-27 SME	Average EU-27 large company
Profit/loss for period (€)	194,624	4,124,827
Total assets (€)	4,258,420	126,434,049
Sales (€)	7,167,799	159,457,817
Share of tangible fixed assets (%)	25.50	29.89
Return on sales (%)	2.72	2.59
Return on equity (%)	15.52	9.50
Equity ratio (%)	29.46	34.34
Return on assets (%)	6.87	6.11
Inventories to capital (%)	20.61	18.14
Costs for personnel to turnover (%)	18.20	20.97

One must keep in mind that the above ratios are only valid for the EU-27 average model firms. The use of country and industry specific company data would produce different financial ratios.

Other important assumptions are as follows:

- Expected economic lifetime for assets: production buildings (50 years); office buildings (50 years); patents and concessions (5 years each); plant (4 years) and machinery (five assets are considered, 5 to 10 years); office furniture and fixtures (9 years); financial assets (all zero); stocks (zero).
- Rates of price increase: consumer price index (2.2%); price index for basic material (4.8%); price index for wages (0.8%); price index for investment goods (2.3%).[5]
- Interest rates for creditors and debtors: short term credit (3%); long term credit (3.9%); short term debt (5.9%); long term debt (5.1%).[6]

Since these assumptions in some cases do not represent the reality that individual companies captured by the AMADEUS database are faced with, it is unavoidable that the structure of the implemented EU model firms slightly differs from the EU-27 average model companies shown in Appendix 4. However, as the structure of the companies is very similar, significant distortions in the results can be ruled out.

2.5.2 Data Base and Applied Aggregation Methods

2.5.2.1 Financial Data Derived from the AMADEUS Database

Pre-tax financial data was extracted from AMADEUS database. The AMADEUS database provides financial and supplementary information for about 6.74 million companies in the European Union. Not all of these companies are included in the

[5] See ECB, ECB and Eurostat calculations, 2006.

[6] See ECB, MFI interest rate statistics, December 2006; OECD, Financial indicators MEI, 2006.

study, however. One reason for this is that the AMADEUS database also comprises companies with legal forms (e.g. partnerships) and in industries (e.g. mining) that are not relevant for the study. Furthermore, publicly owned companies are not addressed in the study, but are covered by the AMADEUS database. In addition, some companies have to be excluded because the minimum data set required for the study is not available (for further details see section 2.5.2.2). Altogether this leads to a reduction in the number of companies used in the study, in total 1,147,483 companies make up the relevant data sample (see Table 16).[7]

Table 16: Determination of the companies used in the study

Steps	Number
All companies in the AMADEUS database	6,636,823
Of this number, companies with relevant legal forms	6,192,918
Of this number, companies which are not publicly owned	6,182,972
Of this number, companies in relevant industries	4,539,415
Total companies with relevant data (= companies used in the study)	1,147,483

The determination of EU-average companies is based here on Update 125 of February 2005, comprising financial data for the years 1994-2004. The structure of the financial information in AMADEUS (income statement and balance sheet, with applicable annotations) is presented in Table 17. The study uses EU tax legislation in the 27 member states as of the year 2006. Although it would have been desirable to employ company data from 2006, the existing AMADEUS database version provides data only up to 2004. Furthermore, the data at hand is only adequate for the years up to and including 2003. Table 18 provides an overview of the data. In this pre-sample, no restrictions with regard to relevant industries are included.

Moreover, we have to take into account that data for 2002 and 2003 were negatively impacted by an economic downturn. Therefore, it was decided to base the calculations on financial data for 2001. The years 2002 and 2003 were characterised by weak economic activity (in these years the Ifo Economic Climate Indicator registered average quarterly values for the euro zone of 85.4 and 78.0, respectively).

7 The reported numbers cover companies belonging to the manufacturing, construction, commerce, service/trade and transport industries.

Table 17: Financial information in the AMADEUS database

Number	Items of the financial information according to the AMADEUS format	Annotation
	Income Statement	
1	Operating Revenue	Turnover and stock movements as well as other capitalised costs
2	Sales	Turnover resulting from operative activities
3	Costs of goods sold	
4	Gross profit	1 – 3
5	Other operating expenses	
6	Operating profit/loss	4 – 5
7	Financial revenue	
8	Interest paid	
9	Other financial expenses	
10	Financial profit/loss	7 – 8 – 9
11	Profit/loss before tax	6+10
12	Taxation	Income taxes and other taxes
13	Profit/loss after tax	11 – 12
14	Extraordinary revenue	
15	Extraordinary expenses	
16	Extraordinary and other profit/loss	14 – 15
17	Profit/loss for period	13+16
	Balance Sheet	
1	Fixed assets	2+3+4
2	Intangible fixed assets	
3	Tangible fixed assets	
4	Other fixed assets (incl. financial fixed assets)	Primarily consisting of shareholdings and other financial fixed assets
5	Current assets	6+7+8
6	Stocks	
7	Debtors	
8	Other current assets	
9	Total assets	1+5
10	Shareholders funds	11+12
11	Capital	
12	Other shareholder funds (incl. reserves)	
13	Non-current liabilities	14+15
14	Long-term debt	
15	Other non-current liabilities (incl. provisions)	Primarily consisting of provisions
16	Current liabilities	17+18+19
17	Loans	
18	Creditors	
19	Other current liabilities	
20	Total shareholders funds and liabilities	10+13+16

Table 18: Number of companies for which relevant data is provided by AMADEUS (all industries)

Year	2004	2003	2002	2001	2000	1999
EU-27	69,127	1,468,194	1,673,139	1,423,813	1,237,262	1,104,774
EU-15	69,008	1,251,712	1,478,333	1,264,052	1,095,151	988,734
EU-12	119	216,482	194,806	159,761	142,111	116,040

However, strong econonomic activity was experienced in 1999 and 2000 (the Ifo quarterly average in these years was 94.1 and 116.5). The year 2001 (87.1) approximates the long-term average (90.82) and can thus be said to represent balanced economic conditions. The level of economic activity is likely to influence the values of the reported financial data and consequently the EU-average companies.

Figure 2: Ifo Economic Climate Indicator for the euro area (1990-2008)

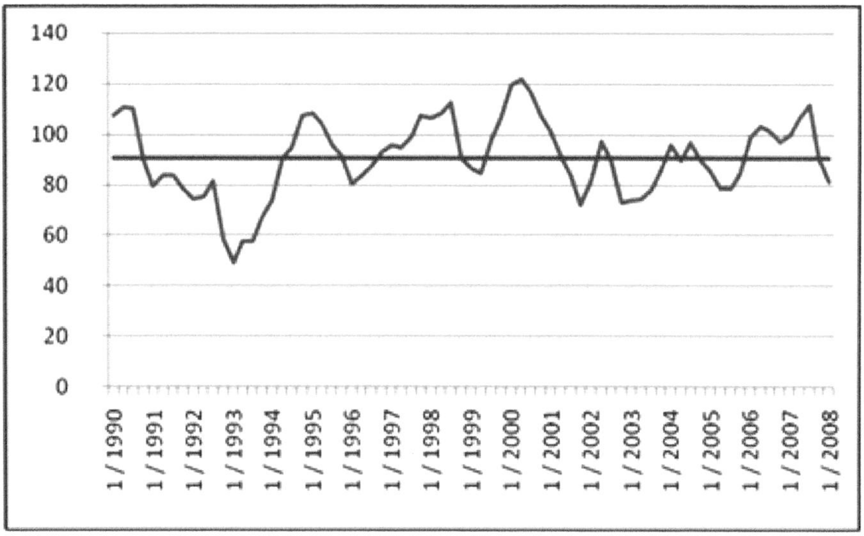

Source: Ifo Institute, available at www.ifo.de

The computation of EU-average companies is primarily based on balance sheet and income statement data derived from the AMADEUS database. The framework for our computations is in line with the latest CCTB Working Document.[8] Therefore, the scope of companies included in the sample for the determination of EU-average companies is restricted to legal forms as recorded by the Parent Subsidiary Directive.[9] With respect to the terms of reference for this report, the

[8] Common Consolidated Corporate Tax Base Working Group (CCCTB WG), CCCTB: Possible elements of a technical outline, CCCTB/WP057\doc\en, Brussels 2007.

[9] Council Directive of 23 July 1990 on the common system of taxation applicable in the case of parent companies and subsidiaries of different Member States (90/435/EEC), OJ L 225, 22.9.1990, p. 6.

analysis is based on companies belonging to the following industries: manufacturing, construction, commerce, service/trade and transport. In accordance with the Commission's Steering Group, the energy sector is additionally considered in the sensitivity analysis. The classification of industries is consistent with the NACE codes, as presented in Table 19. As described above, public sector companies are not examined in the study and have thus been excluded. The size determination of large companies as well as of small and medium-sized companies is made in accordance with the Commission's recommendation.[10]

Table 19: Classification of industries

Industry	Sub-sections of NACE Rev. 1.1
Manufacturing	15-37
Construction	45
Commerce	50-52
Service Trade	71-74 without 7415, 90-93
Transport	60-63
Energy	40

2.5.2.2 Organisation of Data

Complete and correct data are of course required for an accurate analysis. For this reason, companies which do not provide all the information needed to determine the financial ratios are removed from the calculations. Companies have to report, as a minimum, the following items: tangible fixed assets, stocks, shareholder funds, balance sheet total, sales, interest paid, cost of employees, profit and loss for the period, and number of employees. Moreover, companies for which obviously flawed data has been reported are excluded from the calculations as well. In order to identify such companies it is necessary to check whether the balance sheet totals on the assets side and on the liabilities side correspond. Deviations up to a threshold of 10% are accepted. If the deviation exceeds this threshold, a check is made as to whether the difference can be traced back to mistakes in the summation of the sub-items. If not, the financial statements of the year in question are completely eliminated. Negative values are not accepted within the balance sheet (except for equity items). Any other deviations between overall values (e.g. fixed assets) and the total of the relevant sub-items (e.g. tangible fixed assets, intangible fixed assets, other fixed assets) are eliminated by proportional increase or decrease of these sub-items. The mathematical accurancy of the income statement is also verified. In the case of flaws, certain items are eliminated from the income statement. Alternatively, the financial statement is omitted as a whole. For both the balance sheet and income statement, missing values are calculated if possible without any ambiguity.

In order to provide the broadest possible data sample, however, estimated values for some items are used. The necessity of employing estimated values

[10] Commission Recommendation of 6 May 2003 concerning the definition of micro, small and medium-sized enterprises (2003/361/EC), OJ L 124, 20.5.2003, p. 36.

results from the fact that certain items of the income statement or balance sheet are entirely absent for some countries. Consequently, without some estimates, additional countries would have to be excluded from further analysis. Estimated values are used with regard to the following variables: number of employees/costs of employees, sales/operating revenue and interest paid/financial expenses. While the number of employees is required to determine the size class of a company, interest paid and sales are necessary for the determination of important financial ratios (profit and interest paid to balance sheet total and profit to sales).

For the estimation of these variables, average ratios between variable pairs are used. These ratios are determined in a country-specific as well as in an industry-specific manner on the basis of data from AMADEUS.

Table 20: Number of companies in the sample

Country	Number of large companies	Number of small and medium-sized companies	Total number
Austria	96	188	284
Belgium	893	41,748	42,641
Bulgaria	0	0	0
Cyprus	0	0	0
Czech Republic	405	2,028	2,433
Denmark	473	8,920	9,393
Estonia	108	16,172	16,280
Finland	387	31,093	31,480
France	3,760	405,239	408,999
Germany	677	3,347	4,024
Greece	324	11,086	11,410
Hungary	235	5,377	5,612
Ireland	8	76	84
Italy	2,224	100,335	102,559
Latvia	147	1,959	2,106
Lithuania	22	585	607
Luxembourg	33	144	177
Malta	12	46	58
Netherlands	336	1,942	2,278
Poland	1,480	6,794	8,274
Portugal	431	12,550	12,981
Romania	1,410	98,198	99,608
Slovakia	145	828	973
Slovenia	0	0	0
Spain	423	200,746	201,169
Sweden	717	79,019	79,736
United Kingdom	4,465	99,852	104,317
EU-12	3,964	131,987	135,951
EU-15	15,247	996,285	1,011,532
EU-27	19,211	1,128,272	1,147,483

Where necessary, country or industry differentiation is ruled out. Alternatively, the ratio is determined on the basis of macroeconomic data taken from the EUROSTAT database. A detailed description how missing variables are estimated is given in Appendix 1.

The aforementioned requirements concerning the quality of data as well as the necessary adjustments to the AMADEUS data lead to a sample size of 1,147,483 companies in 24 member states[11] of the European Union. Of this number, 19,211 are large and 1,128,272 were small and medium-sized companies. The geographic distribution of these companies is presented in Table 20.

In order to exclude possible outliers which may have a negative impact on average values, company data is removed when the ratios "return to sales" and "return to assets" exceed the 90%-quantile or fall below the 10%-quantile. If the ratios "interest paid to sales" or "costs for personnel to turnover" exceed the 90%-quantile or fall below the 10%-quantile the company is not considered in the calculation of the respective ratio.[12]

2.5.2.3 Determination of the Model Firms

Average Model Firms for EU-27

When preparing data, a key goal is to provide consistent information on the structure of EU-average income statements and EU-average balance sheets in order to accurately represent the companies in the EU member states. On the one hand, it is necessary to consider an appropriate method to ensure that no inconsistencies arise. On the other hand, it is important that the structure of model EU-average companies is not unduly influenced by a small number of member states or companies. If the average balance sheet and income statement is determined as the average of absolute figures for the items, large companies would strongly influenced the structure of the EU-average companies. Therefore we decided to determine the items of the financial statements in relation to the "sales" or "total assets" figure for each company and to determine the average for the companies in each country. Consequently, the computation of the EU-average companies is based on country-specific average ratios for the balance sheet items and the income statement items. These country-specific ratios are subsequently aggregated to obtain the EU-average ratios. Finally, these ratios are multiplied with the average values for "sales" and "total assets" averaged out across the EU member states in order to produce the absolute values in euros for the EU-average companies.

The following steps are conducted:

a. Income statement

In order to avoid inconsistencies, two alternative methods are employed: (1) Setting items in direct relation to sales and (2) determining items as residuals or as

---

[11] Bulgaria, Cyprus and Slovenia show no companies in the sample since the data did not meet the requirements.

[12] These ratios are defined as follows: return to sales = profit or loss for period to sales; return to assets = profit or loss for period and interest paid to total assets; costs for personnel to turnover = costs of employees to sales.

a proportion of a residual. To this end the former method is applied to other operating revenue, operating profit/loss, profit/loss before tax, profit/loss after tax, profit/loss for the period and interest paid, whereas all other items (financial revenue, financial profit/loss, taxes and extraordinary income) are determined as residuals. For further division of residuals, we determine the ratios of costs for goods sold to cost of goods sold plus other operating expenses and other financial expenses to interest paid. This procedure leads to consistent income statements. Appendix 2 summarises the determination of the EU-average income statements by showing the relevant formulae.

b. Balance sheet

With regard to the balance sheet, we apply a two step approach. In the first step, the following headline items are set in relation to total assets: fixed assets, current assets, shareholder funds, noncurrent liabilities and current liabilities. In the second step, sub-items (e.g. intangible fixed assets, tangible fixed assets and other fixed assets) are set in relation to the relevant headline items (e.g. fixed assets). In order to avoid inconsistencies in the resulting balance sheets, companies are only considered for the respective step if the values for all required items are available.

This procedure leads to consistent balance sheets. Appendix 3 summarises the determination of the EU-average balance sheets by showing the relevant formulae. The structure, the values in euros and the required financial ratios for the EU-27 companies (large and SME) are presented in Appendix 4. These figures fit well with the data of the implemented model firms (Table 14 and Table 15), which shows that all relevant empirical information was gathered and assembled with great precision.

EU-12, EU-15 and Industry-Specific Model Firms

The approach described for determining the EU-27 companies is applied identically in order to create the EU-12 and EU-15 as well as the industry specific companies. To this end, the data sample is divided by region (EU-12, EU-15) or by industry class according to the NACE industry code. The steps to determine the income statement and the balance sheet are then applied to the relevant sub-samples. The structure, the values in euros and the required financial ratios for these companies (large and SME) are presented in the Appendix 4.

2.5.2.4 Additional Ratios and Figures

The procedure of the European Tax Analyzer computations also requires information on R&D expenses in relation to sales. This information is taken into account in the production plan and is necessary in order to determine the cost of goods. The data in the study is based on EUROSTAT statistics, which identifiy both R&D expenses as well as the volume of sales in the EU member states. The R&D expenses and sales figures are broken down by country and industry based on the NACE sections D, F, G, I and K. The relation between R&D expenses and sales is ascertained per country and industry. The information on R&D expenses is taken on the one hand from the Research and Development section under Science and Technology (2001 data) and on the other hand from the Community Innovation Survey (CIS 2004 data). The data used in the European Tax Analyzer is mainly based on the R&D information from CIS. If no CIS data are available, the data based on the information from the Science and Technology sector are applied. If no data are available at all, the value is set to zero.

In order to simulate the growth of wage payments and company pension schemes over time, it is also necessary to supply the European Tax Analyzer with data on employee wages. This data is obtained from EUROSTAT, Unit F2, Labour Market Statistics (Structure of Earnings Survey 2002). The number of employees is broken down by gender, country, industry and educational background.[13] Hence, it is possible to supply information on the structure of employees with reference to educational level. We are able to calculate the percentage of employees belonging to an educational level for each individual industry as well as across all industries. This information is additionally structured by gender. Moreover, a second data set provides the number of employees broken down by gender, country and company size. Based on this analysis it is also possible to calculate information on the structure of employees in the member states of the European Union (the percentage of male and female employees) depending on the size of companies.[14] Corresponding analyses are carried out as to average annual earnings. This information is broken down by gender, country and size class. Consequently, similar information on the average annual earnings in the member states of the European Union is compiled. Finally, information on the average annual earnings broken down by gender, country, industry and education level is gathered to create data on the structure of average annual earnings depending on education.

The European Tax Analyzer also requires detailed data on property, plant and equipment. Data on fixed assets is important for the production plan. In order to simulate amortisation and depreciation expenses, additional information on the structure of fixed assets is necessary for the computations, i.e. to itemise the components of fixed assets. Hence, the proportion of the items "land and buildings", "plant and machinery" and "fixtures" have to be estimated. Estimates are based on the BACH database for Belgium, Finland, France, Germany, Italy, Portugal and Spain.[15] Alternatively, to the above asset types fall under total assets, total fixed assets and tangible fixed assets. We choose the variation coefficient as the criterion to evaluate which figure leads to the best estimate of asset structure. The analysis is carried out per country, company size and industry. First, the ratios for each industry are averaged over the countries considered (step one). Second, the ratios are averaged out across industries and subsequently across countries

[13] Educational background is defined according to the International Standard Classification of Education (ISCED-97).

[14] Two classes are reported: companies up to 249 employees and companies with 250 employees or more.

[15] Austria and the Netherlands were ruled out due to questionable data.

(step two). The variation coefficient is identified for each step and alternative, i.e. the relation to tangible fixed assets, fixed assets and total assets. Given that the ratio to tangible fixed assets provides the best estimation results, the asset structure is consequently based on this ratio.

In addition, information on the structure of provisions is generated. The analysis is conducted identically. Regarding provisions, a distinction can be drawn between "provisions for pensions" and "other provisions".[16]

The European Tax Analyzer computations require information on the source country of dividend receipts as well. This is important since the tax consequences differ if either the tax exemption method or the tax credit method is applied to avoid double taxation. As a result, the ratio of participations in domestic and foreign companies is required in particular. This information is not included in the balance sheet data. The AMADEUS database, however, provides additional ownership information. Information on direct shareholdings[17] is taken from AMADEUS (see Appendix 5) and aggregated for each country by adding up the shares. Information on shares in domestic and foreign companies in per cent for large as well as for small and medium-sized companies is delivered for each member state. Additionally, the following information is gathered: the average number of shareholdings per company, the average amount of shareholding in per cent, the average equity capital of the affiliated companies, as well as the average financial assets of the shareholders. The two latter items include assessment of the proportion of shareholdings to total financial assets.

Finally, the European Tax Analyzer Model also processes data on warranty claims. This information is not concluded in the AMADEUS database. Moreover, neither statistical institutions[18] nor economic organisation[19] maintain such data. This information, however, is necessary to calculate the provisions for warranty claims. In order to obtain an indication of the approximate level of warranty claims as a percentage of sales, the consolidated accounts of the Dow Jones Stoxx 50 companies[20] are examined. The percentage of warranty claims is averaged and taken as an indication of an appropriate estimated value.

---

[16] In contrast, Austria's data could be included, but Belgium's have to be excluded due to inconsistency.

[17] Ownership information in the AMADEUS database is provided for direct shares and for the shares of the ultimate owner of a company. Indirect shares are not reported.

[18] EUROSTAT as well as the German statistical agency DESTATIS.

[19] For example, the OECD and ICC were contacted.

[20] With the exception of the financial and utilities sectors, as these are excluded from the determination of average model companies in the study.

3 Future Value of the Tax Base and Effective Company Tax Burden

The analysis in this section comprises three steps. First, the options for a Common Corporate Tax Base (CCTB) examined in the study are described. Second, the corporate tax bases and the effective tax burdens under current national tax provisions in each member state are measured. Third, the impacts on the size of the tax bases and on the effective tax burdens resulting from the application of a CCTB are measured and analysed. In this context, the question as to what extent an exclusive harmonisation of the tax base will effectively reduce the current EU-wide differences in effective company tax burdens is also examined. The study therefore also provides evidence of the extend to which CCTB would increase or decrease the EU-wide spread between the national tax bases and the effective tax burdens. Steps two and three are performed at first for a benchmark case of a large company representing an average EU-27 corporation. A second benchmark case represents an average EU-27 SME.

3.1 Scenario of a Common Corporate Tax Base

The tax accounting rules considered here are based on the proposals made by the Working Group of the Common Consolidated Corporate Tax Base (CCCTB). The options for a CCTB assessed in this study were discussed and agreed upon by the study´s steering group. Altogether, eight different elements of the tax base will be evaluated: (A) depreciation rules, (B) valuation of inventories, (C) determination of production costs, (D) R&D costs as part of production costs, (E) provisions for future pension payments, (F) provisions for legal obligations, (G) avoidance of double taxation of dividend income, and (H) loss relief. These options are outlined in the following.

- Depreciation rules for intangible assets, machinery, buildings, furniture and fixture (office equipment) (A): A distinction is made between long-term and short to medium term assets depending on the useful lifetime of each asset. In case of machinery as well as furniture and fixture, pool depreciation is calculated at a rate of 20%. Special rules apply to buildings (individual straight-line depreciation with a rate of 2.5%) and intangible assets (individual straight-line depreciation with a general rate of 6.67% if the useful lifetime doesn't require a different rate).

- Valuation of inventories (B): The weighted average cost method (WAC) was chosen. Accordingly, items in inventory and the cost of goods which are sold in the period are valued with average costs. The average is calculated using the cost of the units in stock at that time.
- Production costs (C): In contrast to current country practice, which occasionally allows accounting for partial costs, all direct costs are treated as production costs.
- Costs for R&D as part of production costs (D): Current practice in some member states requires capitalisation of R&D costs as part of production costs. Some of these member states require the inclusion of costs for development activities related to production only, and some require the inclusion of costs for research activities as well. The considered CCTB option foresees the inclusion of costs for development which can be allocated directly to specific production. Research costs, in contrast, are deemed to be expensed as they are not directly related to production.
- Provisions for future pension payments (E): In many member states, legal requirements prevail concerning discount rates and the estimation of pension costs. The CCTB option assessed here foresees the use of IFRS rules for the calculation of pension provisions. This implies a harmonisation of the discount rate and rules regarding the projection of future pension costs trends (e.g. increases in labour costs).
- Provisions for legal obligations (e.g. warranty claims) (F): In many member states contributions to provisions for future liabilities are not tax deductible. An example for such future liabilities would be costs or payment liabilities which arise out of legal requirements for product warranty. The considered CCTB option proposes treating contributions to such provisions as tax deductible when certain requirements are met, e.g. reliable estimation is possible and the liability is tax deductible itself.
- Avoidance of double taxation of dividends (G): Most member states exempt dividend income from taxation in the case of major shareholding. Five member states apply a limited credit system on such dividends. The CCTB option is to exempt dividends from major shareholding (participation ratio $\geq$ 10% of shares). Exemption of dividends results in a lower tax burden compared to the credit method, if the foreign income tax is lower than the domestic tax. The assumed foreign tax rate is 30%.
- Loss relief (H): The CCTB option is an indefinite carry forward of losses without the possibility for loss carry back within a single company. This option stands in contrast to a limitation of loss carry forward in some member states. There is no cross-border loss relief in the model because the model companies are analysed in isolation, regardless of whether they belong to a multinational group (i.e. there are no consolidation features in the model).

Each of these eight elements (A-H) could be either combined separately or simultaneously in order to define a CCTB. For the assessment of the impact of common tax accounting rules on the size of the tax base and tax burden, it is assumed that all member states uniformly adopt all common rules (Option I).

The outlined tax base modifications result in an identical tax base in all member states. The remaining differences between the effective tax burdens are therefore the result of the different tax systems, kinds of taxes and their interactions as well as the tax rates. In addition, one must bear in mind that the tax bases still differ even if the rules for tax accounting are harmonised. The reason for this is that some member states levy local taxes which are deductible from the tax base as a business expense (e.g. real estate tax and other local taxes like business taxes) and because the amount of local taxes varies between the member states. In the drafting of this report it was agreed with the Commission's steering group that national provisions concerning the deductibility of local taxes would be taken into account, i.e. none of these taxes are excluded from deductibility under the CCTB. Different assumptions concerning the treatment of local taxes will be addressed in sensitivity analyses in the final report.

3.2 Analysis of EU-Average Large Corporations

3.2.1 Benchmark Case Representing a Large Corporation

3.2.1.1 Tax Bases and Tax Burdens Based on Domestic Accounting

In order to estimate the impact of common tax accounting rules on the size of the corporate income tax base and the effective tax burden of companies, the future value of the tax bases and the effective tax burdens resulting from current national tax rules are examined first. The comparison takes into account the tax rules implemented as of fiscal year 2006 in the 27 member states.

Table 21 as well as Figure 3 present the future value of the tax bases at the corporate level of a model firm which shows typical characteristics for an average company in the category large corporation across all 27 member states and all considered industries (benchmark case). Details of the model firm are described in section 2.5.

There is a remarkable dispersion in the future values of the tax bases across member states. Future values of the tax bases range from €41.70 million in Hungary to €104.98 million in Cyprus over the simulation period of 10 years. The average tax base is €89.91 million and the standard deviation as a percentage of the average is 15.12%. The large model firm shows a comparably low future value of the tax base in the five old member states Austria, Belgium, France, Germany and Spain as well as in Hungary. In case of Hungary this is the result of generous depreciation rules in combination with relatively high annual payroll tax payments which are deductible for corporate income tax purposes.

Table 21: Comparison of future tax base values (large company, corporate level, 10 periods)

Country	Future Value Tax Base in € Millions	Rank	Deviation from Average in %
HU	41.70	1	-53.6
FR	55.43	2	-38.3
DE	74.05	3	-17.6
BE	78.55	4	-12.6
AT	81.19	5	-9.7
ES	85.05	6	-5.4
SL	89.26	7	-0.7
DK	91.36	8	1.6
LU	93.42	9	3.9
UK	93.45	10	3.9
SE	93.60	11	4.1
LT	93.70	12	4.2
LV	93.84	13	4.4
BG	94.64	14	5.3
PT	94.67	15	5.3
IT	94.72	16	5.4
FI	95.06	17	5.7
RO	95.16	18	5.8
NL	95.66	19	6.4
GR	95.90	20	6.7
CZ	95.97	21	6.7
SK	96.26	22	7.1
PL	97.46	23	8.4
MT	98.18	24	9.2
IE	101.06	25	12.4
EE	103.22	26	14.8
CY	104.98	27	16.8
Ø	89.91		
Standard Deviation	13.59		15.12

The deductibility of other taxes causing high annual tax payments also explains the low level of the future value of the tax base in Austria, Belgium, France, Germany and Spain. Estonia is exceptional in that only distributed earnings are subject to corporate income tax. In order to provide an idea of the impact that a CCTB would have on Estonia in comparison to other EU countries, the calculation for Estonia measures effects on the future value of accounting profits.

In contrast to the countries mentioned above, Cyprus, Ireland, Poland and Slovakia show comparatively high future tax base values as low corporate income tax rates lead to moderate cash outflows. A lower cash outflow of tax payments is associated with higher liquidity available for investments in each period. Consequently, an increase in interest receipts in consecutive periods broadens the respective bases and thus the future values of the tax bases. With respect to Malta, the restrictive national tax accounting rules are responsible for a relatively high future value of tax base.

Figure 3: Comparison of future tax base values according to current taxation practice – Deviation from the EU average in % (large company, corporate level, 10 periods)

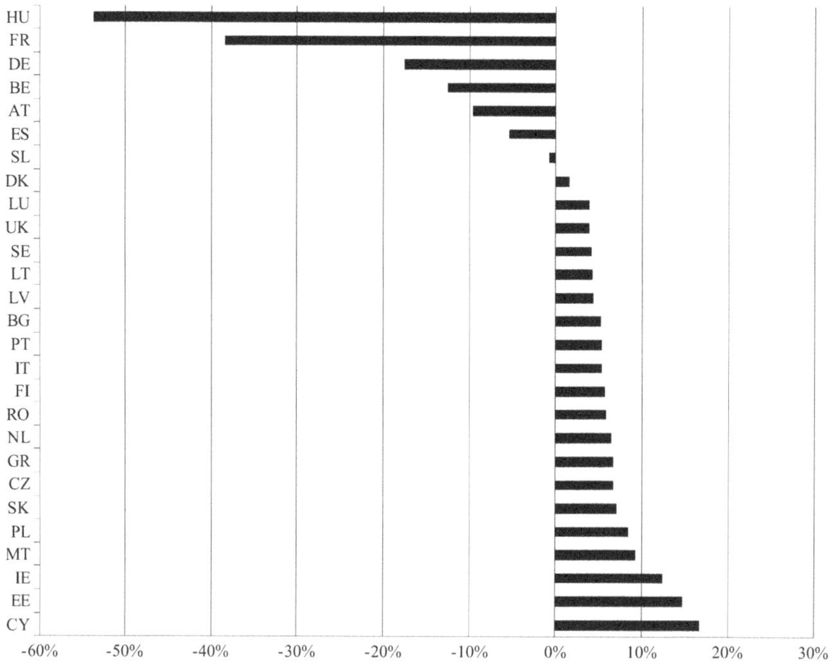

There is also a remarkable dispersion of effective tax burdens across member states (see Table 22 and Figure 4). Tax burdens range from €13.86 million in Ireland to €55.17 million in France over the simulation period of 10 years. The average tax burden is €27.42 million and the standard deviation as a percentage of the average is 34.32%. The large model firm bears a comparably low tax burden in member states which recently joined the EU. The tax burdens in the new member states Bulgaria, Cyprus, the Czech Republic, Estonia, Latvia, Lithuania, Poland, Romania and Slovakia are significantly lower than the EU average. Only Hungary, Malta and Slovenia display an effective tax burden above the EU average. Ireland is the only country among the old member states which ranks in a top position.

The large member states France, Germany, Italy and Spain can be classified as countries imposing a relatively high tax burden on corporations. Smaller member states like the Eastern European countries Bulgaria, Estonia, Latvia, Lithuania, Poland, Romania and Slovakia as well as Ireland rank at the top of the considered countries.

The effective tax burden at the corporate level in countries like the Czech Republic, Slovenia and continental countries like Greece, Luxembourg, the Netherlands, and Portugal as well as in the Scandinavian countries Finland and Sweden is closer to average.

Table 22: Comparison of effective tax burdens (large company, corporate level, 10 periods)

Country	Tax Burden in € Millions	Rank	Deviation from Average in %
IE	13.86	1	-49.5
BG	14.52	2	-47.1
EE	15.63	3	-43.0
RO	15.76	4	-42.5
LV	16.36	5	-40.3
CY	18.35	6	-33.1
SK	19.26	7	-29.7
PL	19.75	8	-27.9
LT	20.44	9	-25.4
CZ	23.38	10	-14.7
FI	26.23	11	-4.3
PT	26.72	12	-2.5
SE	27.19	13	-0.8
GR	27.77	14	1.3
SL	28.85	15	5.2
NL	28.94	16	5.6
LU	29.11	17	6.2
DK	29.40	18	7.3
BE	31.43	19	14.6
UK	31.92	20	16.4
AT	33.05	21	20.6
MT	33.63	22	22.7
ES	37.85	23	38.0
HU	38.09	24	38.9
IT	38.77	25	41.4
DE	38.79	26	41.5
FR	55.17	27	101.2
Ø	27.42		
Standard Deviation	9.41		34.32

A comparison of Table 21 and Table 22 indicates that countries with a higher effective tax burden tend to show a lower future value of the tax base. This result is in line with the explanations used to describe the ranking of future tax base values (see section 2.4).

The effective tax burden is influenced by different kinds of taxes (see Table 23). In general, corporate income tax constitutes the main share of the overall tax burden in all member states, except Hungary. Its share in the overall tax burden ranges from 41.25% in Hungary to 100% in Malta.

Besides corporate income tax, all member states, except Malta and Slovenia, levy real estate tax. The impact of real estate taxes on the overall tax burden is generally not significant. It is comparatively high in Belgium, Denmark, Ireland, Latvia, Lithuania, and in the United Kingdom, however. In these countries, the share of real estate tax in the overall tax burden amounts to more than 9%.

Figure 4: Comparison of effective tax burdens according to current taxation practice – Deviation from the EU average in % (large company, corporate level, 10 periods)

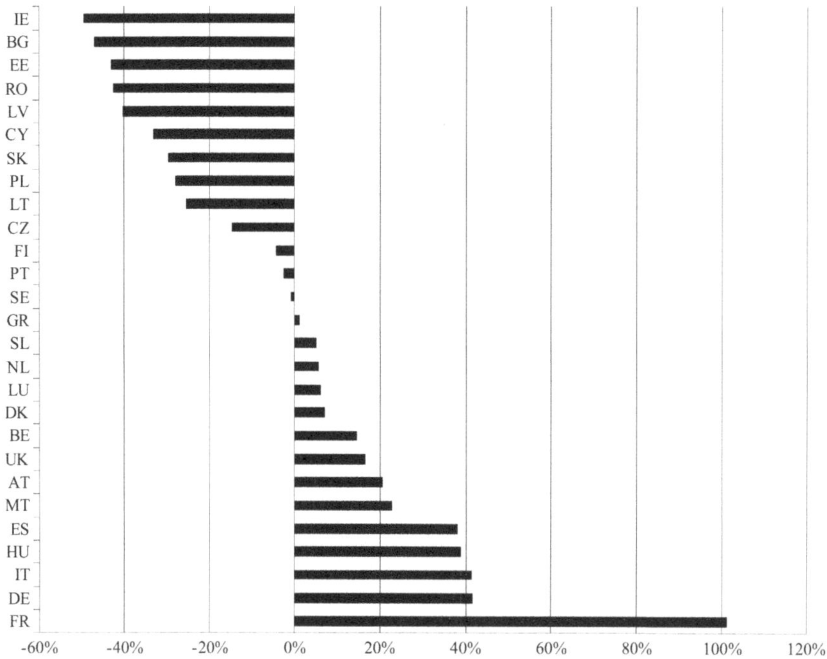

Additional taxes are imposed in Austria, Cyprus, France, Germany, Hungary, Italy, Luxembourg, Spain and Slovenia. Germany, Luxembourg and Italy (*IRAP*) levy a trade tax on income.

As real estate tax in Germany and Italy is negligible, the overall tax burden is almost solely determined by profit taxes. A slightly different picture is given for Austria, Cyprus, France and Slovenia. In these countries, the overall tax burden is substantially determined by non-profit taxes.

All four countries impose a tax on payroll. Its share in the overall tax burden varies between 12.00% in France and 38.01% in Cyprus. France also levies a trade tax on capital (*taxe professionnelle*), which amounts to 26.58% of the overall tax burden.

Table 23. Impact of particular tax categories on the effective tax burden in % (large company)

Country	Real Estate Tax in %	Payroll Tax in %	Trade Tax on Income in %	Trade Tax on Capital in %	Net Wealth Tax in %	Corporate Tax (incl. Surcharges) in %
AT	4.75	23.25				72.00
BE	9.89					90.11
BG	1.84					98.16
CY	4.26	38.01				57.73
CZ	1.11					98.89
DE	1.12		34.19			64.69
DK	9.03					90.97
EE	5.80					94.20
ES	1.23			12.04		86.74
FI	4.12					95.88
FR	2.40	12.00		26.58		59.02
GR	1.88					98.12
HU	3.40		55.35			41.25
IE	9.52					90.48
IT	1.62		17.77			80.62
LT	10.21					89.79
LU	3.02		20.90		0.87	75.22
LV	11.59					88.41
MT						100.00
NL	1.49					98.51
PL	6.81					93.19
PT	2.47					97.53
RO	5.95					94.05
SE	2.51					97.49
SK	4.00					96.00
SL		16.44				83.56
UK	9.76					90.24

3.2.1.2 Tax Bases and Tax Burdens under a CCTB

The changes in the future value of the tax base which would result with the introduction of a CCTB are displayed in Table 24. It is assumed that the above outlined rules regarding depreciation, inventory valuation, determination of production costs, provisions for pensions, provisions for future liabilities, exemption of foreign dividend income and loss relief are implemented simultaneously (Option I).

In all member states, except Cyprus and Ireland, the introduction of a CCTB would increase the tax base (i.e. the future value of the tax base). The increases of the future values of tax bases range from 0.2% in the United Kingdom to 13.1% in Bulgaria. The average increase is 6.20%. Bulgaria, the Czech Republic, Finland, France, Greece, Hungary, Italy, Latvia, Lithuania, Poland, Portugal, Slovakia and Slovenia show an increase in the tax base which is above average.

Table 24. Changes in the future value of the tax base under a CCTB (large company)

Country	**National GAAP**		**CCTB Options (all)**			
	Future Value Tax Base in € Millions	Rank	Future Value Tax Base in € Millions	Rank	Deviation in %	Rank Change
AT	81.19	5	86.02	5	5.9	0
BE[21]	78.55	4	80.93	4	3.0	0
BG	94.64	14	107.00	27	13.1	-13
CY	104.98	27	97.97	13	-6.7	14
CZ	95.97	21	105.51	24	9.9	-3
DE	74.05	3	77.58	3	4.8	0
DK	91.36	8	94.81	8	3.8	0
EE	103.22	26	105.90	26	2.6	0
ES	85.05	6	88.98	6	4.6	0
FI	95.06	17	104.03	18	9.4	-1
FR	55.43	2	60.86	2	9.8	0
GR	95.90	20	104.65	21	9.1	-1
HU	41.70	1	46.82	1	12.3	0
IE	101.06	25	99.50	14	-1.5	11
IT	94.72	16	103.01	17	8.8	-1
LT	93.70	12	104.08	19	11.1	-7
LU	93.42	9	96.92	10	3.7	-1
LV	93.84	13	104.44	20	11.3	-7
MT	98.18	24	101.95	16	3.8	8
NL	95.66	19	97.80	12	2.2	7
PL	97.46	23	104.95	23	7.7	0
PT	94.67	15	104.67	22	10.6	-7
RO	95.16	18	99.86	15	4.9	3
SE	93.60	11	97.69	11	4.4	0
SK	96.26	22	105.69	25	9.8	-3
SL	89.26	7	96.91	9	8.6	-2
UK	93.45	10	93.67	7	0.2	3
Ø	89.91		95.27		6.20	

In 10 countries (Austria, Belgium, Denmark, Estonia, France, Germany, Hungary, Poland, Spain and Sweden) these changes do not translate into a change of the ranking position. Cyprus, Ireland, Italy, Malta, the Netherlands, Romania and the United Kingdom improve their ranking between one and fourteen positions.

[21] For Belgium, the calculations take into account a notional deduction that became effective in 2006. Without this notional deduction, the future value of the tax base under national GAAP amounts to €87.64 million and the introduction of the proposed CCTB results in an increase of the future value of the tax base of 6.35%.

Table 25: Changes in the effective tax burden under a CCTB (large company)

Country	National GAAP		CCTB Options (all)			
	Tax Burden in € Millions	Rank	Tax Burden in € Millions	Rank	Deviation in %	Rank Change
AT	33.05	21	34.26	21	3.6	0
BE	31.43	19	32.24	19	2.6	0
BG	14.52	2	16.07	3	10.7	-1
CY	18.35	6	17.65	5	-3.8	1
CZ	23.38	10	25.18	10	7.7	0
DE	38.79	26	40.15	25	3.5	1
DK	29.40	18	30.37	16	3.3	2
EE	15.63	3	15.63	2	0.0	1
ES	37.85	23	39.37	24	4.0	-1
FI	26.23	11	28.01	11	6.8	0
FR	55.17	27	57.25	27	3.8	0
GR	27.77	14	30.40	17	9.5	-3
HU	38.09	24	38.93	23	2.2	1
IE	13.86	1	13.97	1	0.8	0
IT	38.77	25	41.98	26	8.3	-1
LT	20.44	9	22.18	9	8.5	0
LU	29.11	17	30.14	15	3.5	2
LV	16.36	5	18.18	6	11.1	-1
MT	33.63	22	35.68	22	6.1	0
NL	28.94	16	29.58	14	2.2	2
PL	19.75	8	21.25	8	7.6	0
PT	26.72	12	28.89	13	8.1	-1
RO	15.76	4	17.08	4	8.4	0
SE	27.19	13	28.34	12	4.2	1
SK	19.26	7	20.67	7	7.3	0
SL	28.85	15	30.76	18	6.6	-3
UK	31.92	20	32.73	20	2.5	0
Ø	27.42		28.78		5.15	

The relatively strong impact on the ranking can be attributed to only small differences in the absolute of future tax base value (see Figure 3). For the same reason, Bulgaria, the Czech Republic, Finland, Greece, Italy, Latvia, Lithuania, Luxembourg, Portugal, Slovakia and Slovenia see a worsening of their rank between one and thirteen positions.

The changes to the effective tax burden resulting from a CCTB are displayed in Table 25. Again it is assumed here that the above outlined rules regarding depreciation, inventory valuation, determination of production costs, provisions for pensions, provisions for future liabilities, exemption of foreign dividend income and loss relief are implemented simultaneously (Option I).

In all member states, except Cyprus and Estonia, the introduction of a CCTB would result in a higher effective tax burden. The increases in the effective tax burden ranges from 0.8% in Ireland to 11.1% in Latvia. On average, the effective tax burden increases by 5.15%. Bulgaria, the Czech Republic, Finland, Greece, Italy, Latvia, Lithuania, Malta, Poland, Portugal, Romania, Slovakia and Slovenia all show an above average increase in the tax burden.

However, these changes rarely translate into a change of relative rank. Twelve countries do not change positions. Cyprus, Denmark, Estonia, Germany, Hungary, Luxembourg, the Netherlands and Sweden improve their rank, but only between one and two positions because the differences in the level of effective tax burdens are relatively high (see Figure 3). Bulgaria, Spain, Greece, Italy, Latvia, Portugal and Slovenia worsening of their positions in the ranking, but only between one and three positions.

Overall it can be stated that the introduction of a CCTB would lead to higher future tax bases values as well as to higher effective tax burdens. While the future value of the tax base increases by 6.20% on average, the average effective tax burden increases by 5.15%. The stronger impact to the future value of the tax base is in line with the conclusions derived from the examples in section 2.4. However, this result does not hold true for countries in which the CCTB replaces the tax credit method for dividends with the exemption method. This is the case in Greece, Ireland, Malta, Poland and the United Kingdom. In these countries the exemption of dividends permanently reduces the periodical tax base and thus the future value of the tax base. As opposed to the described effect, the impact of the changed method to avoid double taxation of dividends on the effective tax burden is not significant. This is because, in case of a tax credit system, the inclusion of dividends in the periodical tax base is generally balanced out when a tax credit is granted. Thus the abolishment of the credit method doesn't affect the effective tax burden. It only affects the future value of the tax base. With regard to Ireland this induces a reduction of the future value of tax base and at the same time an increase in the effective average tax burden.

The enlargement of the future value of the tax base and effective tax burden witnessed here would introduce room for manoeuvre for the reduction of nominal tax rates in order to keep the implementation of a CCTB revenue neutral. To what extent tax rate cuts would be possible requires further research beyond this study, however.

So far, the cumulative effects of common tax accounting rules on the future value of the tax base and the effective tax burden have been analysed. In the following, the effects of the different elements of the CCTB considered here (i.e. Options A-G) on the future value of the tax base are evaluated individually. Each simulation is based on a particular element of the tax base being harmonised across the EU while for all other elements domestic accounting rules are still applied. This analysis helps to identify the effect and importance of specific elements of a CCTB.

(1) The first simulation considers an isolated harmonisation of rules governing tax depreciation (Option A).

Depreciation is an important element in determining the size of the tax base. Deviations between current national depreciation rules and common depreciation rules are the result of different depreciation methods and rates. Figure 5 displays the changes in the future value of the tax base stemming from common tax depreciation rules.

Tax depreciation rules following Option A (for a detailed description see section 3.1) lead to a broadening of the tax base and thus to higher future tax base values in all member states. The increase ranges from 0.23% in Belgium to 12.47% in Hungary.

Figure 5: Impact of common rules regarding depreciation on the future value of the tax base in % (large company)

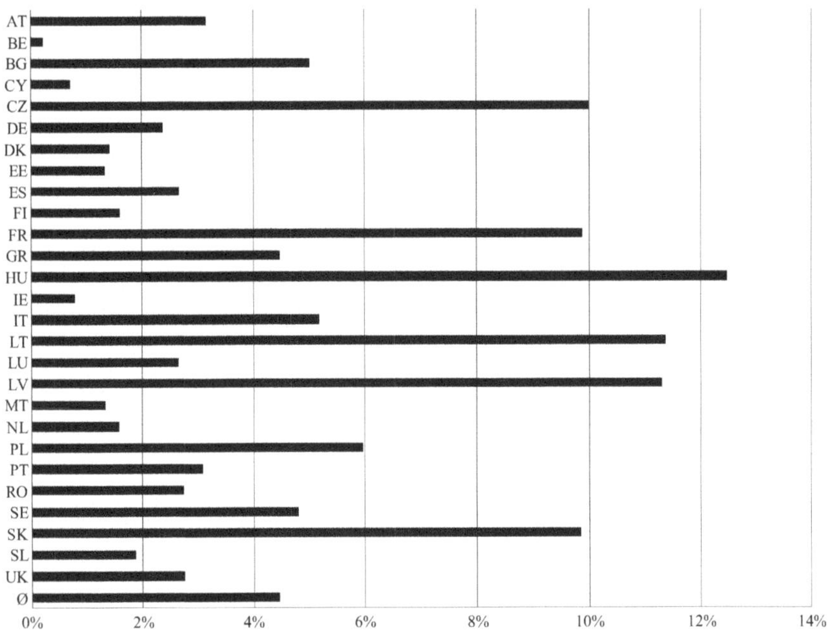

The highest tax base increases are calculated for the Czech Republic, France, Hungary, Latvia, Lithuania and Slovakia. Thus, the current depreciation rules in these countries according to national tax law can be deemed comparably generous, as the introduction of CCTB depreciation rules would lead to a significant broadening of the tax base. In contrast, the current tax depreciation rules in Belgium, Cyprus, Finland, Denmark, Estonia, Ireland, Malta, and in the Netherlands are rather restrictive. In these countries, the future value of the tax base would increase only by 1.59% at the maximum, if common tax depreciation rules were introduced.

Overall, the impact of common tax depreciation rules is of high relevance when it comes to effects on the future value of the tax base. On average, the future value of the tax base increases by 4.47%, revealing depreciation as the CCTB option with the most important impact of the tax base. In isolation, changes in tax depreciation rules as considered here comprise 72.10% (= 4.47/6.20) of the overall EU-average increase in the future value of the tax base with the introduction of a CCTB.

When this 4.47% increase is broken down by the asset categories affected by new depreciation rules, the results, which are displayed in Appendix 7, Table 1, illustrate the key impact of common depreciation rules for machinery and equipment on the future value of the tax base. With the isolated application of the proposed CCTB provisions concerning machinery and equipment, the future value of the tax base increases on average by 4.17%. By contrast, the future value of the tax base only increases by 0.25% if common depreciation rules are applied exclusively to buildings and by 0.04% if the proposed CCTB provisions are only applied to intangibles (see Appendix 7, Table 1).

To sum up, common depreciation provisions for machinery and equipment are responsible for the overwhelming share of the increase in the future value of the tax base observed for Option A.

Consequently, changes in the definition of the proposed depreciation rules on machinery and equipment would considerably influence the future value of the tax base when introducing a CCTB.

To illustrate this influence, a modification of the depreciation rate for pool depreciation on machinery and equipment is considered in Appendix 7, Table 3. It reveals that a change in the depreciation rate for pool depreciation results in high changes of the future value of the tax base under a CCTB and thus in a large deviation between national GAAP and CCTB. If the depreciation rate for the mentioned assets is fixed at 25% instead of 20% (benchmark case), the average increase in the future value of the tax base due to the isolated application of common depreciation rules amounts 1.26%.

This translates into an overall increase in the future value of the tax base of 1.09% if a simultaneous introduction of all CCTB options takes place. Both effects are significantly smaller than in the benchmark case, in which a 20% depreciation rate for pool depreciation is applied.

(2) The second simulation analyses the effect of an isolated harmonisation of methods for simplified valuation of inventories on the future value of the tax base (Option B).

The weighted average costs method (WAC) was chosen as an option for the CCTB. Accordingly, items in inventory and the cost of goods which are sold in the period are valued with the average costs of the units in stock at that time. Given inflation and rising costs over time, as it is assumed for these calculations, inventory is valued moderately at average cost. Sold goods are valued moderately as well at average costs and in tendency below recently higher production costs. However, production costs do not necessarily increase over time. Instead, they may vary from period to period depending on the amount of indirect costs, such as depreciation, and the number of units produced. Therefore, the effects of an introduction of the WAC method may vary. Changes in the future value of the tax base resulting from the introduction of the WAC method are displayed in Figure 6.

Compared to the LIFO method which is used in most member states' national tax laws, the WAC method results in a broader tax base. Sold goods are valued at lower cost, thus increasing taxable profits. This effect is compensated partly in the last period of the simulation when lower hidden reserves for the WAC method lead to a smaller tax base and tax in that period. Austria, Italy, Luxembourg, the Netherlands, Poland and Slovenia, for example show the highest increase in the future value of the tax base when WAC is applied. Compared to countries applying the FIFO method in their national tax law, the tax base with WAC is reduced and the future value of the tax base is therefore lower. In this way, Denmark, Finland and Lithuania show a decrease in the future value of the tax base. There is no change for countries which already apply the WAC method in their national tax law.

Figure 6: Impact of common rules for the simplified valuation of inventory on the future value of the tax base in % (large company)

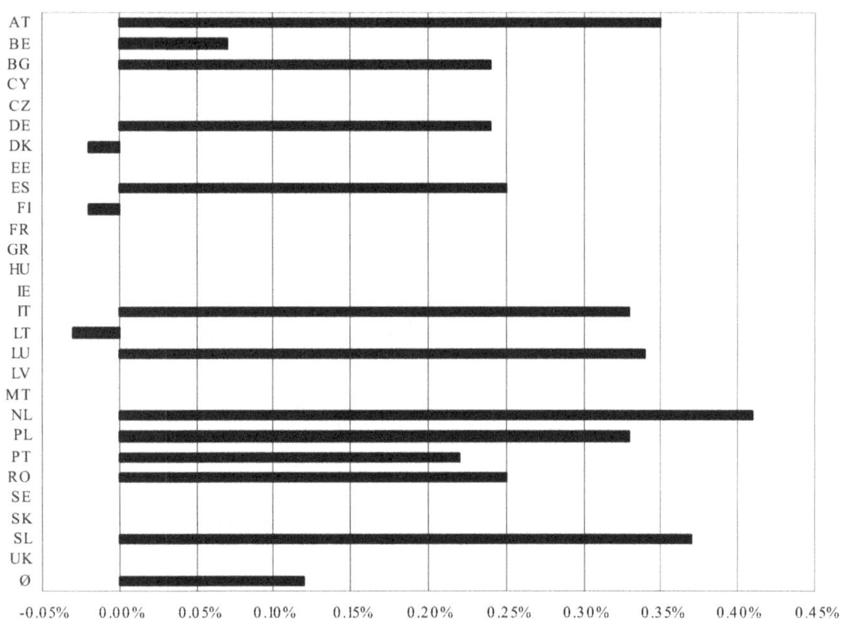

Overall, the impact of the WAC method on the future value of the tax base ranges from -0.03% in Lithuania to 0.41% in the Netherlands. Most countries show an increase of less than 0.1%. Thus, the method used for the assessment of inventory has only a moderate impact on the future value of the tax base. The EU-wide average increase is 0.12%. In isolation this corresponds to 1.94% (= 0.12/6.20) of the overall EU-average increase in the future value of the tax base with the introduction of a CCTB.

(3) The third simulation investigates the effect of common rules for the determination of production costs (Option C).

Depending on the rules for the determination of production costs, expenses are either deductible for accounting and taxation purposes in the period in which they occur or they are capitalised. If the costs are capitalised, they increase the value of the stock of inventory and their tax deduction is thus deferred to the period in which the specific asset is sold. As for the previous options for a CCTB, the tax base is only affected by timing effects. According to Option C, which is in line with the corresponding proposals of the CCCTB Working Group, the costs of inventories should include all costs of purchase, conversion and other direct costs which are needed to bring the inventories to their location and condition. Accordingly, not only direct costs but also indirect costs which are associated with the production process and which can be allocated to individual assets have to be included in production costs and are applied to the CCTB. The results presented in Figure 7 show that the future value of the tax base would change only moderately in most member states.

Figure 7: Impact of common rules regarding the determination of production costs on the future value of the tax base in % (large company)

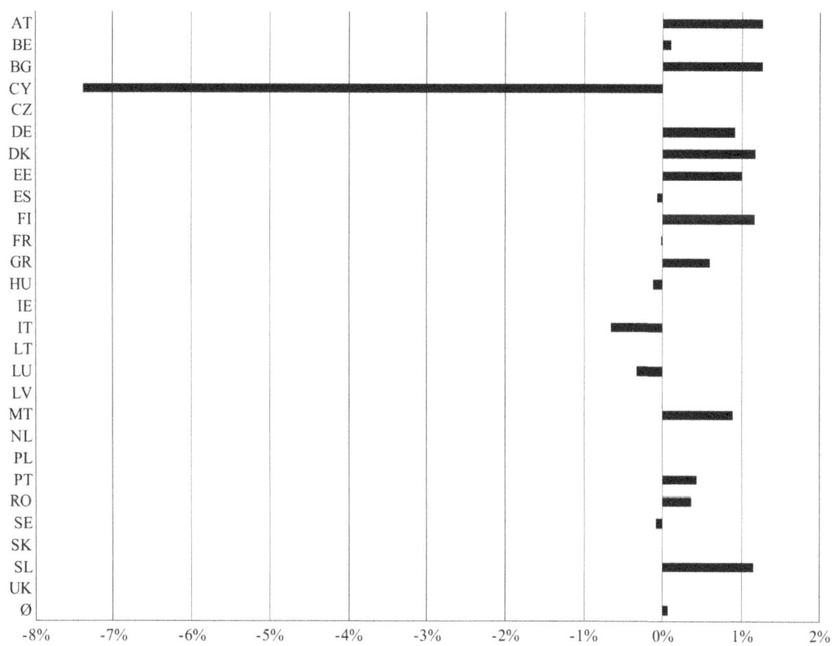

The future values of the tax base in the Czech Republic, France, Ireland, Latvia, Lithuania, the Netherlands, Poland, Slovakia and the United Kingdom do not change at all or only to a very small extent. This indicates that current tax practices in these countries are already in line with the respective CCTB option. Increases in the future value of the tax base are seen for Austria, Belgium,

Bulgaria, Denmark, Estonia, Finland, Germany, Greece, Malta, Portugal, Romania and Slovenia. Under these countries' current tax practices, not all of the costs related to the production of assets are included in production costs. In contrast, the future value of the tax base decreases in Cyprus, Hungary, Luxembourg, Spain, Sweden and Italy. The main reason is that most of these countries demand research and development costs to be capitalised. For the purposes of a CCTB, however, production costs include only those research and development costs which are deemed to be closely related to the production process. Thus, production costs according to current tax law in these countries are higher compared to the production costs under a CCTB. Additional differences in the amount of production costs stem from the capitalisation of taxes on quasi-production factors like real estate (real estate tax), employees (payroll tax) and the expensing of taxes related to earnings like business tax, tax on turnover or value added under the CCTB proposal, which differs from current practices in some countries.

Altogether, there is a negligible impact of the determination of production costs on the future values of the tax bases. The overall EU-average increase is 0.06%. Changes in the determination of production costs as considered here comprise in isolation to 0.98% (= 0.06/6.20) of the overall EU-average increase of the future values of the tax bases in the event of a CCTB.

(4) The next simulation investigates the effect of common rules for the capitalisation of R&D costs within production costs (Option D).

The above simulation showed the effect of expensing or capitalization of production related costs on the future value of the tax base.

Option D considers the inclusion of R&D costs in production costs when these costs are related closely to production. In this option, therefore, R&D costs related to production are included into production costs and reduce the tax base when the underlying goods are sold. The tax base, therefore, is again impacted by a timing effect. The other production cost components remain subject to current national practices.

The results in Figure 8 reveal that there is no considerable impact on the future value of the tax base when production-related R&D costs are considered part of production. Some countries currently consider almost all R&D costs as production costs even if they are not closely related to production, such as basic research or generic development. These countries are Cyprus, Spain, Luxemburg, Malta and Sweden. Their tax bases decrease when the calculation of production costs only permits the inclusion of production-related R&D, as a greater share of R&D expenditures currently fall under production costs for tax purposes. Countries which do already include R&D costs as prescribed by Option D show no change in the future value of the tax base. Countries which allow an expensing of all R&D costs, by contrast, see an increase in the tax base.

The effects of the application of Option D on the future tax base values range between +0.03% in Hungary and -0.46% in Cyprus. The strong effect in Cyprus is caused by its relatively high valuation of assets for taxation purposes due to a comprehensive inclusion of R&D expenditure. The comparison with the economic model leads to a negative result in the last period of the simulation when the valuation for tax purposes is compared to the fair market valuation and hidden reserves or hidden liabilities are included in the tax base. That loss can not be used or carried forward in the last period and is therefore depreciated as described in the model description. That leads to a comparatively strong decrease for Cyprus.

Compared to other CCTB options, the average effect on the future value of the tax base of common rules to include R&D-related expenditure in production costs can be neglected. The overall EU-average decrease in the future value of the tax base amounts to -0.02% and in isolation corresponds to -0.32% (= -0.02/6.20) of the overall EU-average increase in the future value of the tax base with the introduction of a CCTB.

Figure 8: Impact of common rules regarding R&D costs as part of production costs on the future value of the tax base in % (large company)

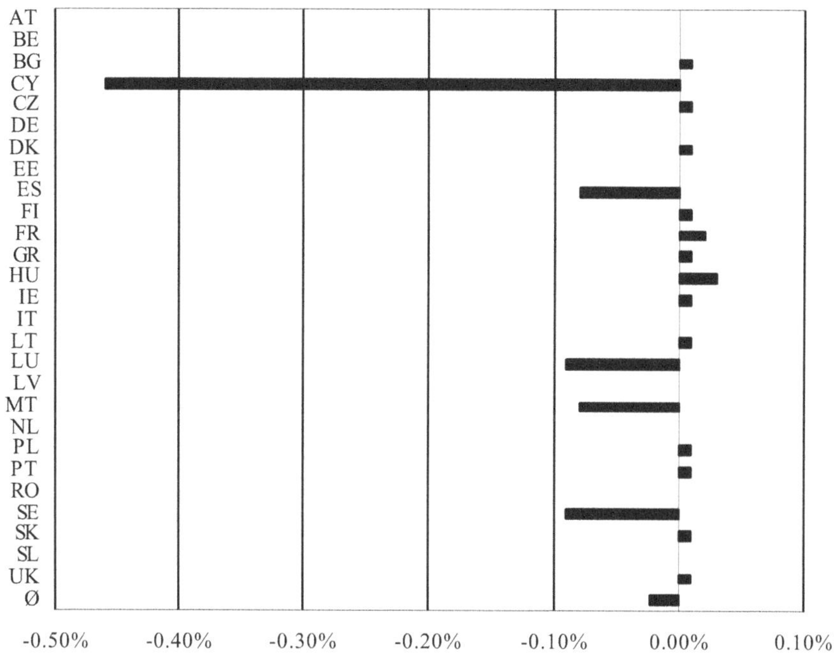

(5) The next simulation deals with the effect of common rules regarding provisions for pensions (Option E).

In the field of accounting for pension liabilities, EU member states' tax practices differ significantly. Funded schemes are common in most member states. With respect to unfunded schemes, only Austria, Germany, Luxembourg and the Netherlands allow for tax-effective pension provisions. The majority of member states require a funded retirement plan in order to deduct contributions from the tax base. The amount of tax-deductible contributions to a pension fund or a pension provision depends on several factors. Again, Option E results in a timing effect for the tax base. The most relevant factors are the future development of labour and pension costs and the discount rate. Based on the principles of IAS 19, the obligation should be calculated using actuarial assumptions, taking into account probabilities of entrance and future salary increases.

Figure 9: Impact of common rules regarding provisions for pensions on the future value of the tax base in % (large company)

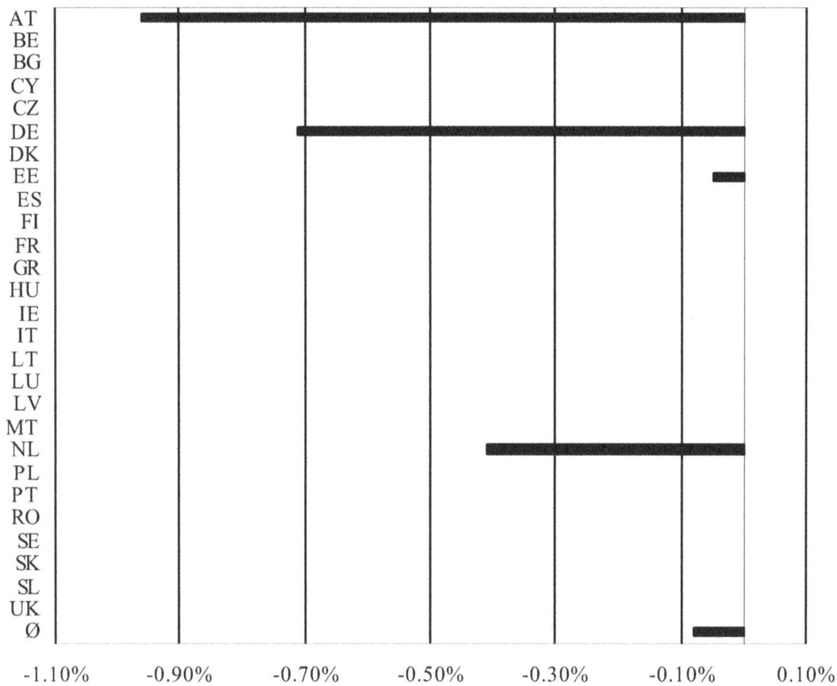

The obligation should be allocated to the expected length of the service period. With respect to the discount rate there are no legal requirements. An important reference point should be the rate of high quality corporate bonds (IAS 19.78). In the model, a discount rate of 3% is assumed for reasons of transparency. This corresponds with the short term credit interest rate. In most member states where funded schemes prevail tax practice is in line with these requirements. The simulations indicate that common tax accounting rules concerning pensions based on IAS, which is the underlying assumption of Option E, would result in a change in the future value of the tax base only in Austria, Germany, Estonia and the Netherlands (see Figure 9). In these four countries, common tax accounting rules in the field of pension provisions would lead to a reduction of the future value of the tax base. This result stems mainly from different discount rates. Austria and Germany require a discount rate of 6%. The discount rate in the Netherlands is fixed at 4%. Estonia requires the determination of the pension liability for employees beginning at the age of 28, instead of 25, as is considered here. Furthermore, in Austria and Germany, future increases in labour costs and pension payments cannot be taken into account in advance. Thus, the obligation as determined under national tax law is lower in earlier years than under the common tax accounting rules considered here. By contrast, national tax accounting rules for pension provisions in Luxembourg already correspondent to IFRS.

Overall, the introduction of common rules for the determination of pension liabilities results in an EU-wide average decrease in the future value of the tax base of 0.08%. This moderate decrease comprises -1.29% (= -0.08/6.20) of the overall EU-average change in the future value of the tax base with the introduction of a CCTB.

(6) The effects of provisions for future warranty liabilities are analysed in the following simulation (Option F).

There are many types of future liabilities which are uncertain but probable; product warranties required by law are one such example. There are basically two ways to account for these liabilities. The CCTB option considered here is to treat contributions to such accruals as tax deductible. The other option is to treat these contributions as non deductible. About half of the member states treat these contributions as tax deductible. If tax deductible, costs can be recognised on an accruals basis before they have to be paid. This lowers the taxable base before the liability is effectively due to pay.

Figure 10: Impact of common rules regarding provisions for warranty payments on the future value of the tax base in % (large company)

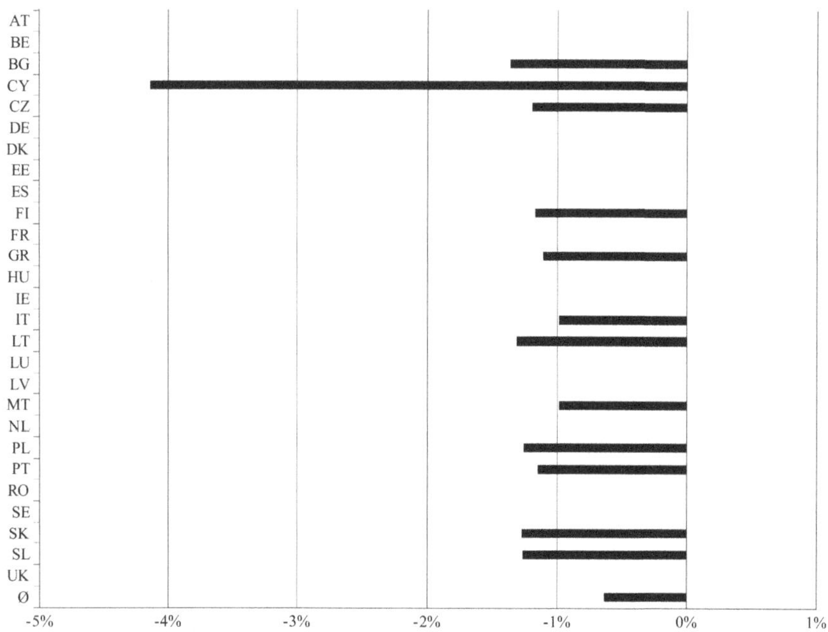

That leads to earlier tax effective deductions. Due to timing advantages, accruals for future liabilities therefore result in a lower future value of the tax base. Countries allowing no tax effective provision for warranty payments according to national tax law are therefore faced with a smaller tax base when Option F is applied (see Figure 10). The maximum reduction is 4.13% in Cyprus. Yet Finland, Greece, Lithuania, Poland, Portugal, Slovakia and Slovenia also show a significant decrease in their tax bases. Greece, Italy and Malta show the smallest decrease out of those countries which have no provision in their national tax law.

Overall, the introduction of common accounting rules concerning provisions for future warranty liabilities results in a considerable EU-wide average decrease in the future value of the tax base of -0.63%. This decrease in isolation corresponds to -10.16% (= -0.63/6.20) of the overall EU-average change in the future value of the tax base with the introduction of a CCTB.

(7) Another CCTB option is the avoidance of double taxation of dividend income by applying the exemption method for dividend income from major shareholdings (Option G).

According to present tax law, Greece, Ireland, Malta, Poland and the United Kingdom grant a limited tax credit for dividends from major shareholdings. Option G for a CCTB as considered here is to exempt dividends from major shareholdings (participation ratio ≥ 10% of shares).

Figure 11: Impact of common rules regarding exemption of foreign dividend income on the future value of the tax base in % (large company)

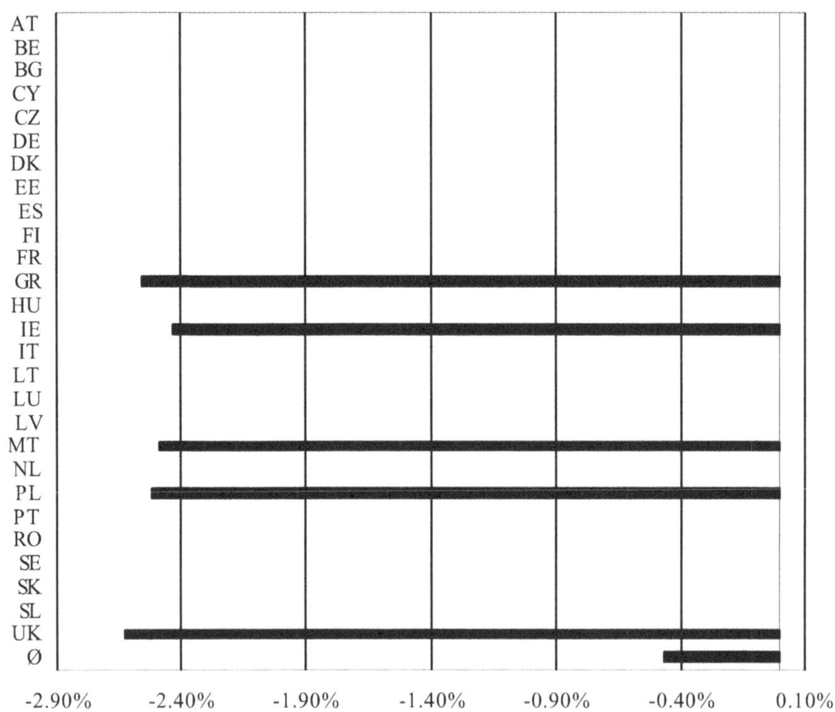

Compared to the credit method, exemption of foreign dividends results in a lower periodical tax base because dividends are excluded from taxation (see Figure 11). In contrast to the previous options for a CCTB there is now a permanent effect on the tax base which explains the decrease in the future value of the tax base in the countries concerned. CCTB Option G therefore has negative effects in Greece, Ireland, Malta, Poland and the United Kingdom. The tax base reduction ranges from -2.43% in Ireland to -2.63% in the United Kingdom.

Compared to other CCTB options, the average effect on the future value of the tax base resulting from an introduction of the exemption method for foreign dividend income is considerable. The overall EU-average decrease in the future value of the tax base amounts to -0.47% and in isolation comprises to -7.58% (= -0.47/6.20) of the overall EU-average change in the future value of the tax base with the introduction of a CCTB.

(8) The effects of loss carry forward are analysed in the following simulation (Option H).

The large model firm considered in this base case scenario is a profitable company and shows no losses from regular activities during the simulation period of 10 years. The isolated application of CCTB Option H for an indefinite loss carry forward therefore does not by itself cause a change in the future value of the tax base of the model firm.

To conclude, the introduction of a CCTB as considered here has a considerable impact on the future value of the tax base and the effective tax burden for the large company benchmark case (see Table 26 and Table 27 for details). The introduction of a CCTB would lead to higher future tax base values as well as to higher effective tax burdens. While the future tax base value increases by 6.20%[22] on average in the EU-27 countries, the average effective tax burden increases by 5.15%.

When the CCTB rules are simulated, the countries most affected in terms of the future value of the tax base and effective tax burden are Bulgaria (13.06%/10.70%), Latvia (11.30%/11.15%) and Lithuania (11.08%/8.50%). In the case of Hungary the introduction of a CCTB leads to a strong increase in the future value of the tax base (12.29%) but to a comparably small increase in the effective tax burden (2.23%). This is primarily attributable to the extraordinary importance of additional taxes aside from the corporate income tax. Cyprus is the only country which is affected negatively in terms of both the future value of the tax base (-6.68%) and the effective tax burden (-3.82%).

The CCTB option which exerts the greatest impact on tax bases and tax burdens is depreciation (A). The implementation of the CCTB depreciation rules considered here would in isolation make up 72.10% of the EU-27 average overall increase of the future value of the tax base for all proposed measures. The Czech Republic (9.98%), France (9.89%), Hungary (12.47%), Latvia (11.30%), Lithuania (11.36%) and Slovakia (9.84%) face higher tax bases due to modifications of depreciation rules.

---

[22] Thereof an increase of 5.26% can be attributed to the EU-15 countries and an increase of 7.41% can be attributed to the EU-12 countries.

Of the CCTB options which have the greatest impact on the future value of the tax base, Option F, concerning provisions for future warranty liabilities, ranks second in significance. It accounts for -10.16% of the overall EU-average increase. Countries most affected by this option are: Cyprus (-4.13%), Finland (-1.17%), Greece (-1.11%), Lithuania (-1.30%), Poland (-1.25%), Portugal (-1.14%), Slovakia (-1.27%) and Slovenia (-1.26%). CCTB rules concerning the avoidance of double taxation (G) also cause relevant changes in the future value of the tax bases and explain on average -7.58% of the average increase. Countries affected most are Greece (-2.56%), Ireland (-2.43%), Malta (-2.49%), Poland (-2.52%) and the United Kingdom (-2.63%). The option to choose weighted average cost (WAC) valuation for inventory (B) comprises 1.94% of the overall effect. The valuation of pension schemes based on IAS/IFRS (E) only causes -1.29% of the overall decrease and is thus of minor importance.

Table 26: Future value (in € millions) of the tax base for large benchmark case (large company, EU-27) under national tax law and deviation (in %) caused by each particular CCTB option A-H and by a simultaneous application all CCTB options (I)

Country	National GAAP	A	B	C	D	E	F	G	H	I
AT	81.19	3.15	0.35	1.26	0.00	-0.96	0.00	0.00	0.00	5.94
BE	78.55	0.23	0.07	0.10	0.00	0.00	0.00	0.00	0.00	3.03
BG	94.64	5.02	0.24	1.26	0.01	0.00	-1.36	0.00	0.00	13.06
CY	104.98	0.70	0.00	-7.38	-0.46	0.00	-4.13	0.00	0.00	-6.68
CZ	95.97	9.98	0.00	-0.01	0.01	0.00	-1.19	0.00	0.00	9.94
DE	74.05	2.38	0.24	0.90	0.00	-0.71	0.00	0.00	0.00	4.78
DK	91.36	1.42	-0.02	1.16	0.01	0.00	0.00	0.00	0.00	3.77
EE	103.22	1.32	0.00	1.00	0.00	-0.05	0.00	0.00	0.00	2.60
ES	85.05	2.66	0.25	-0.08	-0.08	0.00	0.00	0.00	0.00	4.63
FI	95.06	1.59	-0.02	1.16	0.01	0.00	-1.17	0.00	0.00	9.43
FR	55.43	9.89	0.00	-0.02	0.02	0.00	0.00	0.00	0.00	9.80
GR	95.90	4.48	0.00	0.60	0.01	0.00	-1.11	-2.56	0.00	9.13
HU	41.70	12.47	0.00	-0.13	0.03	0.00	0.00	0.00	0.00	12.29
IE	101.06	0.78	0.00	-0.01	0.01	0.00	0.00	-2.43	0.00	-1.54
IT	94.72	5.19	0.33	-0.66	0.00	0.00	-0.98	0.00	0.00	8.75
LT	93.70	11.36	-0.03	-0.01	0.01	0.00	-1.30	0.00	0.00	11.08
LU	93.42	2.66	0.34	-0.33	-0.09	0.00	0.00	0.00	0.00	3.75
LV	93.84	11.30	0.00	0.00	0.00	0.00	0.00	0.00	0.00	11.30
MT	98.18	1.32	0.00	0.88	-0.08	0.00	-0.98	-2.49	0.00	3.84
NL	95.66	1.58	0.41	0.00	0.00	-0.41	0.00	0.00	0.00	2.24
PL	97.46	5.97	0.33	-0.01	0.01	0.00	-1.25	-2.52	0.00	7.69
PT	94.67	3.08	0.22	0.42	0.01	0.00	-1.14	0.00	0.00	10.56
RO	95.16	2.74	0.25	0.35	0.00	0.00	0.00	0.00	0.00	4.93
SE	93.60	4.81	0.00	-0.09	-0.09	0.00	0.00	0.00	0.00	4.37
SK	96.26	9.84	0.00	-0.01	0.01	0.00	-1.27	0.00	0.00	9.80
SL	89.26	1.87	0.37	1.14	0.00	0.00	-1.26	0.00	0.00	8.57
UK	93.45	2.75	0.00	-0.01	0.01	0.00	0.00	-2.63	0.00	0.24
Ø	89.91	4.47	0.12	0.06	-0.02	-0.08	-0.63	-0.47	0.00	6.20

In contrast to the above CCTB options, common rules for the determination of production costs (C) explain 0.98% of the overall increase and are thus negligible. The same holds true for option (D), which considers the inclusion of R&D-related costs in production costs, as well as for option (H). This option concerning unlimited loss carry forward has no impact on the tax base when evaluated on an isolated basis. It has an impact, however, if it is applied together with other CCTB options (I).

It has to be kept in mind that the changes caused by the isolated application of single CCTB options can not be summed up to receive the cumulative effects of common tax accounting rules on both the future value of the tax base and effective tax burden. This is because of timing effects caused by interdependencies between different CCTB options that can intensify or weaken the impact of changed tax rules on the size of the tax base. For example, changed depreciation rules lead to changed production costs when depreciation is included in the definition of the production costs. If the proposed CCTB options allow higher depreciation in comparison to domestic accounting but are more restrictive concerning the production cost definition the impact of changed depreciation rules on the size of the tax base is weakened in a scenario where both options are considered simultaneously.

Table 27: Effective tax burden (in € millions) for large benchmark case (large company, EU-27) under national tax law and deviation (in %) caused by each particular CCTB option A-H and by a simultaneous application all CCTB options (I)

Country	National GAAP	A	B	C	D	E	F	G	H	I
AT	33.05	1.94	0.22	0.77	0.00	-0.59	0.00	0.00	0.00	3.65
BE	31.43	0.19	0.06	0.08	0.00	0.00	0.00	0.00	0.00	2.58
BG	14.52	4.91	0.24	1.23	0.01	0.00	-1.33	0.00	0.00	10.70
CY	18.35	0.40	0.00	-4.22	-0.27	0.00	-2.36	0.00	0.00	-3.82
CZ	23.38	9.83	0.00	-0.01	0.01	0.00	-1.17	0.00	0.00	7.66
DE	38.79	2.18	0.22	0.82	0.00	-0.65	0.00	0.00	0.00	3.49
DK	29.40	1.24	-0.02	1.01	0.01	0.00	0.00	0.00	0.00	3.28
EE	15.63	0.00	0.00	0.00	0.00	0.00	0.00	0.00	0.00	0.00
ES	37.85	2.58	0.25	-0.07	-0.07	0.00	0.00	0.00	0.00	4.02
FI	26.23	1.50	-0.02	1.09	0.01	0.00	-1.10	0.00	0.00	6.78
FR	55.17	3.80	0.00	-0.01	0.01	0.00	0.00	0.00	0.00	3.77
GR	27.77	4.49	0.00	0.60	0.01	0.00	-1.11	0.00	0.00	9.49
HU	38.09	2.19	0.00	0.04	0.00	0.00	0.00	0.00	0.00	2.23
IE	13.86	0.91	0.00	-0.01	0.01	0.00	0.00	0.00	0.00	0.81
IT	38.77	6.60	0.97	-0.53	0.00	0.00	-1.70	0.00	0.00	8.27
LT	20.44	10.33	-0.02	-0.01	0.01	0.00	-1.13	0.00	0.00	8.50
LU	29.11	2.52	0.36	-0.40	-0.09	0.00	0.00	0.00	0.00	3.55
LV	16.36	13.06	0.00	0.00	0.00	0.00	0.00	0.00	0.00	11.15
MT	33.63	1.54	0.00	0.90	-0.09	0.00	-1.00	-0.35	0.00	6.11
NL	28.94	1.67	0.40	0.00	0.00	-0.40	0.00	0.00	0.00	2.20
PL	19.75	5.80	0.31	-0.01	0.01	0.00	-1.17	0.00	0.00	7.57
PT	26.72	3.00	0.22	0.41	0.01	0.00	-1.12	0.00	0.00	8.11
RO	15.76	6.65	0.25	1.46	0.00	0.00	0.00	0.00	0.00	8.38
SE	27.19	4.64	0.00	-0.08	-0.08	0.00	0.00	0.00	0.00	4.21
SK	19.26	9.34	0.00	-0.01	0.01	0.00	-1.20	0.00	0.00	7.27
SL	28.85	1.45	0.29	0.88	0.00	0.00	-0.97	0.00	0.00	6.63
UK	31.92	2.62	0.00	-0.02	0.01	0.00	0.00	-0.01	0.00	2.51
Ø	27.42	3.90	0.14	0.15	-0.02	-0.06	-0.57	-0.01	0.00	5.15

The above findings are relevant for an EU-average large company. The results could be different for companies belonging to specific sectors with different economic structures. The impact of this sector's specific balance of assets and liabilities as well as its performance will be investigated in the course of the sensitivity analyses for specific sectors below. Another factor of influence is the size of a company, which translates into different pre-tax data such as structure of assets and liabilities and profitability. The impact of the size of a company on the effective tax burden will be analysed in the following.

3.2.2 Sensitivity Analysis on Economic Model Assumptions

The results presented in section 2.1 are valid for an EU-27 average model firm characterised by the specific financial ratios given in Table 15. These results represent the benchmark case. The objective of this section is to determine how changes in economic model assumptions influence the effect of a simultaneous introduction of all CCTB options. Specifically, the effects of changes in the firm's capital intensity, profitability, labour intensity and inventory intensity are analysed. The following procedure is repeated throughout the analysis: First, the effects of changes in economic model assumptions on the future value of the tax base are determined in absolute terms for both national tax accounting rules and the proposed CCTB provisions. Second, the deviation between the future values of the tax base under national GAAP and a CCTB are evaluated for alternative economic model assumptions.

The analysis makes clear that the effects on the future value of the tax base caused by changes in economic model assumptions is the same under both GAAP and a CCTB. Increasing capital intensity and increasing labour intensity always lead to a decreasing future value of the tax base. Furthermore, increasing profitability and increasing inventory intensity for both accounting systems result in an increasing future value of the tax base.

Focusing on the deviation between the future values of the tax base under national GAAP and a CCTB, an increase in capital intensity leads to an increasing deviation. By contrast, increasing profitability, increasing labour intensity as well as increasing inventory intensity all induce a decreasing deviation between the future values of the tax base under national GAAP and a CCTB. In the following section these results are derived in detail.

3.2.2.1 Capital Intensity

To measure the impact of the model firm's capital intensity on the future value of the tax base in the case of a simultaneous introduction of all CCTB options (Option I), the share of tangible assets to total assets in the benchmark case is both positively and negatively adjusted in 6 scenarios by 2.5%, 5% and 7.5%. In return, long term debts are reduced or increased accordingly to leave the sum of all assets unchanged. Sales are kept constant to maintain a stable profitability.

The effects of the described modification in capital intensity on the future value of the tax base under national GAAP and a CCTB are displayed in Table 28. Under both tax accounting regimes, an increase in capital intensity results in a decrease in the future value of the tax base. This effect can be attributed to the high impact of depreciation rules on the absolute level of the future value of the tax base (see section 3.2.1.2).

Table 28: Average future value of the tax base (EU-27 large company) for different levels of capital intensity under national tax law and CCTB Option I in € millions

Regime	Decrease in share of tangible fixed assets by			Benchmark Case[1]	Increase in share of tangible fixed assets by		
	7.50%	5%	2.50%		2.50%	5%	7.50%
National GAAP	94.57	92.99	91.49	**89.91**	88.41	86.92	85.42
CCTB	99.08	97.78	96.55	**95.27**	94.03	92.82	91.59

[1] For the benchmark case see Table 26.

If, compared to the benchmark case, the proportion of tangible assets to total assets is increased, the share of depreciable assets increases as well, thus yielding a higher depreciation in absolute terms. Hence, all other financial ratios being unchanged, annual tax bases and the future value of the tax base decrease with higher capital intensity. Conversely, a decrease in the share of tangible fixed assets is in both cases associated with lower depreciation and thus with an increase in the future value of the tax base.

Turning to the magnitude of these effects, the results displayed in Table 28 reveal that capital intensity adjustments have a greater absolute and relative impact on the future value of the tax base under national GAAP than under a CCTB. This is because national depreciation rules are less restrictive than the proposed CCTB provisions: Additional depreciable assets are depreciated at higher rates, thus reducing the tax base by a larger extent than under CCTB. Since for the benchmark case the future value of the tax base under national GAAP is already lower than the future value of the tax base under a CCTB the deviation between the considered tax accounting regimes rises with capital intensity, as can be seen from the results displayed in Table 29.

Table 29 displays the difference in per cent between the future value of the tax base under national GAAP and the future value of the tax base under a CCTB (Option I). The deviations are given for the benchmark case as well as six variations of tangible assets to fixed assets discussed above. The results show an increasing deviation with greater capital intensity, and decreasing deviation with lower intensity.[23]

The EU average deviation rises from 6.2% to 7.55% in the case of a capital intensity that is 7.5% above the ratio in the benchmark case. Correspondingly, given lower capital intensity than in the benchmark case, there is a smaller deviation in the future value of the tax base between the CCTB and GAAP regimes. If the share of tangible assets is reduced by 7.5%, the introduction of a CCTB would result in an EU-wide increase in the future value of the tax base of 4.93%.

[23] A positive correlation is also revealed between capital intensity and the magnitude of the deviation between the GAAP and CCTB regimes for the effective tax burden. For detailed results see Appendix 7.1, Table 1.

Table 29: Deviation in the future value of the tax base (EU-27 large company) from national GAAP caused by a simultaneous application all CCTB options (I) for different levels of capital intensity

Country	Decrease in share of tangible fixed assets in % by			Bench-mark Case[1]	Increase in share of tangible fixed assets in % by		
	7.50%	5%	2.50%		2.50%	5%	7.50%
AT	4.72	5.12	5.52	**5.94**	6.37	6.81	7.27
BE	2.01	2.34	2.67	**3.03**	3.40	3.79	4.19
BG	11.22	11.83	12.42	**13.06**	13.70	14.35	15.03
CY	-6.44	-6.52	-6.60	**-6.68**	-6.76	-6.84	-6.93
CZ	8.38	8.89	9.40	**9.94**	10.48	11.03	11.60
DE	3.56	3.97	4.36	**4.78**	5.19	5.61	6.05
DK	2.86	3.16	3.46	**3.77**	4.09	4.41	4.75
EE	2.12	2.16	2.35	**2.60**	2.85	3.10	3.36
ES	3.35	3.77	4.18	**4.63**	5.07	5.52	5.98
FI	7.99	8.47	8.93	**9.43**	9.93	10.44	10.97
FR	7.80	8.45	9.09	**9.80**	10.51	11.24	11.92
GR	7.57	8.08	8.58	**9.13**	9.66	10.21	10.78
HU	9.52	10.40	11.30	**12.29**	13.30	14.37	15.53
IE	-2.06	-1.89	-1.72	**-1.54**	-1.36	-1.18	-0.99
IT	7.37	7.83	8.27	**8.75**	9.23	9.71	10.21
LT	9.34	9.91	10.47	**11.08**	11.68	12.29	12.94
LU	2.85	3.15	3.44	**3.75**	4.06	4.37	4.70
LV	9.53	10.11	10.68	**11.30**	11.91	12.54	13.20
MT	3.03	3.30	3.56	**3.84**	4.12	4.40	4.69
NL	1.46	1.72	1.97	**2.24**	2.51	2.78	3.06
PL	6.24	6.72	7.19	**7.69**	8.19	8.70	9.24
PT	9.02	9.53	10.02	**10.56**	11.09	11.63	12.20
RO	3.26	3.67	4.12	**4.93**	5.26	5.63	6.23
SE	3.34	3.68	4.01	**4.37**	4.73	5.09	5.47
SK	8.24	8.75	9.26	**9.80**	10.34	10.89	11.46
SL	7.41	7.79	8.16	**8.57**	8.97	9.38	9.81
UK	-0.49	-0.25	-0.01	**0.24**	0.50	0.76	1.03
Ø	4.93	5.34	5.74	**6.20**	6.63	7.07	7.55

[1] For the benchmark case see Table 26.

These effects are valid for all countries except Cyprus, where national depreciation rules are comparably restrictive. With respect to relative rankings there is no substantial change due to varying capital intensity: the Czech Republic, Finland, Lithuania, Luxembourg, Slovakia and Slovenia change by one position and Estonia by two positions. For all other countries no change in rank is witnessed.

3.2.2.2 Profitability

Apart from capital intensity, profitability is another factor that influences the impact of a CCTB. To capture this impact, the financial ratio return on sales – a major indication of profitability – is modified with respect to the benchmark case by changing sales revenues. In the following scenario increases and decreases in return on sales of 10%, 20% and 30% are considered. With expenses unchanged, a rise in sales revenues results in an increase of taxable profits and periodical liquidity and thus in a higher future value of the tax base. The tax base is lowered if sales revenues fall below that of the benchmark case. These findings are valid for national tax accounting rules and in the case of a CCTB, as can be seen from the results displayed in Table 30.

Table 30: Average future value of the tax base (EU-27 large company) for different levels of profitability under national tax law and CCTB Option I in € millions

Regime	Decrease in return on sales of			Benchmark Case[1]	Increase in return on sales of		
	30%	20%	10%		10%	20%	30%
National							
GAAP	71.23	77.55	83.51	**89.91**	96.58	102.64	109.16
CCTB	77.65	83.65	89.25	**95.27**	101.53	107.23	113.40

[1] For the benchmark case see Table 26.

For the benchmark case and all variations the future value of the tax base is higher under a CCTB than under national GAAP. However, in relative and absolute terms the increase/decrease in the future value of the tax base with varying profitability is slightly less significant under a CCTB.[24] As a result, the deviation between the future value of the tax base under the proposed CCTB and under national GAAP decreases if profitability exceeds the ratio given for the benchmark case, and vice versa.

Table 31 displays the difference in per cent between the future value of the tax base under national GAAP and CCTB (Option I) regimes. The deviations are given for the benchmark case and six variations of profitability. The results show a decreasing/increasing deviation due to an upward/downward variation of profitability.[25]

On average, companies that exceed the profitability of the benchmark case by 30% experience an enlargement of the future value of the tax base due to the simultaneous introduction of all CCTB options (Option I) of 3.98%. For the benchmark case, in contrast, the deviation from national GAAP amounts to 6.20%. Conversely, an average 9.68% increase is induced by a CCTB if profitability is 30% lower than in the benchmark case.

To give an intuitive explanation of the results, two identical investments differing only in their profitability can be considered. The investment yielding a higher profitability has the same level of expenses as the other investment and therefore does not trigger additional allowances. Hence, the additional income of the high profitability investment is in fact taxed at the statutory tax rate and the relative importance of tax accounting rules shrinks.

---

[24] This effect is caused by hidden liabilities arising under the proposed CCTB, which are devalued in period 10.

[25] The measure effective tax burden also reveals a negative correlation between profitability and deviation between national GAAP and CCTB. For detailed results see Appendix 8.1, Table 2.

Table 31: Deviation in the future value of the tax base (EU-27 large company) from national GAAP caused by a simultaneous application all CCTB options (I) for different levels of profitability

Country	Decrease in % in Return on Sales of			Benchmark Case[1]	Increase in % in Return on Sales of		
	30%	20%	10%		10%	20%	30%
AT	9.39	8.00	6.92	**5.94**	5.07	4.40	3.76
BE	5.30	4.39	3.68	**3.03**	2.45	2.00	1.57
BG	18.41	16.31	14.62	**13.06**	11.66	10.52	9.45
CY	-8.10	-7.55	-7.10	**-6.68**	-6.29	-5.97	-5.66
CZ	14.32	12.60	11.22	**9.94**	8.77	7.84	6.95
DE	7.90	6.68	5.70	**4.78**	3.94	3.28	2.62
DK	6.15	5.21	4.47	**3.77**	3.15	2.66	2.18
EE	4.49	3.75	3.16	**2.60**	2.12	2.00	1.89
ES	7.73	6.51	5.54	**4.63**	3.80	3.14	2.51
FI	13.72	12.04	10.68	**9.43**	8.30	7.38	6.51
FR	14.98	12.90	11.43	**9.80**	8.25	7.12	6.09
GR	13.27	11.65	10.33	**9.13**	8.02	7.13	6.29
HU	26.63	19.13	15.23	**12.29**	9.92	8.19	6.77
IE	-0.63	-0.99	-1.27	**-1.54**	-1.79	-1.98	-1.89
IT	12.74	11.19	9.93	**8.75**	7.68	6.81	5.99
LT	15.94	14.02	12.49	**11.08**	9.80	8.77	7.80
LU	6.04	5.13	4.42	**3.75**	3.14	2.66	2.23
LV	16.24	14.29	12.73	**11.30**	10.00	8.95	7.97
MT	5.95	5.13	4.46	**3.84**	3.27	2.81	2.37
NL	4.10	3.36	2.79	**2.24**	1.74	1.35	1.07
PL	11.49	10.00	8.80	**7.69**	6.68	5.86	5.09
PT	15.14	13.34	11.89	**10.56**	9.35	8.37	7.44
RO	5.15	6.57	5.72	**4.93**	4.21	3.63	3.48
SE	6.83	5.86	5.09	**4.37**	3.72	3.20	2.82
SK	14.18	12.46	11.07	**9.80**	8.64	7.70	6.81
SL	12.29	10.82	9.64	**8.57**	7.60	6.83	6.11
UK	1.64	1.09	0.65	**0.24**	-0.13	-0.42	-0.71
Ø	9.68	8.29	7.20	**6.20**	5.30	4.60	3.98

[1] For the benchmark case see Table 26.

In other words, with rising profitability the share of turnover in the tax base increases against the share of all other components in the determination of the tax base. This result is also valid for the tax base broadening effects induced by a CCTB that have been determined in section 3.2.1.2. To sum up, the tax base effects are of a higher relevance in the case of lower profitability.

3.2.2.3 Labour Intensity

The impact of the model firm's labour intensity on the future value of the tax base in the case of a simultaneous introduction of all CCTB options (Option I) is analysed by raising and lowering the ratio costs for personnel to turnover in two steps by 20%. To keep profitability constant, the rise or fall in wages and salaries is counterbalanced by a corresponding reduction or increase in other costs.

The described modification in the ratio of labour costs affects the future value of the tax base under the GAAP and CCTB regimes in the same direction. Under both tax accounting regimes, an increase in the ratio of labour costs results in a relatively small decrease of the future value of the tax base (see Table 32).

Table 32: Average future value of the tax base (EU-27 large company) for different levels of labour intensity under national tax law and CCTB Option I in € millions

Regime	Decrease of labour intensity		Benchmark Case[1]	Increase of labour intensity	
	20.0%	10.0%		10.0%	20.0%
National GAAP	90.46	90.22	**89.91**	89.56	89.20
CCTB	96.06	95.71	**95.27**	94.78	94.29

[1] For the benchmark case see Table 26.

The main reason for this is that an increased ratio of labour costs increases taxes based on labour expenditure (such as payroll taxes, taxes on value added or certain local business taxes). This holds true for Austria, Cyprus, France, Hungary, Italy and Slovenia. As a consequence, if these taxes are deductible as business expenses, they reduce the corporate tax base. If they are not tax deductible they lower the tax base indirectly by decreasing liquidity, which worsens the financial performance of the company. As there are no material differences between national GAAP and CCTB concerning these taxes, the impact on the tax base is the same for both accounting systems.

For the benchmark case and all variations the future value of the tax base is higher under a CCTB than under national GAAP. However, the changes in the future value of the tax base due to varying labour intensity are less important under the CCTB. Table 33 displays the difference in per cent between the future value of the tax base under national GAAP and the future value of the tax base under CCTB Option I. The deviations are given for the benchmark case and six variations of labour intensity. The results show a slightly decreasing/increasing deviation due to an upward/downward variation of labour intensity.[26]

On average, companies that exceed the labour intensity of the benchmark case by 20% experience an increase in the future value of the tax base of 5.95% with the simultaneous introduction of all CCTB options (Option I). For the benchmark case, in contrast, the deviation from national GAAP amounts to 6.20%. Conversely, an average 6.40% increase is induced by a CCTB if labour intensity is 20% lower than in the benchmark case.

The first reason for the observed effects is a technical one. As the future value of the tax base in the benchmark case is higher under a CCTB than national GAAP, the same absolute changes in the future value of the tax base lead to smaller relative changes. This reason holds true for all countries except Cyprus and Ireland where the future value of the tax base is smaller under a national GAAP.

[26] The effective tax burden also reveals a negative correlation between labour intensity and deviation between national GAAP and CCTB. For detailed results see Appendix 8.1, Table 3.

The second reason for the observed effects can be found in the provisions for pension schemes. Increasing wages and salaries also increase the liability of the firm for pension payments. In countries in which provisions for pensions under national GAAP are below the provisions according to CCTB rules (Austria, Germany and the Netherlands) the firm can deduct higher amounts in favour of the pension liability under a CCTB. Higher labour costs therefore lead to a decreasing future value of the tax base which slightly reduces the differences between the two accounting systems.

Table 33: Deviation (in %) in the future value of the tax base (EU-27 large company) from national GAAP caused by a simultaneous application all CCTB options (I) for different levels of labour intensity

Country	Decrease of labour intensity by		Benchmark Case[1]	Increase of labour intensity by	
	20%	10%		10%	20%
AT	6.02	5.99	**5.94**	5.89	5.84
BE	3.23	3.14	**3.03**	2.91	2.80
BG	13.25	13.17	**13.06**	12.95	12.84
CY	-5.62	-6.10	**-6.68**	-7.33	-7.97
CZ	10.14	10.05	**9.94**	9.82	9.70
DE	5.15	4.98	**4.78**	4.55	4.33
DK	3.93	3.86	**3.77**	3.68	3.59
EE	2.73	2.67	**2.60**	2.52	2.44
ES	4.86	4.75	**4.63**	4.49	4.35
FI	9.64	9.54	**9.43**	9.31	9.19
FR	9.62	9.69	**9.80**	9.89	9.99
GR	9.33	9.24	**9.13**	9.00	8.88
HU	12.54	12.42	**12.29**	12.14	11.99
IE	-1.38	-1.46	**-1.54**	-1.64	-1.73
IT	8.95	8.86	**8.75**	8.63	8.51
LT	11.27	11.18	**11.08**	10.96	10.84
LU	3.90	3.83	**3.75**	3.65	3.56
LV	11.49	11.40	**11.30**	11.18	11.07
MT	3.98	3.92	**3.84**	3.75	3.67
NL	2.48	2.37	**2.24**	2.09	1.95
PL	7.90	7.81	**7.69**	7.57	7.44
PT	10.76	10.67	**10.56**	10.44	10.32
RO	5.29	5.13	**4.93**	4.72	4.50
SE	4.52	4.45	**4.37**	4.28	4.20
SK	10.00	9.91	**9.80**	9.68	9.57
SL	8.51	8.54	**8.57**	8.60	8.64
UK	0.41	0.33	**0.24**	0.14	0.04
Ø	6.40	6.31	**6.20**	6.07	5.95

[1] For the benchmark case see Table 26.

3.2.2.4 Inventory Intensity

In order to measure the effects of varying inventory intensity (i.e. the value of inventory stocks to total capital), the production output is raised and lowered while keeping the volume of sales stable. A variation in the units produced affects variable costs but not the fixed cost components of total production costs.

Table 34: Average future value of the tax base (EU-27 large company) for different levels of inventory intensity under national tax law and CCTB Option I in € millions

Regime	Decrease of inventories to capital by		Benchmark Case[1]	Increase of inventories to capital by	
	9.20%	4.60%		4.60%	9.20%
National					
GAAP	87.49	88.70	**89.91**	91.11	92.31
CCTB	92.92	94.10	**95.27**	96.43	97.60

[1] For the benchmark case see Table 26.

Table 35: Deviation (in %) in the future value of the tax base (EU-27 large company) from national GAAP caused by a simultaneous application all CCTB options (I) for different levels of inventory intensity

Country	Decrease of inventories to capital by		Bench-mark Case[1]	Increase of inventories to capital by	
	9.20%	4.60%		4.60%	9.20%
AT	6.05	5.99	**5.94**	5.90	5.86
BE	3.24	3.13	**3.03**	2.94	2.84
BG	13.43	13.24	**13.06**	12.89	12.73
CY	-6.83	-6.75	**-6.68**	-6.61	-6.54
CZ	10.42	10.18	**9.94**	9.71	9.48
DE	4.94	4.86	**4.78**	4.70	4.63
DK	3.89	3.83	**3.77**	3.72	3.67
EE	2.63	2.61	**2.60**	2.58	2.57
ES	4.93	4.78	**4.63**	4.48	4.35
FI	9.75	9.59	**9.43**	9.28	9.13
FR	10.48	10.11	**9.80**	9.47	9.15
GR	9.45	9.28	**9.13**	8.97	8.82
HU	13.44	12.85	**12.29**	11.76	11.26
IE	-1.45	-1.50	**-1.54**	-1.59	-1.63
IT	9.10	8.92	**8.75**	8.59	8.43
LT	11.62	11.34	**11.08**	10.82	10.56
LU	3.96	3.85	**3.75**	3.65	3.56
LV	11.84	11.57	**11.30**	11.04	10.78
MT	3.96	3.90	**3.84**	3.78	3.72
NL	2.36	2.30	**2.24**	2.19	2.14
PL	8.06	7.87	**7.69**	7.52	7.35
PT	10.89	10.72	**10.56**	10.40	10.26
RO	4.88	4.82	**4.93**	5.04	5.14
SE	4.65	4.51	**4.37**	4.24	4.11
SK	10.28	10.04	**9.80**	9.57	9.34
SL	8.73	8.65	**8.57**	8.49	8.42
UK	0.39	0.31	**0.24**	0.17	0.11
Ø	6.48	6.33	**6.20**	6.06	5.93

[1] For the benchmark case see Table 26.

Hence, with increasing output, production costs per unit decline. The same holds true for total production costs of units sold as lower costs per unit are multiplied with a constant number of units sold. Whereas the production costs of units stocked are capitalised the production costs of units sold enter into the calculation of annual profit, thus affecting the tax base.

Lower production costs for units sold are thus associated with an increase in the tax base as sales remain unchanged. This reasoning is valid when calculating the tax base for both national GAAP and the proposed CCTB. Under both regimes the future value of the tax base increases with increasing inventory intensity, as can be seen from Table 34.

However, as the future value of the tax base in the benchmark case is higher under a CCTB the change due to increasing inventory intensity in per cent is lower than under national GAAP. As a result the deviation between the future value of the tax base under national GAAP and under the proposed CCTB decreases with higher inventory intensity.

Table 35 displays the difference in per cent between the future value of the tax base under national GAAP and the future value of the tax base under CCTB (Option I). The deviations are given for the benchmark case and six variations of inventory intensity. The results show a decreasing or increasing deviation due to an upward or downward variation of inventory intensity.[27]

On average the deviation in the future value of the tax base decreases from 6.20% to 5.93% if inventory intensity exceeds the benchmark case by 9.20%. If the ratio considered is lowered by 9.20% compared to the benchmark case, the effect of a CCTB on the future value of the tax base increases to 6.48%. These effects are valid for all countries. The ranking remains unchanged except for Luxembourg and Slovenia.

3.2.3 Sensitivity Analysis on Specific Sectors

The analysis presented in section 3.2.1 was based on an EU-27 average large company (benchmark case). To enlarge the spectrum of analysis, in the following section companies belonging to different sectors are analysed in isolation. The sectors considered are: construction, commerce, energy, manufacturing, service/trade and transport. The data determining the implemented model firms were again mainly taken from the AMADEUS database. The companies representing these sectors are characterised by a specific set of financial ratios displayed in Table 36. Since the model assumptions in some cases do not represent the actual reality faced by individual companies captured by the AMADEUS database, for model firms from different sectors it is unavoidable that their financial characteristics differ slightly from the EU-27 average sector-specific companies shown in Appendix 4.4.

The sector analysis can be understood as an analysis considering a simultaneous variation of the financial ratios of the benchmark case.

[27] The effective tax burden also reveals a negative correlation between inventory intensity and the magnitude of the GAAP/CCTB deviation. For detailed results see Appendix 8.1, Table 4.

Table 36: Financial ratios of sector-specific companies (period 6)

Financial Ratio	Benchmark Case	Commerce	Construction	Energy	Manufacturing	Service/Trade	Transport
Profit/loss for period (€)	**4,124,827**	4,100,087	2,589,102	14,038,918	5,087,719	2,569,769	991,788
Total assets (€)	**126,434,049**	106,491,860	92,198,048	507,777,252	158,673,640	103,393,623	161,494,787
Sales (€)	**159,457,817**	235,488,844	100,372,294	296,484,315	169,088,711	102,688,578	144,381,685
Share of tangible fixed assets (%)	**29.89**	22.37	19.03	42.85	33.66	25.16	40.51
Return on sales (%)	**2.59**	1.74	2.58	4.74	3.01	2.50	0.69
Return on equity (%)	**9.50**	13.75	9.88	6.60	8.07	7.96	1.82
Equity ratio (%)	**34.34**	28.00	28.44	41.87	39.75	31.24	33.79
Return on assets (%)	**6.11**	6.13	4.65	5.50	5.91	4.57	3.44
Inventories to capital (%)	**18.14**	26.66	18.11	5.10	19.20	6.20	4.14
Costs for personnel to turnover (%)	**20.97**	11.76	22.78	11.51	20.93	43.94	28.32

Table 37: Future value of the tax base (large company) under national tax law (in € millions) and deviation (in %) caused by CCTB for different sectors

Country	Benchmark Case[1]		Commerce		Construction		Energy		Manufacturing		Service/Trade		Transport	
	FV	Dev.	FV	Dev.	FV	Dev.	FV	Dev.	FV	Dev.	FV	Dev.	FV	Dev.
AT	81.19	5.94	78.68	3.30	49.89	4.73	217.24	11.40	110.30	7.23	34.84	9.52	8.65	110.25
BE	78.55	3.03	78.91	0.35	49.95	1.46	145.77	13.52	100.05	4.94	38.37	6.61	2.17	182.50
BG	94.64	13.06	91.34	9.30	58.45	11.51	245.46	19.04	124.77	14.29	52.09	15.50	25.13	81.79
CY	104.98	-6.68	97.97	-5.35	64.36	-7.51	283.00	-3.52	140.95	-6.24	55.84	-13.31	39.48	-22.38
CZ	95.97	9.94	92.53	6.46	59.53	7.99	246.62	16.77	126.77	10.93	51.69	14.77	26.15	72.11
DE	74.05	4.78	71.32	2.43	45.49	3.16	182.72	13.00	96.46	6.69	40.13	6.48	16.31	61.77
DK	91.36	3.77	87.04	2.37	57.54	2.46	217.06	9.27	120.71	5.03	48.38	5.98	18.79	48.98
EE	103.22	2.60	96.73	2.34	63.72	2.62	270.78	4.62	137.00	3.59	57.47	3.40	34.31	23.06
ES	85.05	4.63	81.45	1.89	52.69	2.87	218.86	12.02	112.52	6.39	45.76	7.92	20.90	62.68
FI	95.06	9.43	90.75	7.23	59.13	7.75	239.42	15.63	125.47	10.41	51.43	13.07	27.07	56.64
FR	55.43	9.80	37.13	5.55	34.10	7.67	146.62	18.81	81.80	9.83	19.77	22.18	-7.18	-25.99
GR	95.90	9.13	92.22	5.99	59.47	7.33	246.85	15.13	126.69	10.13	52.94	11.12	30.96	43.71
HU	41.70	12.29	5.15	31.87	27.23	8.39	164.98	10.90	69.14	10.01	20.63	22.39	-10.84	8.34
IE	101.06	-1.54	95.14	-2.00	62.91	-2.50	259.43	1.79	133.95	-0.49	54.65	-0.22	33.06	2.01
IT	94.72	8.75	90.51	6.21	58.58	7.29	245.44	13.81	125.29	9.39	50.93	13.20	27.05	59.78
LT	93.70	11.08	90.72	7.43	59.17	8.25	218.20	23.86	123.40	12.20	49.18	17.62	25.32	60.20
LU	93.42	3.75	89.25	1.86	58.03	2.61	235.82	9.46	123.52	5.03	50.21	6.03	23.31	41.38
LV	93.84	11.30	91.37	7.04	59.00	9.08	225.82	19.34	123.32	12.62	49.99	15.94	25.07	60.45
MT	98.18	3.84	93.04	2.93	60.62	2.74	255.67	8.23	130.04	4.15	54.05	5.12	32.07	24.22
NL	95.66	2.24	90.70	1.01	59.22	1.17	246.08	7.75	126.55	3.63	51.96	3.76	25.88	34.39
PL	97.46	7.69	93.70	4.75	60.87	5.69	238.86	16.41	128.54	8.69	52.83	10.93	25.97	63.40
PT	94.67	10.56	90.75	7.76	58.36	9.41	248.08	14.46	124.94	11.65	52.07	12.88	26.38	67.54
RO	95.16	4.93	90.90	2.98	61.71	-0.76	242.53	12.57	125.33	7.30	51.50	7.56	24.08	58.14
SE	93.60	4.37	89.81	1.92	58.15	3.09	236.46	11.08	123.74	5.82	50.27	6.90	23.98	42.24
SK	96.26	9.80	92.69	6.52	60.03	7.56	240.34	18.42	127.02	10.84	51.49	15.03	25.25	74.28
SL	89.26	8.57	85.76	6.89	54.47	7.74	246.51	11.28	119.97	8.95	43.11	12.81	18.71	72.12
UK	93.45	0.24	89.38	-1.39	59.27	-1.33	211.94	8.06	123.26	1.54	49.57	1.66	19.67	32.84
Ø	89.91	6.20	84.26	4.73	56.00	4.46	228.76	12.34	119.69	7.21	47.45	9.44	21.77	51.72

Therefore, the results of the sensitivity analysis of single economic model assumptions in section 3.2.3 can be used to explain the future values of the tax base induced by the sector-specific model firms. In this context it has to be kept in mind that a simultaneous variation of the financial ratios implies an interaction of the different effects identified within the sensitivity analysis of economic model assumptions. Table 37 displays for the considered sector-specific companies and the benchmark case the future value of the tax base under national GAAP as well as the deviation caused by the introduction of a CCTB Option I.

Commerce

Table 36 displays slightly lower profits for the average company representing the commerce sector than for the benchmark case. As a result, the future value of the tax base – while of a comparable level – is lower for the average commerce company (see Table 37).

In all countries except Cyprus and Ireland the introduction of a CCTB results in an increase in the future value of the tax base. On average the increase amounts to 4.73%, compared to 6.20% in the benchmark case. For this reason, the impact of a CCTB on the model commerce-sector company is lower than in the benchmark case. However, while both company types do not vary much in size, they differ in their specific financial ratios displayed in Table 36. Capital intensity of the average commerce company amounts to 22.37%, thus falling below the capital intensity of the benchmark case. It has been shown in section 3.2.2.1 that a low capital intensity correlates with a smaller impact on the future value of the tax base with the introduction of a CCTB. Likewise, according to the sensitivity analysis in section 3.2.2.4, high inventory intensity also correlates with a smaller impact on the future value of the tax base when a CCTB is introduced. At 26.66%, inventory intensity for the average commerce company exceeds the respective ratio of the benchmark case (18.14%).

It has to be kept in mind that the financial ratios are not varied in isolation. Therefore, the effects induced by the specific profitability and labour intensity of the commerce sector have to be accounted for. At 1.74% the profitability of the average commerce company is below the benchmark case. The sensitivity analysis on profitability in section 3.2.2.2 revealed a negative correlation between profitability and the impact of the introduction of a CCTB on the future value of the tax base. Hence, the low profitability of the average commerce company potentially raises the deviation in the future value of the tax base between the GAAP and CCTB regimes. The same reasoning holds true for labour intensity, since a negative correlation between labour intensity and the impact of the introduction of a CCTB on the future value of the tax base has been derived in section 3.2.2.4. However, the potential increase of the future value of the tax base in the event of a CCTB due to lower profitability and lower labour intensity is overshadowed by the opposite effect induced by low capital and high inventory intensity.

To sum up, the specific capital intensity and inventory intensity of an average commerce company imply a smaller increase in the future value of the tax base in the event of a CCTB. This effect is only partially cancelled out by the opposite effects induced by sector-specific profitability and labour intensity.[28]

Construction

As indicated in Table 36, the model firm representing the construction sector shows lower annual profits than the benchmark case. Consequently, the future value of the tax base is below that of the benchmark case when national GAAP is applied (Table 37). The introduction of the proposed CCTB results in an increase in the future value of the tax base in all countries except for Cyprus, Ireland and Romania. With an average increase of 4.46% the tax base broadening effect for an average company in the construction sector is smaller than for the benchmark case model firm. Again, the specific setting of financial ratios is responsible for the observed result. With respect to profitability and inventory intensity the comparison of financial ratios displayed in Table 36 reveals a high similarity between the benchmark case and the average company representing the commerce sector. Profitability amounts to 2.58% (against 2.59% in the benchmark case) and inventory intensity amounts to 18.11% (against 18.14% in the benchmark case). These financial ratios therefore cannot explain the weaker impact of the proposed CCTB on the construction sector.

However, the average company in the construction sector and the benchmark case differ notably in terms of capital intensity and also slightly in term of labour intensity. With regard to capital intensity the financial ratio is 19.03%, and, therefore, about ten percentage points below the respective ratio of the benchmark case. The positive correlation between capital intensity and the impact of the proposed CCTB on the future value of the tax base that has been identified in section 3.2.2.1 implies a decreasing deviation between the future values of the tax base under national GAAP and a CCTB for capital intensity below the benchmark case. This finding is in line with the results displayed in Table 37. Moreover, it has been shown within the sensitivity analysis that a labour intensity above the respective ratio of the benchmark case is in isolation associated with a higher increase of the future value of the tax base in the event of a CCTB. Yet, compared to the impact of capital intensity, the impact of labour intensity is only of minor importance.

With profitability and inventory intensity stable and labour intensity of minor importance, the lower impact of the proposed CCTB on the future value of the tax base compared to the benchmark case can primarily be attributed to the low capital intensity of the construction sector.[29]

Energy

Viewing the financial ratios displayed in Table 36, the energy sector clearly stands out from the other sectors considered. The average company from the energy sector is characterised by particularly high profits, total assets and sales. Consequently, the level of the future value of the tax base under national GAAP is

[28] The results for the effective tax burden are displayed in Appendix 9, Table 1 and confirm the conclusions for the commerce sector.

[29] The results for the effective tax burden are displayed in Appendix 9, Table 1 and confirm the conclusions for the construction sector.

much higher for the average energy firm than for the benchmark case (Table 37). The harmonisation of tax accounting provisions according to the proposed CCTB results in an average increase in the future value of the tax base of 12.34%. A lower future value of the tax base is only witnessed for Cyprus. Taking into account that the future value of the tax base under national GAAP already is at a high level, the strong relative increase is associated with a particular high absolute increase.

First of all, this result can be traced back to the high capital intensity of the average energy sector company, which, at 42.85%, is much higher than the benchmark case (29.89%). Due to this considerable difference in capital intensity special importance should be attached to the positive correlation between capital intensity and the increase in the future value of the tax base caused by the strong impact of depreciation rules.

To some extent the effect is even strengthened by the average energy company's low inventory intensity (5.10% versus 18.14% in the benchmark case) and low labour intensity (11.51% versus 20.97% in the benchmark case). Low values here are associated with a higher CCTB impact, as shown in sections 3.2.2.3 and 3.2.2.4. However, high capital intensity remains the main driver of the significant increase in the deviation between future values of the tax base under the national GAAP and CCTB regimes.

The described effect is partially counteracted by the average energy company's high profitability (4.74% versus 2.59% in the benchmark case). In isolation, a higher profitability results in a lower increase in the future value of the tax base in with the introduction of a CCTB. However, for the average energy-sector company this impact is dominated by the countervailing effect (i.e. capital intensity) described above.

To sum up, when compared to the benchmark case, the high capital intensity of the energy sector results in a higher future value of the tax base with the introduction of a CCTB. This effect is counteracted to a certain extent by the comparably high profitability of the energy sector.[30]

Manufacturing

Compared to the benchmark case, the average company from the manufacturing sector has higher annual profits (see Table 36). Therefore, the future value of the tax base is higher when national GAAP is applied (see Table 37).

In all countries except Cyprus and Ireland the introduction of a CCTB results in a substantial increase in the future value of the tax base. On average, the future value of the tax base increases by 7.21% in the event of a CCTB. Again, this result can be attributed to the interaction of the financial ratios displayed in Table 36. In particular, the capital intensity of the model company from the manufacturing sector (33.66%) exceeds that of the benchmark company (29.89%) by around 4 percentage points. Hence, the positive correlation between capital intensity and a higher CCTB impact explains to a great extent the deviation between the future

[30] The results for the effective tax burden are displayed Appendix 9, Table 1 and confirm the conclusions for the energy sector.

value of the tax base under the GAAP and CCTB regimes. The described positive impact is counterbalanced by slightly higher profitability (3.01% versus 2.59% in the benchmark case), as higher profitability weakens the impact of a CCTB on the future value of the tax base (see 3.2.2.2).

The inventory intensity of the average manufacturing company is slightly higher than that of the benchmark company (19.20% versus 18.14% in the benchmark case). Increased inventory intensity tends to lower the impact of a CCTB on the future value of the tax base. However, the effect resulting from a change in inventory intensity is small and the difference in inventory intensity between the manufacturing and benchmark companies is small as well. Labour intensity in the manufacturing sector and for the benchmark case is almost the same (20.93% versus 20.97% in the benchmark case). Thus, there is no considerable impact on the increase in the future value of tax base stemming from labour intensity.

To sum up, in the case of the manufacturing sector, the impact of higher capital intensity on the deviation between future value of the tax base under the national GAAP and CCTB regimes is of major importance. The effects induced by higher profitability and higher inventory intensity counterbalance the effect of higher capital intensity to a certain extent.[31]

Service/Trade

The financial ratios displayed in Table 36 indicate that the average company representing the service sector has lower profits than the benchmark company. Consequently, the future value of the tax base under national GAAP as displayed in Table 37 is considerably lower than in the benchmark case.

With a CCTB, all countries except for Cyprus and Ireland experience an increase in the future value of the tax base. On average, the future value of the tax base increases by 9.44%.

Considering the specific constellation of financial ratios displayed in Table 36, the observed effect can partially be explained by lower profitability and lower inventory intensity that are, in isolation, both associated with a higher CCTB impact on the future value of the tax base. However, the effect of lower profitability can be deemed relatively small as the financial ratio for the service sector (2.50%) falls only slightly below that of the benchmark case (2.59%). Inventory intensity, in contrast, is considerably lower in the service sector (6.20% versus 18.14% in the benchmark case), thus explaining, in isolation, an increase in the future value of the tax base in the event of a CCTB. This reasoning is in line with the findings in section 3.2.2.4.

However, the described effect is partially counteracted by an effect induced by lower capital intensity and higher labour intensity compared to the benchmark case. The capital intensity of the service sector is 25.16%, compared to 29.89% in the benchmark case (see Table 36). Due to the positive correlation between capital intensity and the impact of the proposed CCTB on the future value of the tax base that exists in isolation (section 3.2.2.1), lower capital intensity implies a smaller

[31] The results for the effective tax burden are displayed in Appendix 9, Table 1 and confirm the conclusions for the manufacturing sector.

difference between the considered future values of the tax base. Moreover, it is striking that labour intensity in the service sector is almost twice as high as that of the benchmark case. In isolation, a higher labour intensity is associated with a lower impact of changes in tax accounting regulations on the future value of the tax base. This effect, however, should not be overestimated since labour intensity is of minor importance for the absolute level of the future value of the tax base (section 3.2.2.3).

To sum up, the effect derived from lower profitability and especially from lower inventory intensity in the service sector is not dominated by the opposite effect induced by lower capital intensity and higher labour intensity. Moreover, since the future value of the tax base under national GAAP is very low, the absolute change due to the specific setting of financial ratios translates to a comparatively higher relative effect.[32]

Transport

Compared to the benchmark case, the transport sector has considerably lower annual profits (see Table 36). Hence, a lower future tax base value results when national GAAP is applied (see Table 37). In France and Hungary, the future value of the tax base is even reduced when compared to the benchmark case. This can be attributed to the impact of non-profit taxes that are deductible from the tax base.

In all countries except Cyprus the introduction of a CCTB results in a substantial increase in the future value of the tax base. On average, the future value of the tax base increases by 51.72% in the event of a CCTB. This result can mainly be attributed to the comparably high capital intensity of the company model representing the transport sector. At 40.51%, capital intensity in this sector exceeds that of the benchmark case (29.89%) by almost 11 percentage points. Hence the positive correlation between capital intensity and impact of the CCTB explains for a large part the high deviation between the future value of the tax base under the national GAAP and CCTB regimes. The described positive impact is strengthened by the low profitability (0.69% versus 2.59% in the benchmark case) and low inventory intensity (4.14% versus 18.14% in the benchmark case) of the average transport company, as both of these values are correlated with an increase in the deviation between the future value of the tax base under national GAAP and CCTB regimes (section 3.2.2.2 and 3.2.2.4).

Labour intensity (28.32%) for the average transport company exceeds that of the benchmark case (20.97%). Taking into account that section 3.2.2.3 revealed a negative correlation of labour intensity and the impact of a CCTB, the given specification of the ratio indicates a decrease of the deviation between the future value of the tax base under the national GAAP and CCTB regimes. However, it has been shown within the sensitivity analysis that the impact of labour intensity on the deviation between the future value of the tax base under national GAAP and a CCTB is of minor importance. Therefore, this effect is dominated by the opposite effects described above when the simultaneous variation of countervailing financial factors takes place.

[32] The results for the effective tax burden are displayed in Appendix 9, Table 1 and confirm the conclusions for the service/trade sector.

To sum up, for the average transport company the introduction of a CCTB has a higher impact on the future value of the tax base than in the benchmark case. This can be traced back to higher capital intensity, lower profitability and lower inventory intensity compared to the benchmark case.

Moreover, there is a technical reason for the strong relative change: Since the future value of the tax base under national GAAP is very low, the absolute increase due to the specific constellation of financial ratios translates into a particular high relative change.[33]

Conclusion

The main findings for the sensitivity analyses carried out for sector-specific large model companies can be summarized as follows:

- All sector-specific EU-27 large model companies witness an increase in the future value of the tax base with the introduction of a CCTB.
- There is a considerable variation among sectors in the increases witnessed for the future values of the tax base. The increases vary between 4.46% in the construction sector and 51.72% in the transport sector
- Aside from the commerce and the construction sectors, the average increase in the future value of the tax base exceeds the increase for the benchmark company.
- As was the case for the benchmark company, it turns out that capital intensity and thus the impact of differing depreciation rules in the event of a CCTB is the most relevant factor explaining the increase in the future value of the tax base.

3.2.4 Consideration of EU-15/EU-12 Average Large Corporation

The analysis presented in section 3.2.1 is based on an EU-27 average large company and represents the benchmark case. In the following the analysis is extended with two additional model companies representing EU-15 and EU-12 large companies (see Table 38). As was the case for the EU-27 average company, data are derived from the AMADEUS databases, as described in section 2.5. The companies differ in the structure of their balance sheet and income statement thus yielding different financial ratios. Although the considered EU-12, EU-15 and EU-27 companies are all categorised as large corporations, they differ considerably in size in terms of profits, sales and total assets. Consequently, the following analysis will provide additional information on the impact a CCTB would have on different company sizes.

The EU-15 average large model company only applies to the respective subgroup of countries formerly named the EU-15 member states. Likewise, the EU-12 average large model company only applies to the EU-12 accession countries.

The following analysis comprises three steps and is carried out separately for the EU-15 and EU-12 average large companies. First, the future value of the tax

[33] The results for the effective tax burden are displayed in Appendix 9, Table 1 and confirm the conclusions for the transport sector.

base and the effective tax burden stemming from the current national tax provisions in each member state are considered. Second, the impacts on the size of the future value of the tax base and on the effective tax burden resulting from the isolated introduction of tax accounting rules in the event of a CCTB (Option A-H) are measured and analysed. Finally, in the third step, the simultaneous introduction of all proposed CCTB options is evaluated. A detailed description of the proposed CCTB provisions is given in section 3.1.

To avoid repeating information previously presented in section 3.2.2, the explanation of observed effects will be kept brief, provided the effects correspond to that described for the EU-27 average company.

Table 38: Financial ratios for the benchmark case (EU-27 large company) in comparison to EU-15 and EU-12 large model firms

Financial Ratio	EU-27	EU-15	EU-12
Profit/loss for period (€)	**4,124,827**	5,190,886	1,344,662
Total assets (€)	**126,434,049**	177,384,948	35,042,958
Sales (€)	**159,457,817**	228,539,993	42,527,194
Share of tangible fixed assets (%)	**29.89**	24.44	38.20
Return on sales (%)	**2.59**	2.27	3.16
Return on equity (%)	**10.50**	9.28	9.34
Equity ratio (%)	**34.34**	31.53	41.10
Return on assets (%)	**6.19**	5.61	6.66
Inventories to capital (%)	**18.14**	16.83	18.88
Costs for personnel to turnover (%)	**20.97**	21.03	21.06

3.2.4.1 EU-15 Average Large Corporation

The second column of Table 39 displays the future value of the tax base under national GAAP for the EU-15 average large company. As was the case for EU-27 average large company, there is a remarkable dispersion of the future values of the tax base across member states. The future values of the tax base range from €68.34 million in France to €133.11 million in Ireland. The average future value of the tax base amounts to €115.72 million. Therefore, it exceeds the future value of the tax base of the benchmark case by €25.81 million. The main reason for this effect is the higher profits of the EU-15 model firm (see Table 38).

(1) The first simulation considers an isolated harmonisation of rules governing tax depreciation (Option A).

It has been shown for the EU-27 average large corporation in section 3.2.2 that depreciation rules are highly relevant when determining the size of the tax base. Column A of Table 39 displays the change in the future value of the tax base stemming from the common tax depreciation rules in the case of a CCTB. For all countries the change due to the isolated introduction of the proposed tax depreciation rules is positive, indicating a broadening of the tax base. Depending on the specific national depreciation provisions, the tax base broadening effect is larger in some countries than in others: France, Greece, Italy and Sweden experience the highest increase in the future value of the tax base, whereas the increase is smallest in Belgium and Ireland.

On average, the future value of the tax base increases by 2.57%.[34] In isolation, common depreciation rules correspond to 65.06% (= 2.57/3.95) of the overall EU-average increase in the future value of the tax base, thus revealing depreciation as the option with the most important impact on the future tax base values.

(2) The second simulation analyses the effect of an isolated harmonisation of methods for simplified valuation of inventories on the future value of the tax base (Option B).

Changes in the future value of the tax base resulting from the introduction of the WAC method in the case of a CCTB are displayed in column B of Table 39. Countries applying the LIFO method in their national tax accounting rules experience an increase in the future value of the tax base due to the introduction of the WAC method. A decrease in the future value of the tax base, in contrast, is seen for those countries applying the FIFO method according to their national GAAP. There is no change for countries which already apply the WAC method in their national tax law. Overall, the impact of the WAC method on the future value of the tax base ranges from -0.02% in Denmark and Finland to 0.41% in the Netherlands.

On average, the future value of the tax base increases by 0.16%.[35] In isolation, this corresponds to 4.05% (= 0.16/3.95) of the overall EU-average increase in the future value of the tax base. As was the case for the EU-27 average large corporation, the assessment of inventory only exerts moderate impact on the future value of the tax base.

(3) The third simulation investigates the effect of common rules for the determination of production costs (Option C).

The results of an isolated harmonisation of production costs are displayed in column C of Table 39. The highest increase in the future value of the tax base is witnessed for Austria, at 1.13%. France, Ireland, Italy, Luxembourg, Spain and Sweden show a decrease in the future value of the tax base ranging from -0.01% to -0.58%. In most countries the future value of the tax base only changes to a very small extent, indicating that the current national tax practice is very similar to the proposed CCTB provision. On average, the future value of the tax base increases by 0.27% with the isolated harmonisation of rules determining production costs.[36] This average increase corresponds in isolation to 6.8% (= 0.27/3.95) of the overall EU-average increase in the future value of the tax base in the event of a simultaneous introduction of all CCTB options. To sum up, for the EU-15 countries, the proposed CCTB provisions on the determination of production costs have a moderate impact on the future value of the tax base.

---

[34] Under Option A the effective tax burden increases by 2.12% (Table 40, column A).

[35] Under Option B the effective tax burden increases by 0.19% (Table 40, column B).

[36] Under Option C the effective tax burden increases by 0.23% (Table 40, column C).

(4) The next simulation investigates the effect of common rules for the capitalisation of R&D costs within production costs (Option D).

The results displayed in column D of Table 39 reveal no considerable impact of common rules for the capitalisation of R&D costs on the future value of the tax base. In the majority of countries the future value of the tax base does not change at all or by not more than 0.1%. On average, the future value of the tax base decreases by -0.01%.[37] In isolation, this corresponds to -0.25% (= -0.01/3.95) of the overall EU-average increase in the future value of the tax base in the event of a CCTB. Hence, the conclusion drawn for the EU-27 average large company that the effect of harmonised rules for the capitalisation of R&D is negligible also holds true for the EU-15 company and the countries it represents.

(5) The next simulation deals with the effect of common rules regarding provisions for pensions (Option E).

As can be seen from column E of Table 39 the proposed provisions for pension schemes only affect the future value of the tax base in Austria, Germany and the Netherlands. In all other countries, the national tax accounting rules concerning pension schemes are in line with the proposed CCTB provisions. On average, the results reveal a decrease in the future value of the tax base of -0.16%.[38] This moderate decrease corresponds in isolation to -4.05% (= -0.16/3.95) of the overall EU-average change in the future value of the tax base in the event of a CCTB. For this option the results again confirm the findings for the EU-27 average company.

(6) The effects of provisions for future warranty liabilities are analysed in the following simulation (Option F).

The changes in the future value of the tax base due to the application of the proposed provisions concerning warranty liabilities are displayed in column F of Table 39. This option either does not translate into a change in the future value of the tax base at all or causes a decrease. The decrease ranges from -1.09% in Italy to -1.30% in Finland. Overall, the introduction of the proposed provisions for future warranty liabilities causes on average a decrease in the future value of the tax base of -0.33%.[39] This decrease in isolation corresponds to -8.35% (= -0.33/3.953) of the overall EU-average change in the future value of the tax base in the event of a CCTB.

(7) Another CCTB option is the avoidance of double taxation of dividend income by applying the exemption method for dividend income from major shareholdings (Option G).

Column G of Table 39 displays the deviation in the future value of the tax base due to the application of the exemption method to avoid double taxation of dividend income. A change in the future value of the tax base can only be observed for Greece, Ireland and the United Kingdom since all other former EU-15 countries already apply the exemption method under national GAAP. If the tax credit in the above mentioned countries is replaced by the exemption method this change translates into a decrease in the future value of the tax base.

37 Under Option D the effective tax burden decreases by 0.01% (Table 40, column D).

38 Under Option E the effective tax burden decreases by 0.13% (Table 40, column E).

39 Under Option F the effective tax burden decreases by 0.37% (Table 40, column F).

On average, the decrease in the future value of the tax base caused by the implementation of the exemption method in all EU member states amounts to -0.64%.[40] This corresponds to -16.2% (= -0.64/3.95) of the overall EU-average change in the future value of the tax base in the event of a CCTB. This option thus exerts a considerable impact on the future value of the tax base. The same conclusion has been drawn for the EU-27 average large corporation.

(8) The effects of loss carry forward are analysed in the following simulation (Option H).

The large model firm representing EU-15 corporations is a profitable company and shows no losses from regular activities during the simulation period of 10 years. The isolated application of CCTB Option H for an indefinite loss carry forward itself does therefore not result in changes in the future value of the tax base. This also held true for the EU-27 average large corporation.

(9) The effects of a simultaneous introduction of all CCTB options (Option I)

So far, different regulations concerning the computation of taxable income have been harmonised in isolation. Now, the focus will be on a simultaneous introduction of all proposed CCTB options. The results of this calculation are displayed in column I of Table 39. Except for Ireland and the United Kingdom all countries experience a higher future value of the tax base with the simultaneous introduction of all proposed CCTB options. On average the increase in the future value of the tax base amounts to 3.95%. The highest impact is seen for Finland, France and Portugal. In Ireland and the United Kingdom the simultaneous introduction of all CCTB options results in a decrease in the future value of the tax base. With regard to the United Kingdom, the slightly positive impact witnessed for the EU-27 average corporation turns slightly negative in the case of the EU-15 average corporation. This is due to the fact that the tax base broadening effect of depreciation is lower than for an EU-27 average corporation. At the same time the decrease in the future value of the tax base due to the substitution of tax credit with the exemption method is stronger.

To sum up, the future value of the tax base increases by 3.95% when an EU-15 average large corporation is considered.[41] The increase in the future value of the tax base is lower compared to the benchmark EU-27 case (6.20%). This result strengthens the conclusion drawn from the EU-27 average large corporation that the introduction of a CCTB would increase tax bases according to the measured future values but that this increase would be less pronounced in the former EU-15 countries.

As for the benchmark case, the harmonisation of depreciation rules has by far the strongest impact on the tax base. Relevant changes in the future value of the tax base are also caused by CCTB provisions for future warranty liabilities and the CCTB rules concerning the avoidance of double taxation of dividends. In contrast, the impact of common rules for the determination of production costs as well as

[40] Under Option G the effective tax burden remains unchanged on average (Table 40, column G).

[41] A simultaneous introduction of all CCTB options results in an increase of the effective tax burden by 3.47%.

Table 39: Future value of the tax base (in € millions) for EU-15 large company under national tax law and deviation (in %) caused by each particular CCTB option A-H and by a simultaneous application all CCTB options (I)

Country	National GAAP	A	B	C	D	E	F	G	H	I
AT	105.56	2.84	0.39	1.13	0.00	-1.13	0.00	0.00	0.00	4.44
BE	103.95	0.20	0.07	0.08	0.00	0.00	0.00	0.00	0.00	2.00
DE	98.05	2.10	0.27	0.79	0.00	-0.82	0.00	0.00	0.00	2.99
DK	120.30	1.24	-0.02	1.04	0.01	0.00	0.00	0.00	0.00	2.58
ES	111.38	2.36	0.30	-0.07	-0.07	0.00	0.00	0.00	0.00	3.11
FI	124.94	1.40	-0.02	1.04	0.01	0.00	-1.30	0.00	0.00	8.37
FR	68.34	8.87	0.00	-0.02	0.02	0.00	0.00	0.00	0.00	8.78
GR	127.16	3.89	0.00	0.54	0.01	0.00	-1.22	-3.22	0.00	7.04
IE	133.11	0.16	0.00	-0.01	0.01	0.00	0.00	-3.08	0.00	-2.92
IT	123.92	4.16	0.35	-0.58	0.00	0.00	-1.09	0.00	0.00	7.96
LU	122.56	2.35	0.38	-0.21	-0.08	0.00	0.00	0.00	0.00	2.72
NL	125.31	1.16	0.41	0.00	0.00	-0.48	0.00	0.00	0.00	1.20
PT	124.34	2.72	0.28	0.38	0.01	0.00	-1.28	0.00	0.00	9.46
SE	122.85	3.53	0.00	-0.08	-0.08	0.00	0.00	0.00	0.00	3.14
UK	123.96	1.61	0.00	0.00	0.01	0.00	0.00	-3.30	0.00	-1.54
Ø	115.72	2.57	0.16	0.27	-0.01	-0.16	-0.33	-0.64	0.00	3.95

Table 40: Effective tax burden (in € millions) for EU-15 large company under national tax law and deviation (in %) caused by each particular CCTB option A-H and by a simultaneous application all CCTB options (I)

Country	National GAAP	A	B	C	D	E	F	G	H	I
AT	44.02	1.70	0.23	0.68	0.00	-0.68	0.00	0.00	0.00	2.66
BE	40.76	0.17	0.06	0.07	0.00	0.00	0.00	0.00	0.00	1.73
DE	50.37	1.97	0.25	0.74	0.00	-0.76	0.00	0.00	0.00	2.46
DK	38.07	1.10	-0.02	0.92	0.01	0.00	0.00	0.00	0.00	2.28
ES	49.57	2.29	0.29	-0.07	-0.07	0.00	0.00	0.00	0.00	2.80
FI	34.22	1.32	-0.02	0.98	0.01	0.00	-1.23	0.00	0.00	6.06
FR	74.82	2.78	0.00	-0.01	0.00	0.00	0.00	0.00	0.00	2.76
GR	36.45	3.94	0.00	0.55	0.01	0.00	-1.23	0.00	0.00	8.41
IE	17.88	0.15	0.00	-0.01	0.01	0.00	0.00	0.00	0.00	0.14
IT	51.85	5.38	0.94	-0.45	0.00	0.00	-1.85	0.00	0.00	7.38
LU	37.84	2.24	0.41	-0.25	-0.08	0.00	0.00	0.00	0.00	2.61
NL	37.81	1.14	0.40	0.00	0.00	-0.47	0.00	0.00	0.00	1.18
PT	34.98	2.66	0.27	0.37	0.01	0.00	-1.25	0.00	0.00	7.30
SE	35.53	3.42	0.00	-0.08	-0.07	0.00	0.00	0.00	0.00	3.04
UK	41.27	1.49	0.00	-0.02	0.01	0.00	0.00	-0.01	0.00	1.29
Ø	41.70	2.12	0.19	0.23	-0.01	-0.13	-0.37	0.00	0.00	3.47

the inclusion of R&D-related costs in production expenses are of minor importance for the future value of the tax base in the EU-15 countries.

3.2.4.2 EU-12 Average Large Corporation

The second column of Table 41 displays the future value of the tax base under national GAAP for the EU-12 average large company. As for the previous cases there is a remarkable dispersion in future tax base values across member states. The future value of the tax base ranges from €20.54 million in Hungary to €35.40 million in Cyprus. The average future value of the tax base amounts to €31.57 million. Compared to the benchmark case the average future value of the tax base of the model firm for the EU-12 case is lower by €58.34 million. This is mainly caused by the fact that the EU-12 average large company displays financial ratios which are closer to a small than to a typical large company.

(1) The first simulation considers an isolated harmonisation of rules governing tax depreciation (Option A).

Column A of Table 41 displays the change in the future value of the tax base stemming from the common tax depreciation rules under a CCTB. For all countries the change due to the isolated introduction of the proposed tax depreciation rules is positive, indicating a broadening of the tax base. Depending on the specific national depreciation provisions, the tax base broadening effect is larger in some countries than in others: The Czech Republic, Hungary, Latvia, Lithuania and Slovakia experience the highest increase in the future value of the tax base, whereas the increase is smallest in Cyprus.

On average, the future value of the tax base increases by 6.06%.[42] In isolation, common depreciation rules correspond to 83.01% (= 6.06/7.30) of the overall EU-average increase in the future value of the tax base, thus again revealing depreciation as the option with the most important impact on the future value of the tax base.

(2) The second simulation analyses the effect of an isolated harmonisation of methods for simplified valuation of inventories on the future value of the tax base (Option B).

Changes in the future value of the tax base resulting from the introduction of the WAC method in the case of a CCTB are displayed in column B of Table 41. Countries applying the LIFO method in their national tax accounting rules experience an increase in the future value of the tax base due to the introduction of the WAC method. A decrease in the future value of the tax base, in contrast, is witnessed for those countries applying the FIFO method according to their national GAAP. Overall, the impact of the WAC method on the future value of the tax base ranges from -0.02% in Lithuania to 0.29% in Slovenia.

On average, the future value of the tax base increases by 0.08%.[43] In isolation, this corresponds to 1.10% (= 0.08/7.30) of the overall EU-average increase in the future value of the tax base (Option I). As was the case for the EU-27 average large corporation, inventory rule changes only have a moderate impact on the future value of the tax base.

(3) The third simulation investigates the effect of common rules for the determination of production costs (Option C).

The results of an isolated harmonisation of production costs are displayed in column C of Table 41. The highest increase in the future value of the tax base is seen for Bulgaria, at 0.78%, and the strongest decrease in Cyprus, at -6.19%. In

[42] Under Option A the effective tax burden increases by 5.37% (Table 42, column A).

[43] Under Option B the effective tax burden increases by 0.07% (Table 42, column B).

most countries the future value of the tax base does not change at all or only to a very small extent, indicating that the current national tax practice is similar to the proposed CCTB provision. On average, the future value of the tax base decreases by 0.29% with the isolated harmonisation of rules determining production costs.[44] This average decrease corresponds in isolation to -3.97% (= 0.29/7.30) of the overall EU-average increase in the future value of the tax base in the event of a simultaneous introduction of all CCTB options.

(4) The next simulation investigates the effect of common rules for the capitalisation of R&D costs within production costs (Option D).

The results displayed in column D of Table 41 reveal no considerable impact of common rules for the capitalisation of R&D costs on the future value of the tax base. In the majority of countries the future value of the tax base either does not change at all or changes by not more than 0.03%. On average, the future value of the tax base decreases by 0.03%.[45] In isolation, this corresponds to -0.41% (= -0.03/7.3) of the overall EU-average change in the future value of the tax base in the event of a CCTB. Hence, the conclusion drawn for the EU-27 average large company that the effect of harmonised rules for the capitalisation of R&D is negligible holds true as well.

(5) The next simulation deals with the effect of common rules regarding provisions for pensions (Option E).

As can be seen from column E of Table 41, the proposed provisions for pension schemes only affect the future value of the tax base in Estonia. Estonia experiences a decrease in the future value of the tax base of -0.02%. In all other EU-12 accession countries the national tax accounting rules concerning pension schemes are in line with the proposed CCTB provisions. Therefore, on average, the future value of the tax base remains unchanged in the event of the proposed CCTB option.[46] Hence, for the EU-12 accession countries, common rules regarding provisions for pensions are of no importance with regard to the size of the tax base.

(6) The effects of provisions for future warranty liabilities are analysed in the following simulation (Option F).

The changes in the future value of the tax base due to the application of the proposed provisions concerning warranty liabilities are displayed in column F of Table 41. This option either does not translate in a change in the future value of the tax base at all or causes a decrease. The decrease is strongest in Cyprus (-3.59%). Overall, the introduction of the proposed provisions for future warranty liabilities causes on average a decrease of the tax base of -0.88%.[47] This decrease in isolation corresponds to -12.05% (= -0.88/7.30) of the overall EU-average change in the future value of the tax base in the event of a CCTB. As was the case for the EU-27 average corporation, this option exerts the second largest impact in isolation on the future value of the tax base.

---

[44] Under Option C the effective tax burden decreases by 0.13% (Table 42, column C).

[45] Under Option D the effective tax burden decreases by 0.02% (Table 42, column D).

[46] Under Option E the effective tax burden does not change (Table 42, column E).

[47] Under Option F the effective tax burden decreases by 0.83% (Table 42, column F).

(7) Another CCTB option is the avoidance of double taxation of dividend income by applying the exemption method for dividend income from major shareholdings (Option G).

Column G of Table 41 displays the deviation in the future value of the tax base due to the application of the exemption method to avoid double taxation of dividend income. A change of the future value of the tax base can only be determined for Malta and Poland since all other EU-12 countries already apply the exemption method under national GAAP. On average the decrease in the future value of the tax base caused by the implementation of the exemption method in all EU-12 member states amounts to -0.19%.[48] This corresponds to -2.6% (= -0.19/7.30) of the overall EU-average change in the future value of the tax base in the event of a CCTB.

(8) The effects of loss carry forward are analysed in the following simulation (Option H).

The large model firm representing EU-12 corporations is a profitable company and shows no losses from regular activities during the simulation period of 10 years. The isolated application of CCTB Option H for an indefinite loss carry forward itself does therefore not result in changes in the future value of the tax base. This also held true for the EU-27 average large corporation.

(9) The effects of a simultaneous introduction of all CCTB options (Option I)

The results in the case of a simultaneous introduction of the proposed CCTB options are displayed in column I of Table 41. Except for Cyprus all EU-12 countries experience a higher future value of the tax base due to the simultaneous introduction of all proposed CCTB options. On average, the increase in the future value of the tax base amounts to 7.30%.

Table 41: Future value of the tax base (in € millions) for EU-12 large company under national tax law and deviation (in %) caused by each particular CCTB option A-H and by a simultaneous application all CCTB options (I)

Country	National GAAP	A	B	C	D	E	F	G	H	I
BG	32.21	4.72	0.13	0.78	0.01	0.00	-0.72	0.00	0.00	12.17
CY	35.40	0.74	0.00	-6.19	-0.30	0.00	-3.59	0.00	0.00	-5.47
CZ	32.50	9.85	0.00	0.00	0.01	0.00	-0.78	0.00	0.00	9.83
EE	34.31	1.35	0.00	0.45	0.00	-0.02	0.00	0.00	0.00	2.78
HU	20.54	7.93	0.00	-0.10	0.01	0.00	0.00	0.00	0.00	7.81
LT	31.58	11.31	-0.02	0.00	0.01	0.00	-0.96	0.00	0.00	11.09
LV	31.58	11.36	0.00	0.00	0.00	0.00	-1.06	0.00	0.00	11.36
MT	32.93	3.14	0.00	0.59	-0.06	0.00	-0.76	-1.11	0.00	4.98
PL	32.51	6.56	0.26	0.00	0.01	0.00	-0.99	-1.13	0.00	8.95
RO	31.96	3.70	0.24	0.22	0.00	0.00	0.00	0.00	0.00	6.44
SK	32.50	9.83	0.00	0.00	0.01	0.00	-0.80	0.00	0.00	9.81
SL	30.78	2.22	0.29	0.75	0.00	0.00	-0.92	0.00	0.00	7.86
Ø	31.57	6.06	0.08	-0.29	-0.03	0.00	-0.88	-0.19	0.00	7.30

The highest impact is observed in Bulgaria (12.17%), Latvia (11.36%) and Lithuania (11.09%). This is very similar to the findings for the EU-27 benchmark

[48] Under Option G the effective tax burden decreases by 0.01% (Table 42, column G).

case. The simultaneous introduction of all CCTB options results in a decrease in the future value of the tax base only for Cyprus, as was the case for the EU-27 large corporation.

To sum up, the future value of the tax base increases by 7.30% when the effects of CCTB rule changes are modelled on the EU-12 average large corporation.[49] The increase in the future value of the tax base is 1.10 percentage points above the increase for the benchmark case (6.20%) and 3.35 percentage points above the increase for the EU-15 average large corporation. Hence, the impact of the proposed CCTB is strongest in the EU-12 accession countries. Again, the harmonisation of depreciation rules has by far the strongest impact on the tax base. Relevant changes in the future value of the tax base are also caused by CCTB provisions for future warranty liabilities and the CCTB rules concerning the determination of production expenses. In contrast the impact of common rules for pension schemes as well as the inclusion of R&D-related costs in production expenses are of minor importance for the future value of the tax base in the EU-12 countries.

Table 42: Effective tax burden (in € millions) for EU-12 large company under national tax law and deviation (in %) caused by each particular CCTB option A-H and by a simultaneous application all CCTB options (I)

Country	National GAAP	A	B	C	D	E	F	G	H	I
BG	4.95	4.60	0.13	0.76	0.01	0.00	-2.03	0.00	0.00	9.84
CY	5.79	0.45	0.00	-3.78	-0.18	0.00	-2.19	0.00	0.00	-3.34
CZ	7.93	9.69	0.00	0.00	0.01	0.00	-0.77	0.00	0.00	7.56
EE	4.54	0.00	0.00	0.00	0.00	0.00	0.00	0.00	0.00	0.00
HU	10.48	2.51	0.00	0.07	0.00	0.00	0.00	0.00	0.00	2.57
LT	6.99	10.13	-0.02	0.00	0.01	0.00	-0.83	0.00	0.00	8.40
LV	5.59	13.28	0.00	0.00	0.00	0.00	-0.90	0.00	0.00	11.40
MT	11.44	3.21	0.00	0.63	-0.07	0.00	-0.81	-0.15	0.00	5.97
PL	6.74	6.10	0.24	0.00	0.01	0.00	-0.91	0.00	0.00	7.26
RO	5.59	3.39	0.22	0.20	0.00	0.00	0.00	0.00	0.00	5.23
SK	6.54	9.29	0.00	0.00	0.01	0.00	-0.75	0.00	0.00	7.26
SL	9.52	1.76	0.24	0.64	0.00	0.00	-0.78	0.00	0.00	6.35
Ø	7.18	5.37	0.07	-0.13	-0.02	0.00	-0.83	-0.01	0.00	5.71

[49] A simultaneous introduction of all CCTB options results in an increase of the effective tax burden by 5.71%.

3.3 Analysis of EU-Average Small and Medium-Sized Corporations

3.3.1 Benchmark Case Representing a Small and Medium-Sized Corporation

3.3.1.1 Tax Bases and Tax Burdens Based on Domestic Accounting

In the previous section, alternate tax base regimes were considered with reference to an EU-average large company. In the following section, this analysis is extended to a model small and medium-sized corporation.

Table 43: Comparison of future tax base values; national GAAP (SME, corporate level, 10 periods)

Country	Future Value Tax Base in € Millions	Rank	Deviation from Average in %
HU	1.08	1	-66.5
FR	2.36	2	-26.8
DE	2.68	3	-16.7
AT	2.87	4	-11.0
BE	2.94	5	-8.7
ES	3.07	6	-4.7
SL	3.17	7	-1.5
DK	3.29	8	2.1
LU	3.35	9	4.1
UK	3.36	10	4.3
SE	3.36	11	4.4
LT	3.38	12	5.1
IT	3.39	13	5.2
LV	3.40	14	5.5
GR	3.41	15	6.0
NL	3.41	16	6.0
PT	3.41	17	6.0
FI	3.42	18	6.1
BG	3.43	19	6.5
RO	3.44	20	6.8
CZ	3.45	21	7.2
PL	3.46	22	7.4
MT	3.46	23	7.5
SK	3.46	24	7.5
IE	3.54	25	10.0
EE	3.60	26	11.8
CY	3.74	27	16.3
Ø	3.22		
Standard Deviation	0.51		15.80

Figure 12 and Table 43 present future tax base values under national GAAP at the corporate level for a model firm which has typical characteristics for an average company in the category small and medium-sized company (SME) across all 27 member states and all considered industries (SME benchmark case). Details on this benchmark case are described in section 2. Where appropriate, the analysis makes reference to the analysis for the large corporation in order to avoid unnecessary repetition.

Figure 12: Comparison of the future values of the tax base according to current taxation practice – Deviation from the EU average in % (SME, corporate level, 10 periods)

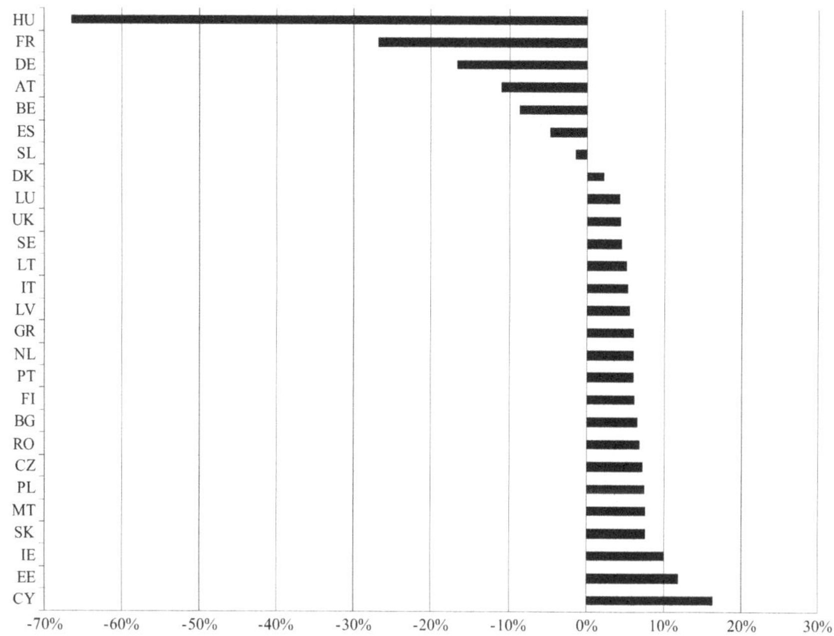

There is a strong dispersion of future tax base values across EU member states. Future tax base values range from €1.08 million in Hungary to €3.74 million in Cyprus over the simulation period of 10 years. The average future value of the tax base is €3.22 million and the standard deviation as a percentage of the average is 15.80%. As was the case with the large model company, the SME model firm shows a comparably low future value of the tax base in the five original member states Austria, Belgium, France, Germany and Spain as well as in Hungary and Estonia. In the case of Hungary this result is caused by generous depreciation rules in combination with relatively high annual payroll tax payments which are deductible for corporate income tax purposes. The deductibility of other taxes causing high annual tax payments also explains the low level of the future value of the tax base in France, Germany, Belgium, Austria and Spain. Estonia represents an exception, as the future value of the tax base is solely determined by the level of dividend distribution as only distributed earnings are subject to corporate income tax.

In contrast to the countries mentioned above, Cyprus, Ireland, Slovakia and Poland show comparatively high future values of the tax bases as low corporate income tax rates lead to moderate cash outflows. A lower cash outflow of tax payments is associated with higher liquidity available for investments in each period. Consequently, an increase in interest receipts in consecutive periods broadens the respective bases and thus the future values of the tax bases. With respect to Malta, restrictive national tax accounting rules are responsible for a relatively high future value of tax base.

There is also a remarkable dispersion of effective tax burdens across member states (see Table 44 and Figure 13). Tax burdens range from €0.49 million in Ireland to €1.70 million in France over the simulation period of 10 years. The average tax burden is €0.96 million and the standard deviation as a percentage of the average is 33.08%.

Table 44: Comparison of effective tax burdens (SME, corporate level, 10 periods)

Country	Tax Burden in € Millions	Rank	Deviation from Average in %
IE	0.49	1	-49.3
BG	0.52	2	-45.5
EE	0.55	3	-42.6
RO	0.56	4	-41.4
LV	0.58	5	-39.5
CY	0.67	6	-30.4
SK	0.69	7	-28.3
PL	0.71	8	-26.7
LT	0.73	9	-24.5
UK	0.78	10	-19.1
CZ	0.84	11	-12.6
FI	0.94	12	-2.6
PT	0.96	13	-0.2
SE	0.97	14	1.1
GR	0.99	15	2.4
NL	1.02	16	6.2
LU	1.03	17	6.8
DK	1.04	18	8.1
SL	1.06	19	9.9
BE	1.13	20	17.4
MT	1.21	21	25.3
AT	1.21	22	25.8
ES	1.30	23	35.0
DE	1.37	24	42.1
IT	1.42	25	47.9
HU	1.52	26	57.5
FR	1.70	27	77.0
Ø	0.96		
Standard Deviation	0.32		33.08

The SME is subject to a comparably low tax burden in those member states which joined the EU recently. The tax burdens in Bulgaria, Cyprus, the Czech Republic, Estonia, Latvia, Lithuania, Poland, Romania and Slovakia are significantly lower than the EU average. Only Hungary, Malta and Slovenia display an effective tax burden above the EU average. Ireland is the only country among the old member states which ranks in a top position.

The large member states France, Germany, Italy and Spain can be classified as countries imposing a relatively high tax burden on corporations. Smaller member states like the Eastern European countries Bulgaria, Estonia, Latvia, Lithuania, Poland, Romania and Slovakia as well as Ireland rank at the top of the considered countries imposing a low tax burden.

The effective tax burdens at the corporate level in countries like the Czech Republic, Slovenia and continental countries like Greece, Luxembourg, the Netherlands, and Portugal as well as in the Scandinavian countries Finland and Sweden are closer to average.

Figure 13: Comparison of effective tax burdens according to current taxation practice – Deviation from the EU average in % (SME, corporate level, 10 periods)

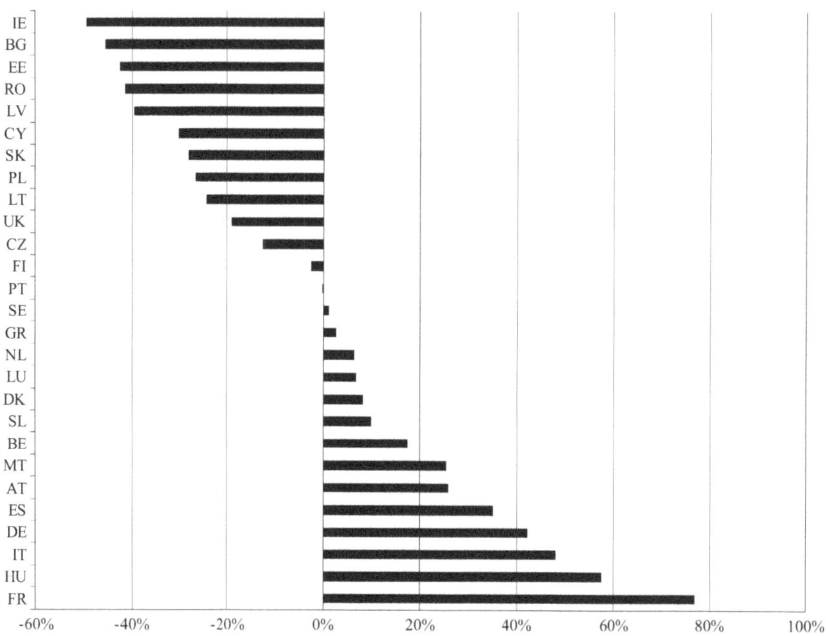

A comparison of Table 43 and Table 44 indicates that countries with a higher relative effective tax burden tend to show a lower relative future value of the tax base. This result is in line with the explanations used to describe the ranking of future tax base values (see section 2.4).

The effective tax burden is influenced by different kinds of taxes (see Table 45). In general, the corporate income tax constitutes the main share of the overall tax burden in all member states, except Hungary. Its share in the overall tax burden ranges from 37% in Hungary to 100% in Malta. Besides corporate income tax, all member states except Malta and Slovenia levy real estate tax. The impact of real estate taxes on the overall tax burden is generally not significant. It is comparatively high in Belgium, Denmark, Ireland, Latvia, Lithuania, and in the United Kingdom, however. In these countries, the share of real estate tax in the overall tax burden amounts to more than 7%.

Additional taxes are levied in Austria, Cyprus, France, Germany, Hungary, Italy, Luxembourg, Spain and Slovenia. Germany, Luxembourg and Italy (*IRAP*) levy a trade tax on income. As real estate tax in Germany and Italy is negligible, the overall tax burden is almost solely determined by profit taxes. A slightly different picture is given for Austria, Cyprus, France and Slovenia. In these countries, the overall tax burden is substantially determined by non-profit taxes. All four countries impose a tax on payroll. Its share in the overall tax burden varies between 16.37% in France and 41.71% in Cyprus. France also levies a trade tax on capital (*taxe professionnelle*), which amounts to 14.50% of the overall tax burden.

Table 45: Impact of particular tax categories on the effective tax burden in % (SME)

Country	Real Estate Tax	Payroll Tax	Trade Tax on Income/ Value Added	Trade Tax on Capital	Net Wealth Tax	Corporate Tax (incl. Surcharges)
AT	4.11	25.47				70.42
BE	8.52					91.48
BG	1.61					98.39
CY	1.82	41.71				56.47
CZ	0.98					99.02
DE	1.01		33.33			65.67
DK	7.92					92.08
EE	5.12					94.88
ES	1.13			12.33		86.54
FI	3.66					96.34
FR	2.47	16.37		14.50		66.66
GR	0.13					99.87
HU	2.71		60.29			37.00
IE	8.56					91.44
IT	1.30		19.77			78.93
LT	9.10					90.90
LU	2.71		20.09		0.84	76.36
LV	10.31					89.69
MT						100.00
NL	1.34					98.66
PL	6.04					93.96
PT	2.18					97.82
RO	5.27					94.73
SE	2.22					97.78
SK	3.55					96.45
SL		17.99				82.01
UK	14.86					85.14

3.3.1.2 Tax Base and Tax Burden in Case of a CCTB

The changes in the future value of the tax base for a SME if all CCTB options (Option I) are applied simultaneously are displayed in Table 46. The result of the calculations for the SME is very similar to those for the large corporation. In all member states, except Cyprus and Ireland, the introduction of a CCTB would increase the tax base (i.e. the future value of the tax base). The increase in the future values of tax base ranges from 0.7% in the United Kingdom to 15.4% in Hungary. On average, the future value of tax base increases by 5.57%. Bulgaria, the Czech Republic, Finland, Greece, Hungary, Italy, Latvia, Lithuania, Malta, Poland, Portugal, Slovakia and Slovenia show an above-average tax base increase.

Table 46: Changes in the future value of the tax base under a CCTB (SME benchmark case)

Country	National GAAP		CCTB Options (all)			
	Future Value Tax Base in € Millions	Rank	Future Value Tax Base in € Millions	Rank	Deviation in %	Rank
AT	2.87	4	2.99	4	4.3	0
BE	2.94	5	2.99	4	1.5	1
BG	3.43	19	3.83	27	11.8	-8
CY	3.74	27	3.49	13	-6.9	14
CZ	3.45	21	3.78	25	9.5	-4
DE	2.68	3	2.76	3	2.9	0
DK	3.29	8	3.36	7	2.4	1
EE	3.60	26	3.67	17	1.8	9
ES	3.07	6	3.15	6	2.6	0
FI	3.42	18	3.73	19	9.2	-1
FR	2.36	2	2.48	2	5.3	0
GR	3.41	15	3.76	23	10.3	-8
HU	1.08	1	1.25	1	15.4	0
IE	3.54	25	3.52	14	-0.8	11
IT	3.39	13	3.69	18	8.8	-5
LT	3.38	12	3.74	20	10.5	-8
LU	3.35	9	3.43	9	2.3	0
LV	3.40	14	3.75	21	10.4	-7
MT	3.46	22	3.65	16	5.4	6
NL	3.41	15	3.46	12	1.3	3
PL	3.46	22	3.77	24	8.8	-2
PT	3.41	15	3.75	21	9.9	-6
RO	3.44	20	3.53	15	2.5	5
SE	3.36	10	3.45	11	2.7	-1
SK	3.46	22	3.79	26	9.5	-4
SL	3.17	7	3.44	10	8.3	-3
UK	3.36	10	3.38	8	0.7	2
Ø	3.22		3.39		5.57	

In six countries (Austria, Germany, France, Hungary, Luxembourg and Spain) these changes do not translate into a change in rank. Belgium, Cyprus, Denmark, Estonia, Ireland, Malta, the Netherlands, Romania and the United Kingdom improve their ranking between one and fourteen positions. The relatively strong impact on the ranking can be attributed to small differences in the absolute level of future values of tax bases (see Table 46). For this same reason, Bulgaria, the Czech Republic, Greece, Italy, Latvia, Lithuania, Poland, Portugal, Sweden, Slovakia and Slovenia worsen their position in the ranking between one and eight positions.

The changes in the effective tax burden in the event of a CCTB are displayed in Table 47. Again it is assumed here that the above outlined rules regarding depreciation, inventory valuation, determination of production costs, provisions for pensions, provisions for future liabilities, exemption of foreign dividend income and loss relief are implemented simultaneously (Option I).

Table 47: Changes in the effective tax burden under a CCTB (SME benchmark case)

Country	National GAAP		CCTB Options (all)			
	Tax Burden in € Millions	Rank	Tax Burden in € Millions	Rank	Deviation in %	Rank
AT	1.21	21	1.24	21	2.6	0
BE	1.13	20	1.16	20	2.8	0
BG	0.52	2	0.57	3	9.4	-1
CY	0.67	6	0.64	5	-3.9	1
CZ	0.84	11	0.90	11	7.1	0
DE	1.37	24	1.40	24	2.5	0
DK	1.04	18	1.06	17	2.2	1
EE	0.55	3	0.55	2	0.0	1
ES	1.30	23	1.33	23	2.8	0
FI	0.94	12	1.00	12	6.6	0
FR	1.70	27	1.75	27	2.6	0
GR	0.99	15	1.08	18	9.2	-3
HU	1.52	26	1.54	26	1.9	0
IE	0.49	1	0.49	1	0.1	0
IT	1.42	25	1.53	25	7.2	0
LT	0.73	9	0.79	9	8.1	0
LU	1.03	17	1.05	16	2.5	1
LV	0.58	5	0.64	5	10.1	0
MT	1.21	21	1.28	22	6.2	-1
NL	1.02	16	1.04	15	1.4	1
PL	0.71	8	0.76	8	7.1	0
PT	0.96	13	1.03	14	7.6	-1
RO	0.56	4	0.60	4	6.7	0
SE	0.97	14	1.00	12	2.8	2
SK	0.69	7	0.74	7	6.8	0
SL	1.06	19	1.12	19	6.2	0
UK	0.78	10	0.79	9	1.8	1
Ø	0.96		1.00		4.45	

The picture is nearly the same as for the large company: in all member states, except Cyprus and Estonia, the introduction of a CCTB would result in a higher effective tax burden. The increase in the effective tax burden ranges from 0.1% in Ireland to 10.1% in Latvia. On average, the effective tax burden increases by 4.45%. Bulgaria, the Czech Republic, Finland, Greece, Italy, Latvia, Lithuania, Malta, Poland, Portugal, Romania, Slovakia and Slovenia all experience an above-average tax burden increase.

However, these changes rarely translate into a change of rank. In SME analysis, 16 countries do not change positions. Cyprus, Denmark, Estonia, Luxembourg, the Netherlands, Sweden and the United Kingdom improve their rank, but only between one and two positions because of the wide distribution in effective tax burdens (see Figure 13). Bulgaria, Greece, Malta and Portugal worsen their position in the ranking, but only between one and three positions.

To sum up, a CCTB leads to higher future tax base values as well as higher effective tax burdens for the model SME, as was the case for the large corporation. While the future value of tax base increases by 5.57% on average, the average effective tax burden increase is 4.45%. Different results occur in countries that apply the tax credit method for dividends (for a detailed explanation see the discussion for the large corporation).

In the next step, the effects of the different elements of the CCTB considered here (i.e. Options A-G) are evaluated in isolation. This means that each simulation is based on the implementation of an individual CCTB option, with existing domestic accounting rules otherwise applied.

(1) The first simulation considers an isolated harmonisation of rules governing tax depreciation (Option A).

Figure 14 displays the changes in the future value of the tax base due to common tax depreciation rules in the event of a CCTB for the SME company.

The picture is very similar to the large company. Tax depreciation in accordance with CCTB Option A leads to a broadening of the tax base and thus to a higher future value of the tax base in all member states. The increase ranges from 0.09% in Belgium to 15.71% in Hungary.

The Czech Republic, Hungary, Latvia, Lithuania and Slovakia show the strongest broadening of the tax base. In contrast, the current tax depreciation rules in Belgium, Cyprus, Denmark, Estonia, Ireland, Malta and the Netherlands are rather restrictive. In these countries, the future value of the tax base would increase only by 1.07% at the maximum if common tax depreciation rules in line with the CCTB proposal were introduced.

Overall, the impact of common depreciation rules is of high relevance when it comes to effects on the future value of the tax base of a SME. The future value of the tax base increases by 4.29% on average. As was the case for the large company, depreciation is the option with the most important impact on the tax base. Changes in tax depreciation rules as considered here in isolation correspond to 77.02% (= 4.29/5.57) of the overall EU-average increase in the future value of the tax base in the event of a CCTB. In this way, CCTB depreciation rules have a larger significance for the model SME than for the average large company (comprising 77.02% versus 72.10% of the overall CCTB change).

When this 4.29% increase is broken down by the asset categories affected by new depreciation rules, the results, which are displayed in Appendix 7, Table 2, illustrate the key impact of common depreciation rules for machinery and equipment on the future value of the tax base. With the isolated application of the proposed CCTB provisions concerning machinery and equipment, the future value of the tax base increases on average by 4.03%. By contrast, the future value of the tax base only increases by 0.23% if common depreciation rules are applied exclusively for buildings and by 0.03% if the proposed CCTB provisions are only applied on intangibles (see Appendix 7, Table 2).

Figure 14: Impact of common rules regarding depreciation on the future value of the tax base in % (SME)

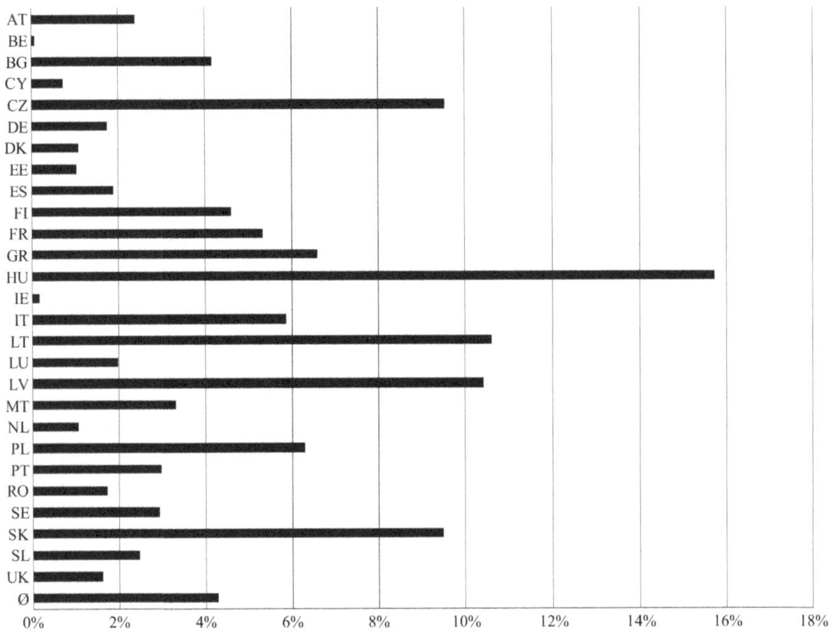

To sum up, the impact of common depreciation provisions for machinery and equipment dominates the increase in the future value of the tax base observed for Option A.

Consequently, changes in the definition of proposed depreciation rules on machinery and equipment considerably influence the future value of the tax base when introducing a CCTB.

To illustrate this influence, a modification of the depreciation rate for pool depreciation on machinery and equipment is considered in Appendix 7, Table 3.[50] It reveals that changes in the depreciation rate for pool depreciation induce large movements in the future value of the tax base. If the depreciation rate for these assets is fixed at 25% instead of 20% (as in the benchmark case), the average increase in the future value of the tax base due to the isolated application of common depreciation rules is considerably lower, at just 1.35%.

These rule changes translate into an overall increase in the future value of the tax base of 1.96% if a simultaneous introduction of all CCTB options takes place. Both effects are significantly smaller than in the benchmark case, where a 20% depreciation rate for pool depreciation is applied.

[50] For detailed results and an interpretation of this modification see Appendix 7, Table 3.

(2) The second simulation analyses the effect of an isolated harmonisation of methods for simplified valuation of inventories on the future value of the tax base (Option B).

The weighted average cost method (WAC) has been selected as an option for the CCTB. Changes in the future value of the tax base resulting from the introduction of the WAC method are displayed in Figure 15.

Compared to the large model company, the effects on the future value of the tax base in the different member states are very similar. The application of the WAC method results in an increasing tax base in most member states since the LIFO method is predominantly applied in national tax law. Austria, Luxembourg, the Netherlands, Poland and Slovenia, for example, show the strongest increase in the future value of the tax base. In the case of countries applying the FIFO method (Denmark, Finland and Lithuania), the overall tax base with WAC is reduced and the future value of the tax base also shrinks accordingly. There is no change for countries which already use the WAC method.

Figure 15: Impact of common rules for the simplified valuation of inventory on the future value of the tax base in % (SME)

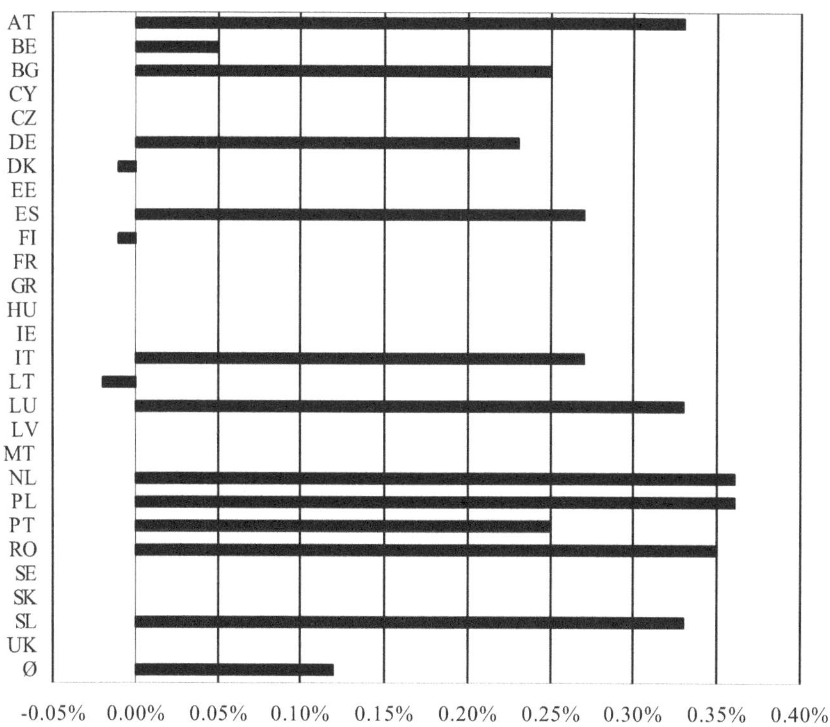

Overall, the impact of the WAC method on the future value of the tax base ranges from -0.02% in Lithuania to 0.36% in Poland. Most countries show an increase in the future value of the tax base of less than 0.3%. The method used for the assessment of inventory has only a moderate impact on the future value of the tax base. The EU-wide average increase is 0.12%. In isolation this corresponds to 2.15% (= 0.12/5.57) of the overall EU-average increase in the future value of the tax base in the event of a CCTB. As the average large company holds fewer goods in inventory versus total assets than the average SME, this rule change stimulates a larger tax base expansion in the SME model case (2.15% compared to 1.94%).

(3) The third simulation investigates the effect of common rules for the determination of production costs (Option C).

The results presented in Figure 16 show that the future value of the tax base changes slightly in most member states if CCTB Option C, which provides a full cost approach for the determination of production costs, is applied.

Figure 16: Impact of common rules regarding the determination of production costs on the future value of the tax base in % (SME)

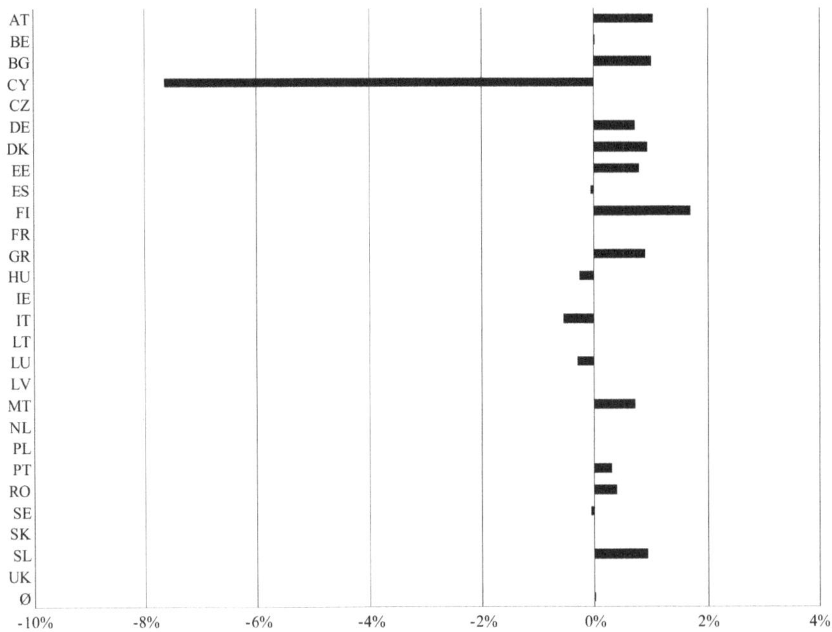

The tax base in Belgium, the Czech Republic, France, Ireland, Latvia, Lithuania, the Netherlands, Poland, Slovakia and the United Kingdom does not change at all or only to a very small extent. This was also the case for the large model company. By contrast, Austria, Bulgaria, Denmark, Estonia, Finland, Germany, Greece, Malta, Romania and Slovenia show significant increases in their future values of the tax bases. The future value of the tax base decreases in Cyprus, Italy, Luxembourg and Hungary. The reasons are similar to those explained for the large company.[51]

[51] See section 3.2.2 for explanation and a detailed analysis.

Altogether, as was the case for the large company, there is a negligible impact of the determination of production costs on the future value of the tax base. The overall EU-average increase in the future value of the tax base amounts to 0.02%. Changes in the determination of production costs as considered here in isolation correspond to 0.36% (= 0.02/5.57) of the overall EU-average increase in the future value of the tax base with the introduction of a CCTB.

(4) The next simulation investigates the effect of common rules for the capitalisation of R&D costs within production costs (Option D).

Option D considers an inclusion of R&D costs into production costs if these costs are related closely to production.

Figure 17: Impact of common rules regarding R&D costs as part of production costs on the future value of the tax base in % (SME)

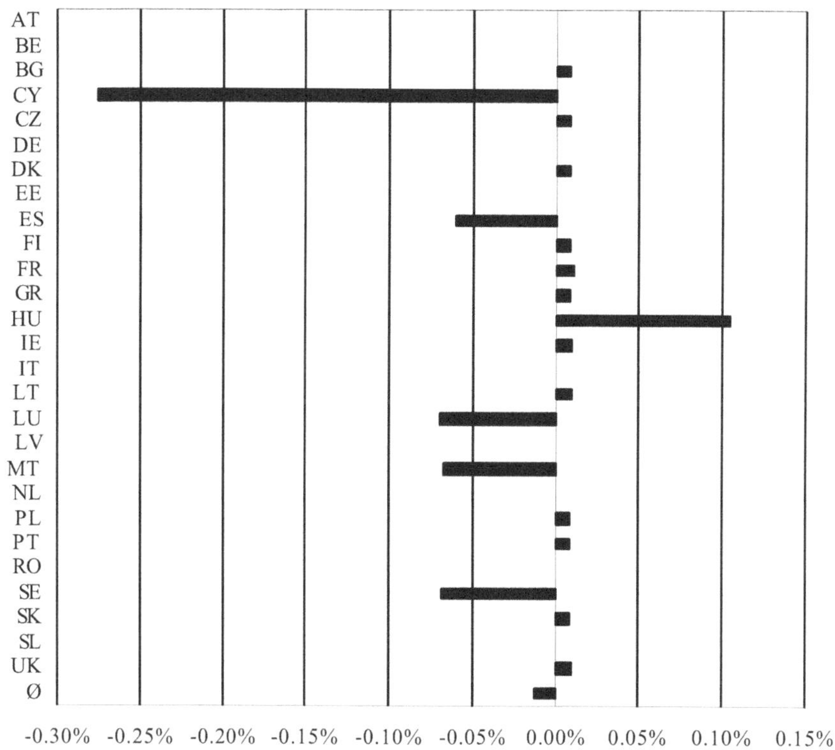

As can be seen from the results in Figure 17, this proposal has no considerable impact on the future value of the tax base. The effects of the application of Option D on the future value of the tax base range between +0.1% in Hungary and -0.28% in Cyprus. These results correspond to the findings for the large company.[52]

[52] See section 3.2.2 for a detailed analysis.

The overall EU-average decrease in the future value of the tax base amounts to -0.01% and in isolation corresponds to -0.18% (= -0.01/5.57) of the overall EU-average change in the future value of the tax base in the event of a CCTB. A similar result was also obtained for the large company (-0.32%). As was the case for the large company, the average effect of common rules to include R&D-related expenditure into the production costs has a negligible effect on the future value of the tax base.

(5) The next simulation deals with the effect of common rules regarding provisions for pensions (Option E).

With respect to accounting for pension liabilities, tax practice in most member states is in accordance with the provisions of CCTB Option E.

Figure 18: Impact of common rules regarding provisions for pensions on the future value of the tax base in % (SME)

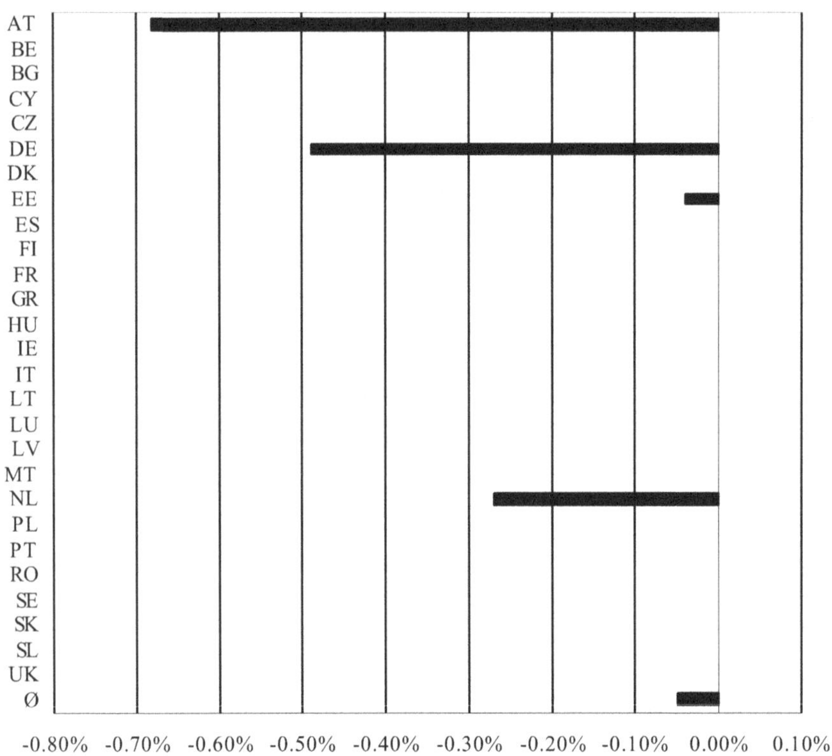

Only the relevant tax provisions in Austria, Estonia, Germany and the Netherlands deviate from Option E, which takes the IFRS as a point of reference. In these four countries, therefore, the introduction of Option E would lead to a reduction in the future value of the tax base (see Figure 18).[53]

[53] See section 3.2.2 for explanation and a detailed analysis.

Overall, the introduction of common rules for the determination of pension liabilities results in an EU-wide average decrease in the future value of the tax base of -0.05%. This very small decrease in isolation corresponds to -0.90% (= -0.05/5.57) of the overall EU-average change in the future value of the tax base in the event of a CCTB. The impact is less significant compared to the large company (-1.29%) since the SME case displays a lower share of costs for personnel of overall costs and thus lower pension obligations.

(6) The effects of provisions for future warranty liabilities are analysed in the following simulation (Option F).

CCTB Option F allows the deduction of contributions to provisions for future warranty liabilities from the tax base. In countries where such contributions are not tax effective according to national tax law, the future value of the tax base would be reduced if this provision were introduced.[54] Figure 19 displays the results.

Figure 19: Impact of common rules regarding provisions for warranty payments on the future value of the tax base in % (SME)

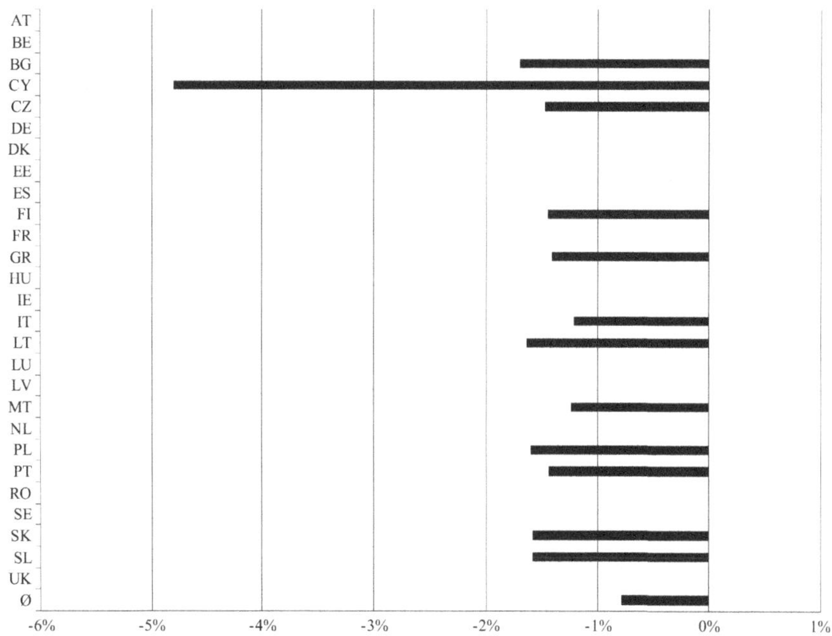

The reduction in the future value of the tax base is highest in Cyprus (-4.80%). As was the case for the large company, Italy (1.21%) shows the lowest reduction among those countries which do not recognise such provisions for tax purposes according to current national law.

[54] See section 3.2.2 for explanation and a detailed analysis.

Overall, the introduction of common accounting rules concerning provisions for future warranty liabilities results in a considerable decrease in the future value of the tax base of -0.78%. This decrease in isolation corresponds to -14.00% (= -0.78/5.57) of the overall EU-average change in the future value of the tax base in the event of a CCTB. Compared to the large company (-10.16%), the provisions are of higher relevance for the SME case mainly because of a higher proportion of accruals for warranties on the balance sheet.

(7) Another CCTB option is the avoidance of double taxation of dividend income by applying the exemption method for dividend income from major shareholdings (Option G).

According to present tax law, Greece, Ireland, Malta, Poland and the United Kingdom grant a limited tax credit for dividends from major shareholdings. CCTB Option G, as considered here, is to exempt dividends from major shareholdings (participation ratio ≥ 10% of shares). Compared to the credit method, exemption of foreign dividends results in a lower periodical tax base because dividends are excluded from taxation.

Figure 20: Impact of common rules regarding exemption of foreign dividend income on the future value of the tax base in % (SME)

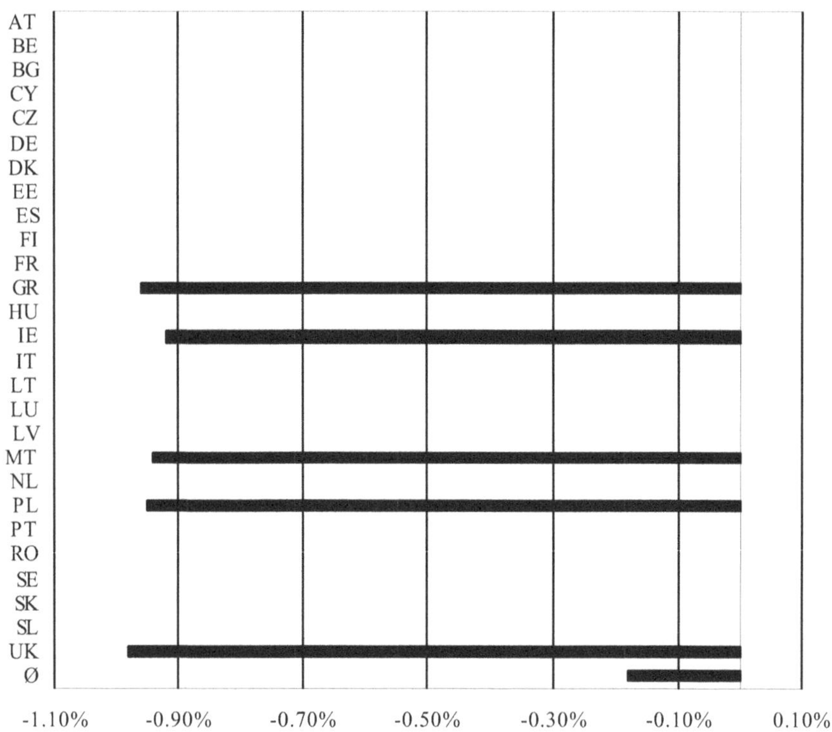

This permanent effect explains the decrease in the future value of the tax base in the countries concerned. CCTB Option G therefore has tax base shrinking effects in Greece, Ireland, Malta, Poland and the United Kingdom, ranging from -0.92% in Ireland to -0.98% in the United Kingdom.

Figure 20 displays the results. Although there is a considerable impact on the tax base in some member states displayed above, the average effect on the future value of the tax base of introducing the exemption method for foreign dividend income is only of minor importance. The overall EU-average decrease in the future value of the tax base is -0.18% and in isolation corresponds to -3.23% (= -0.18/5.57) of the overall EU-average change in the future value of the tax base in the event of a CCTB. Compared to the large company case, this option is less relevant for the SME.

(8) The effects of loss carry forward are analysed in the following simulation (Option H).

Like the large company, the SME model firm considered in the base case scenario is a profitable company and shows no losses from regular activities during the simulation period of 10 years. The isolated application of CCTB Option G for an indefinite loss carry forward itself does therefore not result in changes in the future value of the tax base of the model firm. It has an impact, however, when all CCTB options are applied simultaneously (Option I, see above).

To conclude, the introduction of a CCTB as considered here has a considerable impact on the future value of the tax base and the effective tax burden for the SME benchmark case (see Table 46 and Table 47 for details). The introduction of a CCTB would lead to higher future values of tax base as well as to higher effective tax burdens. While the future value of tax base increases by 5.57%[55] on average, the average effective tax burden increase is 4.45%.

The countries affected most by the simulation of CCTB rules when measured in term of the future value of the tax base and effective tax burden are Bulgaria (11.80%/9.38%), Greece (10.31%/9.20%), Latvia (10.42%/10.06%) and Lithuania (10.48%/8.12%). In the case of Hungary the introduction of a CCTB leads to the highest increase in the future value of the tax base (15.43%), but only to a comparably small increase in the effective tax burden (1.85%). This is mainly caused by the extraordinary importance of additional taxes aside from corporate income tax. Cyprus is the only country which is affected negatively in terms of both the future value of the tax base (-6.91%) and effective tax burden (-3.87%).

In was the case with the large company, the CCTB option which affects the future value of the tax base strongest is depreciation (A). In isolation, depreciation account for 77.02% of the overall EU-average increase in the future value of the tax base. The Countries affected strongest by CCTB depreciation rules are the Czech Republic (9.53%), Hungary (15.71%), Latvia (10.42%), Lithuania (10.60%) and Slovakia (9.48%). The CCTB option provision for future warranty liabilities (F) again exerts the second greatest impact on the future value of the tax base, explaining -14% (-10.16% for the large company) of the overall EU-average increase. The reduction in the future value of the tax base is highest in Cyprus (-4.80%) and lowest in Italy (-1.21%). CCTB rules concerning the avoidance of

[55] This figure is a composite of a 4.23% increase for the EU-15 countries and a 7.36% increase in the EU-12 countries

double taxation (G) are third and explain on average 3.23% (7.58% for the large company) of the average increase. CCTB Option G has negative effects in Greece (-0.96%), Ireland (-0.92%), Malta (-0.94%), Poland (-0.95%) and the United Kingdom (-0.98%). The option to choose weighted average cost (WAC) valuation for inventory (B) comprises 2.15% of the overall effect.

In contrast to the above CCTB options, the common rules for the determination of the production costs (C) explain 0.36% of the overall increase and are negligible. The same holds true for Option D, which considers the inclusion of R&D-related costs in production costs, as well as for Option H. This option concerning unlimited loss carry forward has no impact on the tax base when evaluated in isolation. It has an impact, however, if is applied together with other CCTB options (I).

It has to be kept in mind that the above findings are relevant for an EU-average SME and cannot be generalised. In comparison to the large company, Options A-G influence the future value of the tax base of the SME in the same direction. However, the weights of the factors determining the effective tax burden differ slightly. While Options A and F have a significantly higher impact on the change in the future value of the tax base in the case of a SME, Option G is of negligible importance.

Figure 21: Proportion of EU-27 average overall increase of the future value of the tax base for option A to H

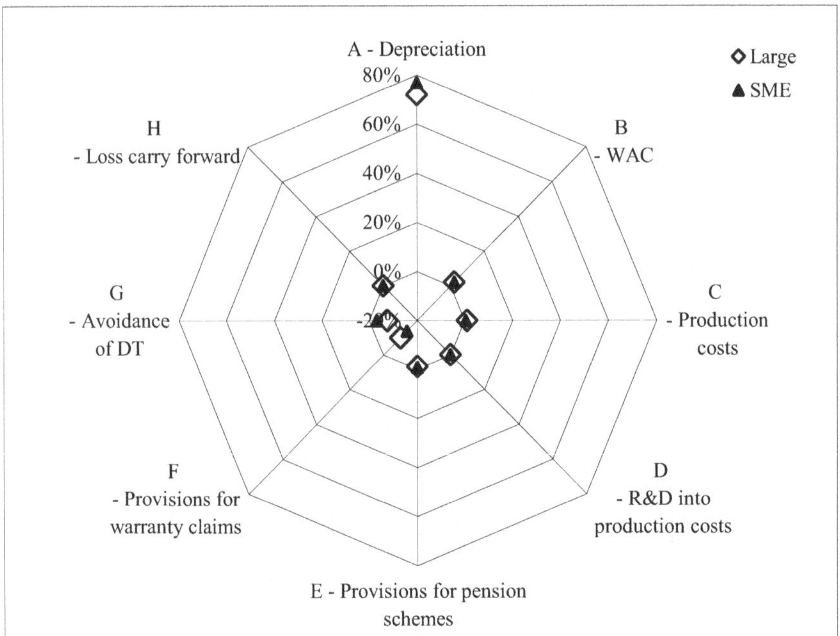

The radar chart in Figure 21 compares the effects derived for the SME with the corresponding effects derived in section 3.2 for the large company. In this way, the radar chart illustrates the impact on the future value of the tax base for the EU-27 large company and the SME that results from an adoption of the single options in isolation. The impact is measured as the proportion of the increase in the tax base resulting from each single option against the increase in the tax base resulting from all options combined. The scale ranges from -20% (centre point) to 80% (outermost web ring-line). The eight rays from the centre point represent the single CCTB options, A to H. The greater the impact of an isolated variation in increasing the tax base, the further the identification mark is located from the centre of the radar chart. If the identification mark is located near the centre, the isolated variation exerts a negative impact on the tax base, i.e. the variation leads to a decrease.

Table 48: Future value of tax base (in € millions) for EU-27 SME (benchmark case) under national tax law and deviation (in %) caused by each particular CCTB option A-H and by a simultaneous application all CCTB options (I)

Country	National GAAP	A	B	C	D	E	F	G	H	I
AT	2.87	2.40	0.33	1.03	0.00	-0.68	0.00	0.00	0.00	4.32
BE	2.94	0.09	0.05	0.01	0.00	0.00	0.00	0.00	0.00	1.52
BG	3.43	4.18	0.25	1.01	0.01	0.00	-1.70	0.00	0.00	11.80
CY	3.74	0.72	0.00	-7.63	-0.28	0.00	-4.80	0.00	0.00	-6.91
CZ	3.45	9.53	0.00	-0.01	0.01	0.00	-1.47	0.00	0.00	9.51
DE	2.68	1.75	0.23	0.71	0.00	-0.49	0.00	0.00	0.00	2.92
DK	3.29	1.07	-0.01	0.94	0.01	0.00	0.00	0.00	0.00	2.36
EE	3.60	1.04	0.00	0.78	0.00	-0.04	0.00	0.00	0.00	1.77
ES	3.07	1.90	0.27	-0.06	-0.06	0.00	0.00	0.00	0.00	2.64
FI	3.42	4.61	-0.01	1.70	0.01	0.00	-1.45	0.00	0.00	9.21
FR	2.36	5.33	0.00	-0.01	0.01	0.00	0.00	0.00	0.00	5.29
GR	3.41	6.58	0.00	0.90	0.01	0.00	-1.41	-0.96	0.00	10.31
HU	1.08	15.71	0.00	-0.27	0.10	0.00	0.00	0.00	0.00	15.43
IE	3.54	0.16	0.00	-0.01	0.01	0.00	0.00	-0.92	0.00	-0.77
IT	3.39	5.86	0.27	-0.54	0.00	0.00	-1.21	0.00	0.00	8.82
LT	3.38	10.60	-0.02	-0.01	0.01	0.00	-1.63	0.00	0.00	10.48
LU	3.35	1.98	0.33	-0.30	-0.07	0.00	0.00	0.00	0.00	2.26
LV	3.40	10.42	0.00	0.00	0.00	0.00	0.00	0.00	0.00	10.42
MT	3.46	3.32	0.00	0.72	-0.07	0.00	-1.23	-0.94	0.00	5.37
NL	3.41	1.06	0.36	0.00	0.00	-0.27	0.00	0.00	0.00	1.32
PL	3.46	6.30	0.36	-0.01	0.01	0.00	-1.60	-0.95	0.00	8.84
PT	3.41	2.98	0.25	0.29	0.01	0.00	-1.44	0.00	0.00	9.92
RO	3.44	1.73	0.35	0.39	0.00	0.00	0.00	0.00	0.00	2.51
SE	3.36	2.94	0.00	-0.07	-0.07	0.00	0.00	0.00	0.00	2.69
SK	3.46	9.48	0.00	-0.01	0.01	0.00	-1.58	0.00	0.00	9.46
SL	3.17	2.47	0.33	0.92	0.00	0.00	-1.58	0.00	0.00	8.25
UK	3.36	1.61	0.00	-0.01	0.01	0.00	0.00	-0.98	0.00	0.67
Ø	3.22	4.29	0.12	0.02	-0.01	-0.05	-0.78	-0.18	0.00	5.57

The influence of the isolated variations is similar for the large company and the SME. In both cases Option A causes the greatest increase in the tax base. Option F and G have a notable influence as well and in isolation lead to a decrease in the tax base. The influence of Option F is stronger for the small and medium-sized company, whereas the large company shows a stronger impact with respect to Option G. The isolated variation of the other options exerts only minor influence and is similar for the large company and the SME.

Table 49: Tax burden (in € millions) for EU-27 SME (benchmark case) under national tax law and deviation (in %) caused by each particular CCTB option A-H and by a simultaneous application all CCTB options (I)

Country	National GAAP	A	B	C	D	E	F	G	H	I
AT	1.21	1.44	0.19	0.63	0.00	-0.36	0.00	0.00	0.00	2.63
BE	1.13	0.85	0.20	0.21	0.00	0.00	0.00	0.00	0.00	2.80
BG	0.52	4.10	0.25	0.99	0.01	0.00	-1.66	0.00	0.00	9.38
CY	0.67	0.39	0.00	-4.27	-0.16	0.00	-2.69	0.00	0.00	-3.87
CZ	0.84	9.40	0.00	-0.01	0.01	0.00	-1.52	0.00	0.00	7.12
DE	1.37	1.70	0.21	0.69	0.00	-0.43	0.00	0.00	0.00	2.48
DK	1.04	1.00	-0.01	0.85	0.01	0.00	0.00	0.00	0.00	2.16
EE	0.55	0.00	0.00	0.00	0.00	0.00	0.00	0.00	0.00	0.00
ES	1.30	2.18	0.28	-0.06	-0.06	0.00	0.00	0.00	0.00	2.77
FI	0.94	4.45	-0.01	1.63	0.01	0.00	-1.44	0.00	0.00	6.60
FR	1.70	2.57	0.00	0.00	0.01	0.00	0.00	0.00	0.00	2.56
GR	0.99	6.91	0.00	0.90	0.01	0.00	-1.41	0.00	0.00	9.20
HU	1.52	1.80	0.00	0.05	0.01	0.00	0.00	0.00	0.00	1.85
IE	0.49	0.16	0.00	-0.01	0.01	0.00	0.00	0.00	0.00	0.14
IT	1.42	6.30	0.70	-0.43	0.00	0.00	-2.17	0.00	0.00	7.18
LT	0.73	9.89	-0.02	-0.01	0.01	0.00	-1.45	0.00	0.00	8.12
LU	1.03	2.02	0.35	-0.36	-0.08	0.00	0.00	0.00	0.00	2.46
LV	0.58	12.10	0.00	0.00	0.00	0.00	0.00	0.00	0.00	10.06
MT	1.21	3.38	0.00	0.75	-0.07	0.00	-1.31	-0.13	0.00	6.21
NL	1.02	1.00	0.35	0.00	0.00	-0.24	0.00	0.00	0.00	1.40
PL	0.71	6.02	0.33	-0.01	0.01	0.00	-1.49	0.00	0.00	7.07
PT	0.96	3.11	0.25	0.29	0.01	0.00	-1.40	0.00	0.00	7.62
RO	0.56	5.92	0.34	0.90	0.00	0.00	0.00	0.00	0.00	6.68
SE	0.97	3.01	0.00	-0.07	-0.07	0.00	0.00	0.00	0.00	2.76
SK	0.69	9.02	0.00	-0.01	0.01	0.00	-1.57	0.00	0.00	6.83
SL	1.06	1.83	0.24	0.71	0.00	0.00	-1.24	0.00	0.00	6.19
UK	0.78	1.91	0.00	-0.01	0.01	0.00	0.00	0.00	0.00	1.80
Ø	0.96	3.79	0.14	0.12	-0.01	-0.04	-0.72	0.00	0.00	4.45

3.3.2 Sensitivity Analysis on Economic Model Assumptions

The results presented in section 3.3.1 are valid for an EU-27 average SME model firm characterised by the specific financial ratios given in Table 15. These results represent the benchmark case. The objective of this section is to determine how changes in economic model assumptions influence the effect of a simultaneous introduction of all CCTB options. To this end, the effects of changes in the firm's capital intensity, profitability, labour intensity and inventory intensity are analysed. The following procedure is repeated throughout the analysis: First, the effects of changes in economic model assumptions on the future value of the tax base are determined in absolute terms for both national tax accounting rules and CCTB provisions. Second, the deviation between the future values of the tax base under national GAAP and a CCTB are evaluated for changing economic model assumptions.

The results show that the effects witnessed for the EU-27 average large company also hold true for the considered EU-27 average SME: changes in economic model assumptions cause the same direction of change in the tax base under both the national GAAP and CCTB regimes. Increasing capital intensity and increasing labour intensity always lead to a decreasing future value of the tax base. Furthermore, increasing profitability and increasing inventory intensity for both accounting systems result in an increasing future value of the tax base.

Focussing on the deviation between the future values of the tax base under national GAAP and a CCTB, increasing capital intensity leads to increasing differences. By contrast, increasing profitability, increasing labour intensity as well as increasing inventory intensity induce a decreasing deviation between the future values of the tax base under national GAAP and a CCTB. In the following section these results are presented in detail.

3.3.2.1 Capital Intensity

To measure the impact of the model firm's capital intensity on the future value of the tax base in the case of a simultaneous introduction of all CCTB options (Option I), the share of tangible assets to total assets is alternatively raised or lowered by 2.5% and 5% with respect to the benchmark case. In addition, long term debts are reduced (or increased) accordingly to leave the sum of all assets unchanged. Sales are kept constant to maintain a stable profitability.

The described modification in capital intensity affects the future value of the tax base under national GAAP and a CCTB as displayed in Table 50.

Table 50: Average future value of the tax base (EU-27 SME) for different levels of capital intensity under national tax law and CCTB Option I in € millions

Regime	Decrease in share of tangible fixed assets by		Benchmark Case[1]	Increase in share of tangible fixed assets by	
	5%	2.50%		2.50%	5%
National					
GAAP	3.31	3.27	**3.22**	3.18	3.13
CCTB	3.47	3.43	**3.39**	3.36	3.32

[1] For the benchmark case see Table 46.

Under both tax accounting regimes, an increase in capital intensity results in a decrease in the future value of the tax base. This effect can be attributed to the high impact of depreciation rules on the absolute level of the future value of the tax base (see section 3.2.1.2). If, compared to the benchmark case, the amount of tangible assets is increased, the share of depreciable assets increases too, thus yielding a higher depreciation in absolute terms. Hence, all other financial ratios being unchanged, annual tax bases and the future value of the tax base decrease with greater capital intensity. Conversely, a decrease in the share of tangible fixed assets is in both cases associated with lower depreciation and consequently with an increase in the future value of the tax base.

Turning to the size of the effects, the results displayed in Table 50 reveal a higher absolute and relative impact of capital intensity on the future value of the tax base under national GAAP than under a CCTB. This result is due to the fact that national depreciation rules are less restrictive than the proposed CCTB provisions: Additional depreciable assets are, therefore, depreciated at higher rates under national GAAP, thus reducing the tax base by a larger extent than under a CCTB.

Table 51: Deviation (in %) in the future value of the tax base (EU-27 SME) from national GAAP caused by a simultaneous application all CCTB options (I) for different levels of capital intensity

Country	Decrease in share of tangible fixed assets by		Benchmark Case[1]	Increase in share of tangible fixed assets by	
	5%	2.50%		2.50%	5%
AT	3.71	4.01	**4.32**	4.64	4.98
BE	1.04	1.27	**1.52**	1.77	2.05
BG	10.87	11.33	**11.80**	12.28	12.80
CY	-6.78	-6.85	**-6.91**	-6.98	-7.05
CZ	8.69	9.09	**9.51**	9.92	10.37
DE	2.29	2.60	**2.92**	3.22	3.54
DK	1.91	2.13	**2.36**	2.59	2.84
EE	1.71	1.74	**1.77**	1.81	1.92
ES	2.01	2.32	**2.64**	2.96	3.31
FI	8.45	8.82	**9.21**	9.60	10.02
FR	4.46	4.87	**5.29**	5.73	6.21
GR	9.43	9.87	**10.31**	10.77	11.26
HU	13.18	14.30	**15.43**	16.38	17.44
IE	-0.76	-0.76	**-0.77**	-0.62	-0.46
IT	8.07	8.44	**8.82**	9.19	9.60
LT	9.57	10.02	**10.48**	10.96	11.47
LU	1.91	2.04	**2.26**	2.49	2.73
LV	9.50	9.96	**10.42**	10.89	11.40
MT	4.90	5.13	**5.37**	5.61	5.87
NL	1.06	1.12	**1.32**	1.52	1.74
PL	8.03	8.43	**8.84**	9.26	9.72
PT	9.12	9.52	**9.92**	10.33	10.78
RO	0.67	0.98	**2.51**	2.82	3.13
SE	2.33	2.43	**2.69**	2.95	3.23
SK	8.63	9.04	**9.46**	9.88	10.34
SL	7.64	7.94	**8.25**	8.57	8.91
UK	0.31	0.45	**0.67**	0.90	1.14
Ø	4.89	5.19	**5.57**	5.91	6.27

[1] For the benchmark case see Table 46.

Since for the benchmark case the future value of the tax base under national GAAP is already lower than the future value of the tax base under a CCTB the deviation between the tax accounting regimes rises with a higher capital intensity, as can be seen from the results displayed in Table 51.[56]

This table shows the difference in per cent between the future value of the tax base under national GAAP and under CCTB Option I. The deviations are given for the benchmark case as well as for the four variations of tangible assets to fixed assets discussed above. The results show an increasing deviation with greater capital intensity, and decreasing deviation with lower intensity.

The EU average deviation rises from 5.57% to 6.27% when capital intensity is 5% above that of the benchmark case. Correspondingly, given lower capital intensity than in the benchmark case, there is a smaller deviation in future tax base values between the GAAP and CCTB regimes. If the share of tangible assets is reduced by 5%, the introduction of a CCTB would result in an EU-wide increase in the future value of the tax base of 4.89%.

These effects are valid for all countries except Cyprus, where national depreciation rules are comparably restrictive. With respect to the ranking there is no substantial change with varying capital intensity: the Czech Republic, Finland, Lithuania, Luxembourg, Slovakia and Slovenia change by one position and Estonia by two positions. For all other countries a variation in capital intensity does not translate in a change in rank.

3.3.2.2 Profitability

Apart from capital intensity, profitability is another factor that influences the impact of a CCTB. To capture this impact, the financial ratio return on sales – a major indication of profitability – is modified with respect to the benchmark case by changing sales revenues. In the following analysis, alternating increases and decreases in return on sales of 10%, 20% and 30% are considered. Expenses being stable, a rise in sales revenues results in an increase of taxable profits and periodical liquidity and thus in a higher future value of the tax base. The tax base is lowered if sales revenues fall below that of the benchmark case. These findings are valid for national tax accounting rules and in the case of a CCTB, as can be seen from the results displayed in Table 52.

Table 52: Average future value of the tax base (EU-27 SME) for different levels of profitability under national tax law and CCTB Option I in € millions

Regime	Decrease in return on sales by			Benchmark Case[1]	Increase in return on sales by		
	30%	20%	10%		10%	20%	30%
National GAAP	2.33	2.63	2.92	**3.22**	3.54	3.83	4.15
CCTB	2.55	2.83	3.11	**3.39**	3.70	3.98	4.28

[1] For the benchmark case see Table 46.

[56] The effective tax burden also reveals a positive correlation between capital intensity and the magnitude of the GAAP/CCTB deviation. For detailed results see Appendix 8.2 Table 1.

For the benchmark case and all variations the future value of the tax base is higher under a CCTB than under national GAAP. However, in relative and absolute terms the increase/decrease in the future value of the tax base with varying profitability is slightly less significant under a CCTB.[57] As a result, the deviation between the future value of the tax base under the proposed CCTB and under national GAAP decreases if profitability exceeds the ratio given for the benchmark case, and vice versa.

Table 53 displays the difference in per cent between the future value of the tax base under the GAAP and CCTB (Option I) regimes. The deviations are given for the benchmark case and six variations of profitability.

Table 53: Deviation (in %) in the future value of the tax base from national GAAP caused by a simultaneous application all CCTB options (I) for different levels of profitability (SME case)

Country	Decrease in Return on Sales by			Benchmark Case[1]	Increase in Return on Sales by		
	30%	20%	10%		10%	20%	30%
AT	8.78	6.95	5.51	**4.32**	3.34	2.62	2.40
BE	4.08	3.02	2.22	**1.52**	0.93	0.50	0.15
BG	19.04	16.10	13.79	**11.80**	10.10	8.74	7.50
CY	-9.02	-8.18	-7.50	**-6.91**	-6.39	-5.96	-5.56
CZ	15.77	13.24	11.23	**9.51**	8.03	6.85	5.77
DE	6.43	5.15	3.99	**2.92**	2.08	1.92	1.77
DK	5.33	4.11	3.17	**2.36**	1.82	1.68	1.56
EE	4.04	3.03	2.23	**1.77**	1.63	1.51	1.40
ES	6.32	4.92	3.70	**2.64**	1.95	1.82	1.69
FI	15.42	12.91	10.91	**9.21**	7.75	6.59	5.53
FR	9.77	7.96	6.54	**5.29**	4.04	3.11	2.28
GR	16.83	14.20	12.10	**10.31**	8.78	7.56	6.43
HU	67.58	37.40	21.91	**15.43**	10.86	7.95	5.87
IE	0.92	0.24	-0.31	**-0.77**	-0.70	-0.65	-0.61
IT	13.94	11.87	10.33	**8.82**	7.40	6.28	5.24
LT	17.36	14.57	12.36	**10.48**	8.89	7.62	6.46
LU	5.11	3.94	3.05	**2.26**	1.84	1.71	1.59
LV	17.21	14.45	12.28	**10.42**	8.82	7.55	6.38
MT	8.76	7.55	6.39	**5.37**	4.49	3.78	3.13
NL	3.76	2.76	2.00	**1.32**	1.04	0.96	0.89
PL	14.87	12.42	10.49	**8.84**	7.43	6.29	5.24
PT	16.37	13.76	11.68	**9.92**	8.42	7.22	6.12
RO	-0.70	-3.04	-3.10	**2.51**	2.46	2.44	2.46
SE	5.69	4.46	3.51	**2.69**	2.29	2.14	1.99
SK	15.75	13.21	11.19	**9.46**	7.98	6.79	5.70
SL	13.68	11.47	9.72	**8.25**	7.02	6.04	5.16
UK	3.01	2.06	1.33	**0.67**	0.34	0.29	0.27
Ø	11.34	8.54	6.69	**5.57**	4.54	3.83	3.21

[1] For the benchmark case see Table 46.

[57] This effect is caused by hidden liabilities arising under the proposed CCTB, which are devaluated in period 10.

As the results show, the deviation grows or shrinks in direct relation to increasing or decreasing profitability.[58] On average, companies that exceed the profitability of the benchmark case by 30% experience an enlargement of the future value of the tax base due to the simultaneous introduction of all CCTB options (Option I) of 3.21%. For the benchmark case, in contrast, the deviation from national GAAP amounts to 5.57%. Conversely, an average 11.34% increase is inducted by a CCTB if profitability is 30% lower than in the benchmark case. Therefore, as seen with the large company, the tax base effects are of a higher relevance in the case of lower profitability.

3.3.2.3 Labour Intensity

The impact of the model firm's labour intensity on the future value of the tax base in the case of a simultaneous introduction of all CCTB options (Option I) is analysed by alternately raising and lowering the ratio costs for personnel to turnover in two steps by 20%. To keep profitability constant, the rise or fall in wages and salaries is counterbalanced by a corresponding reduction or increase of other costs.

The described modification in the ratio of labour costs affects the future value of the tax base under the GAAP and CCTB regimes in the same direction. Under both tax accounting regimes, an increase in the ratio of labour costs results in a relatively small decrease in the future value of the tax base (see Table 54).

Table 54: Average future value of the tax base (EU-27 SME) for different levels of labour intensity under national tax law and CCTB Option I in € millions

Regime	Decrease in labour intensity		Benchmark Case[1]	Increase in labour intensity	
	20%	10%		10%	20%
National GAAP	3.24	3.23	**3.22**	3.21	3.19
CCTB	3.42	3.41	**3.39**	3.37	3.35

[1] For the benchmark case see Table 46.

The main reason for this is that an increased ratio of labour costs increases taxes based on labour expenditure (such as payroll taxes, taxes on value added or certain local business taxes). This holds true for Austria, Cyprus, France, Hungary, Italy and Slovenia.

As a consequence, if these taxes are deductible as business expenses, they reduce the corporate tax base. If they are not tax deductible they lower the tax base indirectly by decreasing liquidity, which worsens the financial performance of the company. As there are no material differences between national GAAP and CCTB concerning these taxes, the impact on the tax base is the same for both accounting systems.

[58] The effective tax burden also reveals a negative correlation between profitability and the magnitude of the GAAP/CCTB deviation. For detailed results see Appendix 8.2, Table 2.

For the benchmark case and all variations the future value of the tax base is higher under a CCTB than under national GAAP. However, the changes in the future value of the tax base due to varying labour intensity are less important under the CCTB.

Table 55 displays the difference in per cent between the future value of the tax base under national GAAP and the future value of the tax base under CCTB Option I. The deviations are given for the benchmark case and four variations of labour intensity. The results show the deviation slighthly decreasing or increasing with rising or falling labour intensity.[59]

Table 55: Deviation (in %) in the future value of the tax base (EU-27 SME) from national GAAP caused by a simultaneous application all CCTB options (I) for different levels of labour intensity

Country	Decrease in labour intensity of		Benchmark Case[1]	Increase in labour intensity of	
	20%	10%		10%	20%
AT	4.45	4.39	**4.32**	4.26	4.19
BE	1.78	1.66	**1.52**	1.37	1.22
BG	12.08	11.95	**11.80**	11.67	11.51
CY	-5.73	-6.26	**-6.91**	-7.64	-8.37
CZ	9.79	9.65	**9.51**	9.37	9.21
DE	3.32	3.14	**2.92**	2.68	2.43
DK	2.57	2.47	**2.36**	2.25	2.13
EE	1.77	1.77	**1.77**	1.78	1.78
ES	2.95	2.80	**2.64**	2.47	2.29
FI	9.49	9.36	**9.21**	9.07	8.91
FR	5.34	5.32	**5.29**	5.25	5.16
GR	10.61	10.47	**10.31**	10.17	10.00
HU	15.20	15.29	**15.43**	15.30	15.04
IE	-0.58	-0.67	**-0.77**	-0.77	-0.77
IT	9.10	8.96	**8.82**	8.66	8.48
LT	10.78	10.64	**10.48**	10.35	10.19
LU	2.47	2.37	**2.26**	2.15	2.03
LV	10.70	10.57	**10.42**	10.28	10.11
MT	5.56	5.47	**5.37**	5.27	5.16
NL	1.59	1.46	**1.32**	1.17	1.06
PL	9.14	9.00	**8.84**	8.69	8.52
PT	10.22	10.08	**9.92**	9.77	9.61
RO	2.94	2.74	**2.51**	2.40	2.32
SE	2.90	2.80	**2.69**	2.58	2.51
SK	9.74	9.61	**9.46**	9.32	9.16
SL	8.25	8.25	**8.25**	8.28	8.30
UK	0.87	0.78	**0.67**	0.56	0.45
Ø	5.83	5.71	**5.57**	5.43	5.28

[1] For the benchmark case see Table 46.

On average, companies that exceed the labour intensity of the benchmark case by 20% experience an increase in the future value of the tax base of 5.28% with

[59] The effective tax burden also reveals a negative correlation between labour intensity and the magnitude of the GAAP/CCTB deviation. For detailed results see Appendix 8.1, Table 3.

the simultaneous introduction of all CCTB options (Option I). For the benchmark case, in contrast, the deviation from national GAAP amounts to 5.57%.

Conversely, an average 5.83% increase is inducted by a CCTB if labour intensity is 20% lower than in the benchmark case. Explanation for these effects was already provided for the case of the large company (see section 3.2.2.3).

3.3.2.4 Inventory Intensity

In order to measure the effects of varying inventory intensity (i.e. the value of stocks to total capital), the production output is alternately raised or lowered while keeping the volume of sales stable. A variation in the units produced affects variable costs but not the fixed cost components of total production costs. Hence, with increasing output, production costs per unit decline. The same holds true for total production costs of units sold as lower costs per unit are multiplied with a constant number of units sold. Whereas the production costs of units stocked are capitalised, the production costs of units sold enter into the calculation of annual profit, thus affecting the tax base. Lower production costs for units sold are thus associated with an increase in the tax base as sales remain unchanged.

Table 56: Average future value of the tax base (EU-27 SME) for different levels of inventory intensity under national tax law and CCTB Option I in € millions

Regime	Decrease of inventories to capital by		Benchmark Case[1]	Increase of inventories to capital by	
	10.7%	5.3%		5.3%	10.6%
National GAAP	3.12	3.17	**3.22**	3.27	3.32
CCTB	3.29	3.34	**3.39**	3.44	3.49

[1] For the benchmark case see Table 46.

This reasoning is valid when calculating the tax base for national GAAP and the proposed CCTB. Under both regimes the future value of the tax base increases with increasing inventory intensity, as can be seen from Table 56.

However, as the future value of the tax base in the benchmark case is higher under a CCTB the change due to increasing inventory intensity in per cent is lower than under national GAAP. As a result, the deviation between the future value of the tax base under national GAAP and under the proposed CCTB decreases with higher inventory intensity.

Table 57 displays the difference in per cent between the future value of the tax base under national GAAP and the future value of the tax base under CCTB (Option I). The deviations are given for the benchmark case and six variations of inventory intensity. The deviation decreases or increases with rising or falling inventory intensity.[60]

[60] The effective tax burden also reveals a negative correlation between inventory intensity and the magnitude of the GAAP/CCTB deviation. For detailed results see Appendix 8.2, Table 4.

On average the deviation in the future value of the tax base decreases from 5.57% to 5.25% if inventory intensity exceeds the benchmark case by 10.60%.

Table 57: Deviation (in %) in the future value of the tax base (EU-27 SME) from national GAAP caused by a simultaneous application all CCTB options (I) for different levels of inventory intensity

Country	Decrease of inventories to capital by		Benchmark Case[1]	Increase of inventories to capital by	
	10.70%	5.30%		5.30%	10.60%
AT	4.42	4.36	**4.32**	4.29	4.26
BE	1.78	1.65	**1.52**	1.41	1.31
BG	12.20	11.99	**11.80**	11.61	11.41
CY	-7.10	-7.00	**-6.91**	-6.81	-6.73
CZ	10.08	9.78	**9.51**	9.23	8.97
DE	3.07	2.99	**2.92**	2.84	2.76
DK	2.47	2.40	**2.36**	2.31	2.27
EE	1.61	1.69	**1.77**	1.85	1.93
ES	3.01	2.82	**2.64**	2.50	2.36
FI	9.61	9.40	**9.21**	9.03	8.85
FR	5.79	5.55	**5.29**	4.98	4.62
GR	10.80	10.55	**10.31**	10.08	9.87
HU	17.10	16.22	**15.43**	14.47	13.54
IE	-0.63	-0.71	**-0.77**	-0.75	-0.73
IT	9.27	9.04	**8.82**	8.56	8.26
LT	11.13	10.81	**10.48**	10.19	9.90
LU	2.52	2.38	**2.26**	2.16	2.07
LV	11.05	10.73	**10.42**	10.10	9.79
MT	5.58	5.47	**5.37**	5.27	5.17
NL	1.46	1.39	**1.32**	1.26	1.20
PL	9.36	9.11	**8.84**	8.59	8.37
PT	10.35	10.13	**9.92**	9.74	9.58
RO	2.28	2.42	**2.51**	2.73	3.00
SE	3.02	2.86	**2.69**	2.55	2.42
SK	10.03	9.73	**9.46**	9.19	8.92
SL	8.46	8.35	**8.25**	8.16	8.08
UK	0.91	0.81	**0.67**	0.52	0.41
Ø	5.91	5.74	**5.57**	5.41	5.25

[1] For the benchmark case see Table 46.

If the ratio considered is lowered by 10.70% compared to the benchmark case the effect of a CCTB on the future value of the tax base increases to 5.91%.

3.3.3 Sensitivity Analysis on Specific Sectors

The analysis presented in section 3.3.1 was based on an EU-27 average SME (benchmark case). In the following section – as was performed for the large model corporation – companies belonging to different sectors are analysed in isolation. The sector-specific financial ratios are displayed in Table 58.

Table 58: Financial ratios for different sectors

Financial Ratio	Benchmark Case	Commerce	Construction	Energy	Manufacturing	Service/Trade	Transport
Profit/loss for period (€)	194,624	273,218	137,653	241,125	195,088	112,192	153,885
Total assets (€)	4,258,420	4,097,763	2,567,892	12,723,463	4,890,718	3,294,557	4,380,917
Sales (€)	7,167,799	9,579,947	3,821,868	7,682,341	7,450,713	3,392,933	6,157,328
Share of tangible fixed assets (%)	25.50	21.61	22.19	51.95	32.16	28.75	36.00
Return on sales (%)	2.72	2.85	3.60	3.14	2.62	3.31	2.50
Return on equity (%)	15.52	23.62	17.44	4.83	11.37	10.77	12.95
Equity ratio (%)	29.46	28.23	30.74	39.20	35.09	31.63	27.12
Return on assets (%)	6.87	9.01	7.56	4.85	6.88	5.27	6.96
Inventories to capital (%)	20.61	30.13	18.76	4.08	20.18	7.75	3.13
Costs for personnel to turnover (%)	18.20	11.66	23.25	20.98	22.00	31.75	20.62

Table 59: Future value of the tax base (SME case) under national tax law (in € millions) and deviation (in %) caused by CCTB for different sectors

Country	Benchmark Case[1]		Commerce		Construction		Energy		Manufacturing		Service/Trade		Transport	
	FV	Dev.	FV	Dev.	FV	Dev.	FV	Dev.	FV	Dev.	FV	Dev.	FV	Dev.
AT	2.87	4.32	4.60	2.40	1.94	3.93	4.17	31.70	2.96	5.29	1.41	2.70	2.72	9.86
BE	2.94	1.52	4.69	0.21	2.04	1.78	2.63	38.38	2.94	2.05	1.39	1.02	2.80	6.06
BG	3.43	11.80	5.14	4.66	2.31	9.96	5.23	40.23	3.62	13.23	1.90	7.85	3.24	20.05
CY	3.74	-6.91	5.33	-3.72	2.48	-6.80	6.19	3.63	4.06	-9.24	1.99	-10.38	3.71	-6.13
CZ	3.45	9.51	5.17	2.92	2.31	8.40	5.23	38.21	3.68	9.94	1.89	6.64	3.23	18.33
DE	2.68	2.92	4.07	1.81	1.82	2.85	3.92	31.16	2.81	3.19	1.50	1.54	2.47	9.70
DK	3.29	2.36	4.95	1.67	2.24	2.17	4.41	27.24	3.49	2.82	1.72	1.59	3.12	7.36
EE	3.60	1.77	5.27	1.73	2.41	1.47	5.66	19.35	3.89	2.23	2.04	0.29	3.51	5.75
ES	3.07	2.64	4.60	1.30	2.07	3.00	4.64	31.92	3.26	3.06	1.69	1.79	2.89	10.22
FI	3.42	9.21	5.10	3.37	2.30	7.77	5.30	30.80	3.64	9.46	1.85	6.47	3.34	12.53
FR	2.36	5.29	2.96	0.97	1.67	4.80	2.27	58.96	2.21	7.66	1.15	4.38	2.02	12.53
GR	3.41	10.31	5.10	3.80	2.29	8.91	5.21	36.72	3.61	11.59	1.91	5.99	3.24	17.15
HU	1.08	15.43	1.69	3.94	1.28	7.33	2.49	55.46	1.23	12.14	0.94	4.97	1.36	27.44
IE	3.54	-0.77	5.23	-0.43	2.38	-0.27	5.56	13.73	3.81	-0.89	1.93	-1.70	3.44	2.83
IT	3.39	8.82	5.07	2.80	2.27	7.76	5.26	32.88	3.60	8.45	1.86	5.34	3.21	15.35
LT	3.38	10.48	5.11	3.42	2.29	8.87	4.48	50.57	3.58	11.25	1.76	10.01	3.16	19.47
LU	3.35	2.26	5.03	1.26	2.26	2.43	4.94	25.00	3.57	2.82	1.83	1.93	3.16	8.09
LV	3.40	10.42	5.14	3.15	2.30	9.03	4.70	42.96	3.58	11.71	1.80	7.89	3.16	20.00
MT	3.46	5.37	5.12	2.02	2.32	4.64	5.40	23.77	3.71	5.02	1.94	2.17	3.31	8.77
NL	3.41	1.32	5.08	0.80	2.30	1.39	5.18	22.94	3.66	1.40	1.87	1.13	3.24	6.46
PL	3.46	8.84	5.18	2.59	2.33	7.67	5.04	38.01	3.67	9.53	1.88	5.00	3.27	16.24
PT	3.41	9.92	5.10	3.73	2.29	8.59	5.34	33.43	3.62	10.80	1.90	5.48	3.24	16.85
RO	3.44	2.51	5.16	1.52	2.33	2.26	5.09	34.10	3.61	4.53	1.88	1.65	3.64	-0.48
SE	3.36	2.69	5.06	1.29	2.26	2.82	5.00	25.96	3.57	3.71	1.83	2.45	3.15	9.34
SK	3.46	9.46	5.18	2.90	2.33	8.19	5.06	41.04	3.69	9.87	1.87	7.62	3.25	17.92
SL	3.17	8.25	4.89	3.59	2.13	6.93	5.03	28.35	3.34	8.75	1.68	6.22	3.03	12.52
UK	3.36	0.67	5.06	0.14	2.28	1.02	4.30	26.61	3.54	1.04	1.75	-0.80	3.17	5.97
Ø	3.22	5.57	4.82	1.99	2.19	4.70	4.73	32.71	3.41	5.98	1.75	3.31	3.08	11.49

[1] For the benchmark case see Table 46.

Since the model assumptions in some cases do not represent the actual reality faced by individual companies captured by the AMADEUS database are faced with, also for model firms of different sectors it is unavoidable that their financial characteristics differ slightly from the EU-27 average sector-specific companies shown in Appendix 4.4.

Table 59 displays the future value of the tax base under national GAAP as well as the deviation caused by the introduction of a CCTB (Option I) for both the considered sector-specific companies and the SME benchmark case.

Commerce

Table 58 shows higher profits for the average company representing the commerce sector than for the benchmark case. As a result, the future value of the tax base is comparably higher for the average commerce company (see Table 59).

In all countries except Cyprus and Ireland the introduction of a CCTB results in an increase in the future value of the tax base. On average the increase amounts to 1.99%, compared to 5.57% in the benchmark case. For this reason, the impact of a CCTB on the considered company in the commerce sector is much lower than in the benchmark case. This result can be attributed to the lower capital intensity, higher profitability and higher inventory intensity of the commerce sector company compared to the benchmark case. The described effect is counteracted to a small extent by lower labour intensity.[61]

Construction

As indicated in Table 58 the small and medium-sized average model firm representing the construction sector generates considerably lower annual profits than the benchmark case. Consequently, the future value of the tax base is below the benchmark case when national GAAP is applied (see Table 59). The introduction of the proposed CCTB results in an increase in the future value of the tax base in all countries except for Cyprus and Ireland. With an average increase of 4.70% the tax base broadening effect for the average company of the construction-sector is smaller than for the benchmark case model firm (5.57%). The observed result can be explained by the – compared to the benchmark case – lower capital intensity, higher profitability and higher labour intensity. The described effect is counteracted to some extent by lower inventory intensity.[62]

Energy

The average company representing the energy sector generates higher profits than the benchmark case. The SME's future value of the tax base is therefore higher than the benchmark case under national GAAP (see Table 58, Table 59). The introduction of the proposed CCTB results in an increase in the future value of the tax base in all countries. On average the increase amounts to 32.71%. Taking into account that the future value of the tax base under national GAAP already is at a high level, the strong relative increase is associated with a particular high absolute increase. Above all, this result can be attributed to the – compared to

---

[61] The results for the effective tax burden are displayed in Appendix 9 Table 2 and confirm the conclusions for an average SME representing the commerce sector.

[62] The results for the effective tax burden are displayed in Appendix 9 Table 2 and confirm the conclusions for an average SME representing the construction sector.

the benchmark case – higher capital intensity of the energy-sector SME. This effect is strengthened by lower inventory intensity but counteracted to a certain extent by higher profitability and labour intensity.[63]

Manufacturing

The average small and medium-sized company representing the manufacturing sector generates higher profits than the benchmark company (see Table 58). Hence, compared to the benchmark case, the future value of the tax base under national GAAP is higher for the manufacturing-sector SME (see Table 59). In all countries except Cyprus and Ireland the introduction of a CCTB results in an increase in the future value of the tax base. On average the future value of the tax base increases by 5.98% in the event of a CCTB compared to an increase of 3.22% in the benchmark case. The observed result can be explained by the higher capital intensity and lower profitability of the manufacturing-sector SME. The described effect is slightly weakened by higher labour intensity.[64]

Service/Trade

Compared to the benchmark case, the average service-sector small and medium-sized company generates lower profits, as shown in Table 58. Therefore, the future value of the tax base under national GAAP, as displayed in Table 59, is considerably lower than in the benchmark case. In all countries, apart from Cyprus and Ireland, the introduction of the proposed CCTB leads to an increase in the future value of the tax base. On average the increase of the future value of the tax base is 3.31%, thus falling below the increase for the benchmark case. This result can be attributed to the higher profitability and higher labour intensity of the service-sector SME. However, the described effect is partially counteracted by the SME's lower capital intensity and higher labour intensity.[65]

Transport

Compared to the benchmark case, the transport sector has lower annual profits and hence a lower future tax base value when national GAAP is applied. In all countries except Cyprus and Romania the introduction of a CCTB results in an increase in the future value of the tax base. On average the future value of the tax base increases by 11.49% in the event of a CCTB. Above all, this increase can be explained by the – compared to the benchmark case – higher capital intensity, lower profitability and lower inventory intensity of the transport-sector SME. The broadening effect is only slightly counteracted by higher labour intensity.[66]

[63] The results for the effective tax burden are displayed in Appendix 9 Table 2 and confirm the conclusions for an average SME representing the energy sector.

[64] The results for the effective tax burden are displayed in Appendix 9, Table 2, and confirm the conclusions for an average SME representing the manufacturing sector.

[65] The results for the effective tax burden are displayed in Appendix 9, Table 2, and confirm the conclusions for an average SME representing the service/trade sector.

[66] The results for the effective tax burden are displayed in Appendix 9, Table 2, and confirm the conclusions for an average SME representing the transport sector.

Conclusion

The main findings of the sensitivity analysis carried out for sector-specific SMEs can be summarised as follows:

- All EU-27 sector-specific small and medium-sized model companies witness an increase in the future value of the tax base with the introduction of a CCTB. This was also the finding for the EU-27 sector-specific large model companies.
- Viewed by sector, there is considerable variation in the size of the tax base increase inducted by a CCTB. This increase varies from 1.99% in the commerce sector to 32.71% in the energy sector. However, compared to the sector-specific large model company analysis, the magnitude of the variation between sectors is smaller in the SME case.
- In the manufacturing and transport sectors the average increase in the future value of the tax base exceeds that of the benchmark SME.
- As was the case for the benchmark SME, capital intensity and thus the impact of differing depreciation rules in the event of a CCTB is the most relevant factor explaining the increase in the future value of the tax base.

3.3.4 Consideration of EU-15/EU-12 Average SMEs

In this section, the analysis for the EU-27 average SME is extended by two additional company models representative of small and medium-sized companies in the EU-15 and EU-12 member states. Although the considered EU-12, EU-15 and EU-27 corporations are categorised as SMEs, they vary considerably in terms of profits, sales and total assets. Table 60 displays the financial ratios of the different model firms.

The EU-15 average SME is based on company data derived from the EU-15 member states. Likewise, data for the EU-12 model SME are derived from company data originating from the EU-12 accession countries.

Table 60: Financial ratios of the EU-27, EU-15 and EU-12 model SMEs

Financial Ratio	EU-27	EU-15	EU-12
Profit/loss for period ()€	**194,624**	237,440	123,948
Total assets (€)	**4,258,420**	4,803,963	2,994,283
Sales (€)	**7,167,799**	8,570,250	4,548,708
Share of tangible fixed assets (%)	**25.50**	23.19	31.81
Return on sales (%)	**2.72**	2.77	2.72
Return on equity (%)	**15.52**	16.54	13.45
Equity ratio (%)	**29.46**	29.88	30.77
Return on assets (%)	**6.87**	7.18	7.04
Inventories to capital (%)	**20.61**	19.59	22.01
Costs for personnel to turnover (%)	**18.20**	21.52	13.21

3.3.4.1 EU-15 Average SME

The second column of Table 61 displays the future value of the tax base under national GAAP. As was the case for the EU-27 small and medium-sized benchmark, there is a remarkable dispersion of future values of the tax base across member states. The future values of the tax base range from €2.60 million in France to €4.32 million in the Netherlands and Portugal. The average future value of the tax base is €4.02 million. Compared to the small and medium benchmark, the future value of the tax base for the EU-15 small and medium model company is €0.80 million higher. This is attributable to the higher profits of the EU-15 SME (see Table 60 for financial ratios)

Table 61: Future value of the tax base (in € millions) for EU-15 SME under national tax law and deviation (in %) caused by each particular CCTB option A-H and by a simultaneous application all CCTB options (I)

Country	National GAAP	A	B	C	D	E	F	G	H	I
AT	3.58	2.02	0.34	0.94	0.00	-0.83	0.00	0.00	0.00	2.62
BE	3.79	0.11	0.05	0.02	0.00	0.00	0.00	0.00	0.00	0.34
DE	3.43	1.43	0.23	0.62	0.00	-0.59	0.00	0.00	0.00	1.76
DK	4.19	0.88	-0.01	0.86	0.01	0.00	0.00	0.00	0.00	1.71
ES	3.88	1.55	0.26	-0.05	-0.05	0.00	0.00	0.00	0.00	1.79
FI	4.33	2.52	-0.01	0.91	0.01	0.00	-1.39	0.00	0.00	6.99
FR	2.60	5.83	0.00	-0.01	0.01	0.00	0.00	0.00	0.00	5.78
GR	4.33	4.14	0.00	0.82	0.01	0.00	-1.06	-0.95	0.00	7.74
IE	4.47	0.14	0.00	-0.01	0.01	0.00	0.00	-0.91	0.00	-0.78
IT	4.28	3.87	0.30	-0.44	0.00	0.00	-1.15	0.00	0.00	6.77
LU	4.25	1.61	0.33	-0.22	-0.06	0.00	0.00	0.00	0.00	1.72
NL	4.32	0.88	0.36	0.00	0.00	-0.32	0.00	0.00	0.00	0.88
PT	4.32	1.83	0.23	0.32	0.01	0.00	-1.36	0.00	0.00	7.63
SE	4.27	2.12	0.00	-0.06	-0.06	0.00	0.00	0.00	0.00	2.06
UK	4.28	1.11	0.00	-0.01	0.01	0.00	0.00	-0.96	0.00	0.15
Ø	4.02	2.00	0.14	0.25	-0.01	-0.12	-0.33	-0.19	0.00	3.14

(1) The first simulation considers an isolated harmonisation of rules governing tax depreciation (Option A).

Column A of Table 61 displays the change in the future value of the tax base with the introduction of CCTB depreciation rules. For all countries the change due to the isolated introduction of the proposed tax depreciation rules is positive, indicating a broadening of the tax base. Depending on the specific national depreciation provisions, the tax base broadening effect is larger in some countries than in others: France, Greece and Italy experience the highest increase in the future value of the tax base whereas the increase is smallest in Belgium, Denmark, Ireland and the Netherlands.

On average the future value of the tax base increases by 2%.[67] In isolation, common depreciation rules correspond to 63.69% (= 2.00/3.14) of the overall EU-average increase in the future value of the tax base, thus revealing depreciation as the option with the most important impact on the future value of the tax base.

[67] Under Option A the effective tax burden increases by 1.80% (Table 62, column A).

(2) The second simulation analyses the effect of an isolated harmonisation of methods for simplified valuation of inventories on the future value of the tax base (Option B).

Changes in the future value of the tax base resulting from the introduction of the WAC method under a CCTB are displayed in column B of Table 61. Overall, the impact of the WAC method on the future value of the tax base ranges from -0.01% in Denmark, Finland and Lithuania to 0.36% in the Netherlands.

On average the future value of the tax base increases by 0.14%.[68] In isolation this corresponds to 4.46% (= 0.14/3.14) of the overall EU-average increase in the future value of the tax base (Option I). As was the case for the EU-27 small and medium model company, the modification of rules governing inventory assessment only exerts a moderate impact on the future value of the tax base.

(3) The third simulation investigates the effect of common rules for the determination of production costs (Option C).

The results of an isolated harmonisation of production costs are displayed in column C of Table 61. The strongest increase in the future value of the tax base is witnessed for Austria, at 0.94%, and the strongest decline in Italy, at -0.44%. In most countries the future value of the tax base changes only to a very small extent. On average the future value of the tax base decreases by 0.25% with harmonised rules governing production costs (this figure was positive for the EU-27 SME).[69] This average decrease corresponds in isolation to -7.96% (= -0.25/3.14) of the overall EU-average increase of the future value of the tax base in the event of a simultaneous introduction of all CCTB options.

(4) The next simulation investigates the effect of common rules for the capitalisation of R&D costs within production costs (Option D).

The results displayed in column D of Table 61 reveal no considerable impact of common rules for the capitalisation of R&D costs on the future value of the tax base. In the majority of countries the future value of the tax base does not change at all or by not more than 0.06%. On average the future value of the tax base decreases by -0.01%.[70] In isolation this corresponds to -0.32% (= -0.01/3.14) of the overall EU-average increase of the future value of the tax base in event of a CCTB. The effect of harmonised rules for the capitalisation of R&D is thus negligible.

(5) The next simulation deals with the effect of common rules regarding provisions for pensions (Option E).

As can be seen from column E of Table 61 the proposed provisions for pension schemes only affect the future value of the tax base in Austria, Germany and the Netherlands. On average the results reveal a decrease in the future value of the tax base of -0.12%.[71] This moderate decrease corresponds in isolation to -3.82% (= -0.12/3.14) of the overall EU-average change in the future value of the tax base in the event of a CCTB.

---

[68] Under Option B the effective tax burden increases by 0.16% (Table 62, column B).

[69] Under Option C the effective tax burden increases by 0.23% (Table 62, column C).

[70] Under Option D the effective tax burden decreases by 0.01% (Table 62, column D).

[71] Under Option E the effective tax burden decreases by 0.08% (Table 62, column E).

(6) The effects of provisions for future warranty liabilities are analysed in the following simulation (Option F).

The changes in the future value of the tax base due to the application of the proposed provisions concerning warranty liabilities are displayed in column F of Table 61. This option either does not translate in a change in the future value of the tax base at all or causes a decrease of the future value of the tax base. The decrease ranges from -1.06% in Greece to -1.39% in Finland. Overall, the introduction of the proposed provisions for future warranty liabilities causes on average a decrease in the future value of the tax base of -0.33%.[72] This decrease in isolation corresponds to -10.51% (= -0.33/3.14) of the overall EU-average change of the future value of the tax base in the event of a CCTB. As was the case for the EU-27 average corporation, this option exerts the second largest impact in isolation on the future value of the tax base.

(7) Another CCTB option is the avoidance of double taxation of dividend income by applying the exemption method for dividend income from major shareholdings (Option G).

Column G of Table 61 displays the deviation in the future value of the tax base due to the application of the exemption method to avoid double taxation of dividend income. A change in the future value of the tax base is only found for Greece, Ireland and the United Kingdom since all other EU-15 countries already apply the exemption method under national GAAP.

On average the decrease in the future value of the tax base caused by the implementation of the exemption method in all EU member states amounts to -0.19%.[73] This corresponds to -6.05% (= -0.19/3.14) in the overall EU-average change of the future value of the tax base in the event of a CCTB. This option thus has a considerable impact on the future value of the tax base.

(8) The effects of loss carry forward are analysed in the following simulation (Option H).

The model firm representing an average EU-15 SME corporation is a profitable company and shows no losses from regular activities during the simulation period of 10 years. The isolated application of CCTB Option H for an indefinite loss carry forward itself does therefore not result in changes in the future value of the tax base of the model firm.

(9) The effects of a simultaneous introduction of all CCTB options (Option I)

So far, different regulations concerning the computation of taxable income have been harmonised in isolation. Now, the focus will be on a simultaneous introduction of all proposed CCTB options. The results of this calculation are displayed in column I of Table 61. Except for Cyprus and Ireland all countries experience a broadening of the future value of the tax base due to the simultaneous introduction of all proposed CCTB options. On average the increase in the future value of the tax base amounts to 3.14%. The highest impact is found for Finland (6.99%), France (5.78%), Greece (7.74%), Italy (6.77%) and Portugal (7.63%). In

---

[72] Under Option F the effective tax burden decreases by 0.44% (Table 62, column F).

[73] Under Option G the effective tax burden remains unchanged on average (Table 62, column G).

Ireland the simultaneous introduction of all CCTB options results in a decrease in the future value of the tax base. Compared to the EU-27 average corporation, the tax base broadening effect of depreciation is lower. At the same time the decrease in the future value of the tax base due to the provisions for warranty liabilities is less pronounced.

Figure 22: Proportional impact of each CCTB option (A-H) on the overall increase in the future value of the tax base (EU-15 large company and SME)

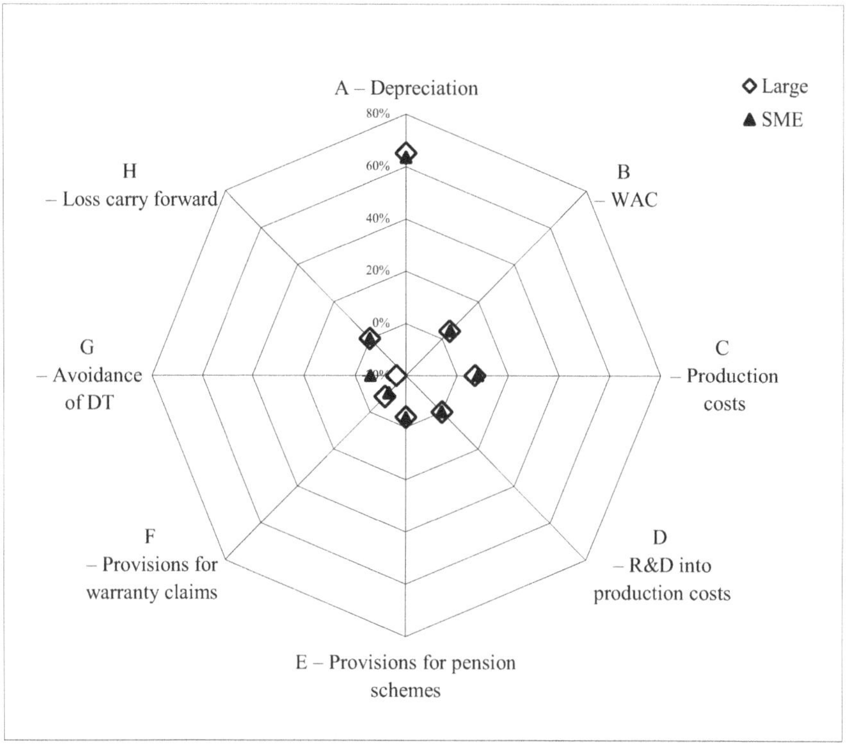

To sum up, the future value of the tax base increases by 3.14% when the effects of introducing a CCTB are modelled on an EU-15 average small and medium size company.[74] This increase is lower compared to the benchmark EU-27 case (5.57%). This result strengthens the conclusion drawn for the EU-27 average SME that the introduction of a CCTB increases tax bases but that this increase is less pronounced in the EU-15 member states. Again, the harmonisation of depreciation rules has the strongest impact on the tax base. Relevant changes in the future value of the tax base are also caused by CCTB provisions for future warranty liabilities, common rules for the determination of production costs and rules concerning the avoidance of double taxation of dividends. In contrast, the impact of common

[74] A simultaneous introduction of all CCTB options results in an increase of the effective tax burden by 2.66%.

rules for the simplified valuation of inventories as well as the inclusion of R&D-related costs in production cost are of minor importance for the future value of the tax base in the EU-15 countries.

The radar chart in Figure 22 compares the effects derived for the EU-15 SME with the respective effects derived in section 3.2.4 for the EU-15 large company. In this way, the radar chart illustrates the relative impact of adopting each CCTB option on the future value of the tax base for both the EU-15 SME and large corporation. Compared to the EU-27 case there are three notable changes.

First, the relative impact of Option A is approximately the same for both the EU-15 large corporation and SME, although this relative impact is much lower in the EU-27 case. Second, for both cases the influence of Option B, C and E is remarkably intensified, whereas the impact is slightly mitigated with respect to Option F. Third, with respect to Option G, there is a notable increase in relative significance, and this effect is even greater for the large company than for the SME.

Table 62: Effective tax burden (in € millions) for the EU-15 SME under national tax law and deviation (in %) caused by each particular CCTB option A-H and by a simultaneous application all CCTB options (I)

Country	National GAAP	A	B	C	D	E	F	G	H	I
AT	1.56	1.16	0.19	0.57	0.00	-0.44	0.00	0.00	0.00	1.59
BE	1.43	0.66	0.16	0.17	0.00	0.00	0.00	0.00	0.00	0.98
DE	1.71	1.42	0.22	0.65	0.00	-0.52	0.00	0.00	0.00	1.83
DK	1.29	0.80	-0.01	0.79	0.01	0.00	0.00	0.00	0.00	1.59
ES	1.69	1.67	0.25	-0.05	-0.05	0.00	0.00	0.00	0.00	1.90
FI	1.17	2.44	-0.01	0.88	0.01	0.00	-1.33	0.00	0.00	5.12
FR	2.45	2.13	0.00	0.00	0.00	0.00	0.00	0.00	0.00	2.11
GR	1.25	4.30	0.00	0.83	0.01	0.00	-1.95	0.00	0.00	7.11
IE	0.60	0.13	0.00	-0.01	0.01	0.00	0.00	0.00	0.00	0.12
IT	1.81	4.42	0.73	-0.34	0.00	0.00	-2.03	0.00	0.00	5.74
LU	1.29	1.62	0.35	-0.26	-0.07	0.00	0.00	0.00	0.00	1.71
NL	1.29	0.83	0.35	0.00	0.00	-0.29	0.00	0.00	0.00	0.87
PT	1.21	1.83	0.23	0.31	0.01	0.00	-1.34	0.00	0.00	5.89
SE	1.23	2.11	0.00	-0.06	-0.06	0.00	0.00	0.00	0.00	2.04
UK	0.96	1.47	0.00	-0.01	0.02	0.00	0.00	-0.05	0.00	1.27
Ø	1.40	1.80	0.16	0.23	-0.01	-0.08	-0.44	0.00	0.00	2.66

3.3.4.2 EU-12 Average SME

The first column of Table 63 displays the future value of the tax base under national GAAP. As was the case for the EU-27 SME, there is a remarkable dispersion in future tax base values across member states.

The future values of the tax base range from €0.84 million in Hungary to €2.83 million in Cyprus. The average future value of the tax base is €2.48 million. Compared to the SME benchmark, the future value of the tax base for the EU-12 model SME is €0.74 million lower. This is attributable to the lower profits of the EU-12 SME (see Table 60 for financial ratios).

(1) The first simulation considers an isolated harmonisation of rules governing tax depreciation (Option A).

Column A of Table 63 displays the change in the future value of the tax base with the introduction of CCTB depreciation rules. For all countries the change due to the isolated introduction of the proposed tax depreciation rules is positive, indicating a broadening of the tax base. Depending on the specific national depreciation provisions, the tax base broadening effect is larger in some countries than in others: the Czech Republic, Hungary, Latvia, Lithuania and Slovakia experience the highest increase in the future value of the tax base whereas the increase is smallest in Cyprus and Malta.

On average the future value of the tax base increases by 5.10%.[75] In isolation, common depreciation rules correspond to 80.44% (= 5.10/6.34) of the overall EU-average increase in the future value of the tax base, thus revealing depreciation as the option with the most important impact on the future value of the tax base.

Table 63: Future value of the tax base (in € millions) for EU-12 SME under national tax law and deviation (in %) caused by each particular CCTB option A-H and by a simultaneous application all CCTB options (I)

Country	National GAAP	A	B	C	D	E	F	G	H	I
BG	2.60	4.21	0.28	1.17	0.01	0.00	-1.42	0.00	0.00	10.44
CY	2.83	0.93	0.00	-5.06	-0.40	0.00	-3.06	0.00	0.00	-4.13
CZ	2.62	7.81	0.00	-0.01	0.01	0.00	-1.24	0.00	0.00	7.77
EE	2.74	1.18	0.00	0.91	0.00	-0.02	0.00	0.00	0.00	2.07
HU	0.84	13.91	0.00	-0.14	0.03	0.00	0.00	0.00	0.00	13.71
LT	2.56	8.99	-0.02	-0.01	0.01	0.00	-1.37	0.00	0.00	8.80
LV	2.57	8.79	0.00	0.00	0.00	0.00	0.00	0.00	0.00	8.79
MT	2.63	0.88	0.00	0.74	-0.08	0.00	-1.04	-0.62	0.00	4.30
PL	2.62	3.80	0.40	-0.01	0.01	0.00	-1.34	-0.63	0.00	7.36
RO	2.64	1.26	0.21	0.29	0.00	0.00	0.00	0.00	0.00	2.44
SK	2.63	7.80	0.00	-0.01	0.01	0.00	-1.33	0.00	0.00	7.76
SL	2.50	1.63	0.38	1.04	0.00	0.00	-1.29	0.00	0.00	6.75
Ø	2.48	5.10	0.10	-0.09	-0.03	0.00	-1.01	-0.10	0.00	6.34

(2) The second simulation analyses the effect of an isolated harmonisation of methods for simplified valuation of inventories on the future value of the tax base (Option B).

Changes in the future value of the tax base resulting from the introduction of the WAC method under a CCTB are displayed in column B of Table 63. Overall, the impact of the WAC method on the future value of the tax base ranges from -0.02% in Lithuania to 0.38% in Slovenia.

On average the future value of the tax base increases by 0.10%.[76] In isolation this corresponds to 1.57% (= 0.10/6.34) of the overall EU-average increase in the future value of the tax base (Option I). As was the case for the EU-27 SME, modification of rules governing inventory assessment only exerts a moderate impact on the future value of the tax base.

[75] Under Option A the effective tax burden increases by 4.52% (Table 64, column A).

[76] Under Option B the effective tax burden increases by 0.10% (Table 64, column B).

(3) The third simulation investigates the effect of common rules for the determination of production costs (Option C).

The results of an isolated harmonisation of production costs are displayed in column C of Table 63. The strongest increase in the future value of the tax base is witnessed for Bulgaria, at 1.17%, and the strongest decline in Cyprus, at -5.06%. In most countries the future value of the tax base does change only to a very small extent. On average the future value of the tax base decreases by -0.9% due to the harmonisation of production cost.[77] This average decrease corresponds in isolation to -1.42% (= -0.09/6.34) of the overall EU-average increase in the future value of the tax base in the event of a simultaneous introduction of all CCTB options. In line with the findings for the EU-27 average SME corporation, the proposed CCTB provision for the determination of production costs induces only slight changes in the future value of the tax base.

(4) The next simulation investigates the effect of common rules for the capitalisation of R&D costs within production costs (Option D).

The results displayed in column D of Table 63 reveal no considerable impact of common rules for the capitalisation of R&D costs on the future value of the tax base. In the majority of countries the future value of the tax base does not change at all or by not more than 0.01%. On average the future value of the tax base decreases by -0.03%.[78] In isolation this corresponds to -0.47% (= -0.03/6.34) of the overall EU-average increase of the future value of the tax base in event of a CCTB. The effect of harmonised rules for the capitalisation of R&D is thus negligible.

(5) The next simulation deals with the effect of common rules regarding provisions for pensions (Option E).

As can be seen from column E of Table 63 the proposed provisions for pension schemes only affect the future value of the tax base in Estonia, which experiences a decrease in the future value of the tax base of -0.02%. On average, for the EU-12 countries, the future value of the tax base remains unchanged.[79]

(6) The effects of provisions for future warranty liabilities are analysed in the following simulation (Option F).

The changes in the future value of the tax base due to the application of the proposed provisions concerning warranty liabilities are displayed in column F of Table 63. This option either does not translate into a change in the future value of the tax base at all or causes a decrease in the future value of the tax base. This decrease is strongest in Cyprus at -3.06%. Overall, the introduction of the proposed provisions for future warranty liabilities causes on average a decrease in the future value of the tax base of -1.01%.[80] This decrease in isolation corresponds to -15.93% (= -1.01/6.34) of the overall EU-average change in the future value of the tax base in the event of a CCTB. As was the case for the EU-27 average

[77] Under Option C the effective tax burden increases by 0.17% (Table 64, column C).

[78] Under Option D the effective tax burden decreases by 0.02% (Table 64, column D).

[79] Under Option E the effective tax burden remains unchanged on average (Table 64, column E).

[80] Under Option F the effective tax burden decreases by 0.90% (Table 64, column F).

corporation, this option exerts the second largest impact in isolation on the future value of the tax base.

(7) Another CCTB option is the avoidance of double taxation of dividend income by applying the exemption method for dividend income from major shareholdings (Option G).

Column G of Table 63 displays the deviation in the future value of the tax base due to the application of the exemption method to avoid double taxation of dividend income. A change in the future value of the tax base is only found for Malta and Poland since all other EU-12 countries already apply the exemption method under national GAAP.

On average the decrease in the future value of the tax base caused by the implementation of the exemption method in all EU member states amounts to -0.10%.[81] This corresponds to -1.58% (= -0.10/6.34) of the overall EU-average change in the future value of the tax base in the event of a CCTB. This option thus has a small impact on the future value of the tax base for the EU-12 countries.

(8) The effects of loss carry forward are analysed in the following simulation (Option H).

The model firm representing an average EU-12 SME corporation is a profitable company and shows no losses from regular activities during the simulation period of 10 years. The isolated application of CCTB Option H for an indefinite loss carry forward itself does therefore not result in changes in the future value of the tax base of the model firm.

(9) The effects of a simultaneous introduction of all CCTB options (Option I)

So far, different regulations concerning the computation of taxable income have been harmonised in isolation. Now, the focus will be on a simultaneous introduction of all proposed CCTB options. The results of this calculation are displayed in column I of Table 63. Except for Cyprus and Ireland all countries experience a broadening of the future value of the tax base due to the simultaneous introduction of all proposed CCTB options. On average the increase in the future value of the tax base amounts to 6.34%. The highest impact is found for Hungary (13.71%), Bulgaria (10.44%), Latvia (8.80%) and Lithuania (8.79%). This is in line with the findings for the EU-27 model SME. In Cyprus the simultaneous introduction of all CCTB options results in a decrease in the future value of the tax base. This is mainly because, compared to the EU-27 SME, the tax base broadening effect of depreciation is lower.

To sum up, the future value of the tax base increases by 6.34% when the effects of introducing a CCTB are modelled on an EU-12 average SME.[82] This increase almost equals the increase in the future value of the tax base of the benchmark case and is considerably above the increase observed for the EU-15 small and medium corporation (3.12%). Thus, the impact of the proposed CCTB is strongest in the EU-12 accession countries. Again, the harmonisation of depreciation rules has the strongest impact on the tax base. Relevant changes in the future value of

[81] Under Option G the effective tax burden decreases by 0.01% (Table 64, column G).

[82] A simultaneous introduction of all CCTB options results in an increase of the effective tax burden by 5.18%.

Figure 23: Proportional impact of each CCTB option (A-H) on the overall increase in the future value of the tax base (EU-12 large company and SME)

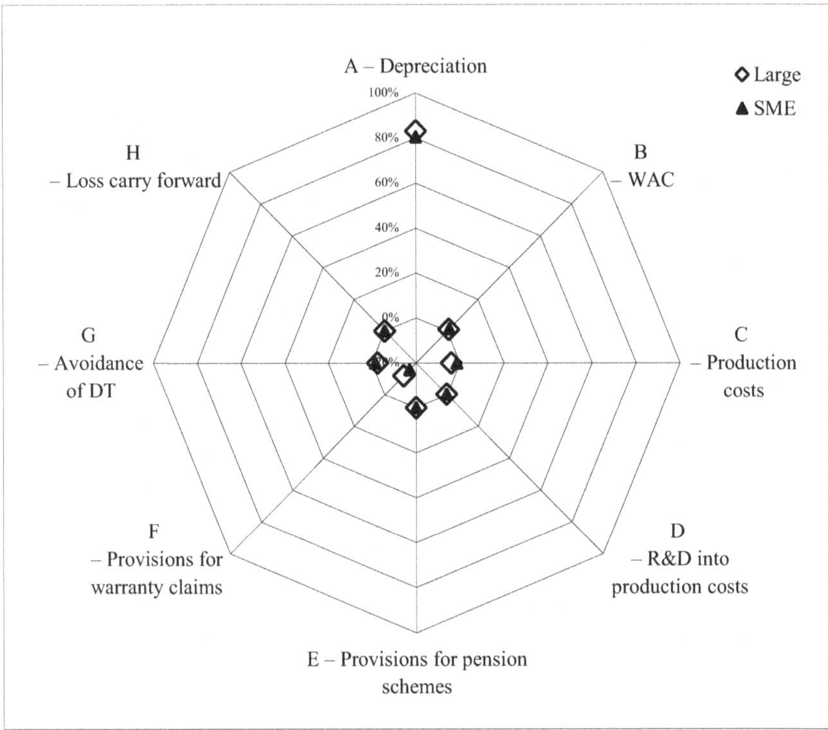

Table 64: Effective tax burden (in € millions) for the EU-12 SME under national tax law and deviation (in %) caused by each particular CCTB option A-H and by a simultaneous application all CCTB options (I)

Country	National GAAP	A	B	C	D	E	F	G	H	I
BG	0.40	4.28	0.27	1.20	0.01	0.00	-1.44	0.00	0.00	8.92
CY	0.43	0.51	0.00	-3.35	-0.27	0.00	-2.06	0.00	0.00	-2.84
CZ	0.64	7.66	0.00	-0.01	0.01	0.00	-1.27	0.00	0.00	6.07
EE	0.42	0.00	0.00	0.00	0.00	0.01	0.00	0.00	0.00	0.01
HU	1.16	1.95	0.00	0.03	0.01	0.00	0.00	0.00	0.00	1.97
LT	0.56	8.15	-0.02	-0.01	0.01	0.00	-1.23	0.00	0.00	6.83
LV	0.45	11.21	0.00	0.00	0.00	0.00	0.00	0.00	0.00	9.82
MT	0.92	1.18	0.00	1.09	-0.09	0.00	-1.10	-0.09	0.00	5.77
PL	0.54	3.73	0.37	-0.01	0.01	0.00	-1.28	0.00	0.00	6.05
RO	0.43	6.95	0.21	2.23	0.00	0.00	0.00	0.00	0.00	8.14
SK	0.53	7.32	0.00	-0.01	0.01	0.00	-1.31	0.00	0.00	5.80
SL	0.75	1.33	0.31	0.91	0.00	0.00	-1.12	0.00	0.00	5.64
Ø	0.60	4.52	0.10	0.17	-0.02	0.00	-0.90	-0.01	0.00	5.18

the tax base are also caused by CCTB provisions for future warranty liabilities, common rules for a simplified valuation of inventories and rules concerning the avoidance of double taxation of dividends. In contrast, the impact of common provisions for pension schemes as well as the inclusion of R&D-related costs in production costs are of minor importance for the future value of the tax base in the EU-12 countries.

The radar chart in Figure 23 compares the effects derived for the EU-12 SME with the respective effects derived in section 3.2.4 for the EU-12 large company. In this way, the chart illustrates the relative impact of adopting each CCTB option on the future value of the tax base for both the EU-12 large corporation and the small and medium corporation.

Compared to the EU-27 case there are four notable changes. Again, the impact of Option A is approximately the same for both the EU-12 large corporation and SME, and this relative impact is higher in the EU-27 case. The relative impact of Option C is lower for both the EU-12 large company and SME. The negative impact on the tax base of Option F is intensified for both model companies. Finally, with respect to Option G, the impact is roughly the same for both the EU-12 large corporation and SME, and is lower compared to the EU-27 case.

3.3.5 Relationship Between Key Accounting Ratios and Overall Tax Base Effect

To obtain a comprehensive picture of the overall tax base effect of a CCTB, it is useful to analyse the tax base increase in relation to key financial ratios (such as return on sales) using statistical methods.

To this end, we employed a multiple linear regression model (standard OLS model). The combined impact of several independent variables on a dependent variable is modelled as a linear function:

$$y = c + p_1 x_1 + p_2 x_2 + p_3 x_3 \ldots + \varepsilon$$

with

$c = Constant$

$x_i = Variable\, i$

$p_i = Parameter\, i$

$\varepsilon = Error\, term$

The parameters p_i express the relationship between the single factors x_i and the dependent variable y. The dependent variable in this study is measured as the average relative increase in the future value of the tax base for the average model companies that results from adopting all CCTB options combined (hereafter referred to as the increase in the tax base). The following key accounting ratios are the independent variables used to explain this increase in the tax base: return on sales, return on assets, return on equity, capital intensity, proportions on the assets side (intangible assets, tangible assets and financial assets to fixed assets on the one hand and to total assets on the other hand), stocks to balance sheet total, equity ratio, provisions for warranty claims to total assets and labour intensity. Analyses were conducted based on the financial ratios of eighteen different model companies (EU-27, EU-15 and EU-12 large company/SME, as well as sector-specific analyses).

In order to use a multiple linear regression model, independent variables must be independent from one another. This precondition, however, is not completely fulfilled in the case of accounting ratios. Nevertheless, the above-mentioned ratios can be grouped according to obvious interdependencies, i.e. return figures, proportions on the assets side and proportions on the liabilities side, as well as labour intensity. Each group is represented by an independent variable that has been applied to the model. Due to the existence of multicollinearity, however, one exception had to be made for the proportions on the liabilities side (equity ratio or provisions for warranty claims to total assets). As a result, the variables that best fit the multiple linear regression model above are: return on sales, capital intensity and labour intensity. The quality of this model is measured as the coefficient of determination R^2 which expresses the variance of the values estimated by the model in relation to the variance of the values observed. Hence, the R^2 value can range from zero to one and here it amounts to 0.715 at a significance level of one percent. This value thus indicates the good validity of the model.[83] The parameters of the multiple linear regression analysis are presented in Table 65.

Table 65: Results of the multiple regression analysis

Variable	Regression coefficient
Return on sales	-7.953*
Capital intensity	1.109*
Labour intensity	0.171

* denote significance level of one per cent

The parameter for return on sales indicates that the higher the return on sales, the less pronounced the increase in the tax base, whereas the parameter for capital intensity expresses a positive relationship. The return on sales is associated with the increase in the tax base to a quite considerable degree, whereas the relationship between the tax base and capital intensity is comparatively moderate. Two conclusions can be drawn with respect to the accounting ratios concerned. First, applying CCTB rules results in a comparatively strong increase in the tax base when less profitable companies or industries are concerned. Second, the higher the proportion of tangible assets, the stronger the tax base increases, implying a relatively strong effect with respect to capital-intensive companies or industries. The parameter for labour intensity is not significant and hence its influence cannot reliably be interpreted. The model implies that the estimated values for return on sales and capital intensity can indicate the tendency and strength of these factors. The small sample size does not, however, allow concrete forecasts to be made

[83] It has to be noted that the small sample size increases the influence of random deviations; a value near 1 therefore cannot be expected.

with respect to the tax base. Nevertheless, the applied multiple linear regression model is basically an appropriate instrument for analysing the relationship between the increase in the tax base and the accounting ratios examined.

3.4 Consideration of Recent National Tax Reforms

The analysis so far has been based on the tax regimes of the EU-27 member states which were effective in 2006. To supplement the analysis, in this section major tax reforms are considered.

Table 66: Overview of major tax changes in France, Germany, Italy, the Netherlands and Spain

	Tax rates	Tax base
France	▪ Apprenticeship tax rate decreased from 0.62% to 0.5%. ▪ Tax rate for vocational increased from 1.5% to 1.6%. ▪ Social solidarity tax rate on turnover decreased from 0.16% to 0.13%.	
Germany	▪ Corporate tax rate decreased from 25% to 15%. ▪ The uniform base rate of the business tax decreased from 5% to 3.5%.	▪ Business tax is no longer deductible from its own and from the corporate tax base. ▪ Declining balance depreciation was abolished in favour of straight line depreciation. ▪ Deduction of net interest expenditures was limited to 30% of EBITDA subject to certain conditions. ▪ Business tax: broadened add-back of 25% was introduced for all interest payments and deemed financing parts of expenditures for using assets other than capital (rents, leases, license fees).
Italy	▪ Business tax rate (IRAP) decreased from 4.25% to 3.9%. ▪ Corporate tax rate reduced from 33% to 27.5%.	▪ Deduction of costs for personnel working in R&D from IRAP tax base was introduced. ▪ Expenditures for R&D are now deductible in the year they occur and do not have to increase production costs. ▪ Accelerated depreciation was abolished. ▪ Depreciation rates for patents and licenses were increased to 50%. ▪ Deduction of net interest expenditures was limited to 30% of EBITDA.

	Tax rates	Tax base
Netherlands	▪ Corporate tax rates were reduced and split so that 20% (up to €40k), 23% (between €40k and €200k) and 25.5% (above €200k) apply.	▪ Introduction of limitation of loss carry-forward to nine years.
Spain	▪ Corporate tax rate was reduced: For companies with less €8 million in turnover, 25% tax on profits up to €120k, 30% on all additional profits. For companies with greater than €8 million in turnover, 30% on all profits.	▪ LIFO method for the valuation of inventory was abolished.

We however focus on the reforms in Germany, France, Italy, the Netherlands and Spain which have become effective in 2007 and 2008. Table 66 summarises the most relevant elements of the tax reforms in these countries.

Large Corporation

Table 67: Future value of the tax base (in € millions) for the EU-27 large company under national GAAP and deviation (in %) to CCTB when recent tax reforms are considered in France, Germany, Italy, the Netherlands and Spain

Country	National GAAP	A	B	C	D	E	F	G	H	I
AT	81.19	3.15	0.35	1.26	0.00	-0.96	0.00	0.00	0.00	5.94
BE	78.55	0.23	0.07	0.10	0.00	0.00	0.00	0.00	0.00	3.03
BG	94.64	5.02	0.24	1.26	0.01	0.00	-1.36	0.00	0.00	13.06
CY	104.98	0.70	0.00	-7.38	-0.46	0.00	-4.13	0.00	0.00	-6.68
CZ	95.97	9.98	0.00	-0.01	0.01	0.00	-1.19	0.00	0.00	9.94
DE	**93.66**	**2.58**	**0.28**	**0.99**	**0.00**	**-0.76**	**0.00**	**0.00**	**0.00**	**4.18**
DK	91.36	1.42	-0.02	1.16	0.01	0.00	0.00	0.00	0.00	3.77
EE	103.22	1.32	0.00	1.00	0.00	-0.05	0.00	0.00	0.00	2.60
ES	**85.77**	**5.13**	**0.00**	**-0.09**	**-0.09**	**0.00**	**0.00**	**0.00**	**0.00**	**4.45**
FI	95.06	1.59	-0.02	1.16	0.01	0.00	-1.17	0.00	0.00	9.43
FR	**55.98**	**9.74**	**0.00**	**-0.02**	**0.01**	**0.00**	**0.00**	**0.00**	**0.00**	**9.65**
GR	95.90	4.48	0.00	0.60	0.01	0.00	-1.11	-2.56	0.00	9.13
HU	41.70	12.47	0.00	-0.13	0.03	0.00	0.00	0.00	0.00	12.29
IE	101.06	0.78	0.00	-0.01	0.01	0.00	0.00	-2.43	0.00	-1.54
IT	**99.40**	**0.71**	**1.02**	**-0.63**	**0.01**	**0.00**	**-1.99**	**0.00**	**0.00**	**0.18**
LT	93.70	11.36	-0.03	-0.01	0.01	0.00	-1.30	0.00	0.00	11.08
LU	93.42	2.66	0.34	-0.33	-0.09	0.00	0.00	0.00	0.00	3.75
LV	93.84	11.30	0.00	0.00	0.00	0.00	0.00	0.00	0.00	11.30
MT	98.18	1.32	0.00	0.88	-0.08	0.00	-0.98	-2.49	0.00	3.84
NL	**96.28**	**1.68**	**0.43**	**0.00**	**0.00**	**-0.43**	**0.00**	**0.00**	**0.00**	**2.68**
PL	97.46	5.97	0.33	-0.01	0.01	0.00	-1.25	-2.52	0.00	7.69
PT	94.67	3.08	0.22	0.42	0.01	0.00	-1.14	0.00	0.00	10.56
RO	95.16	2.74	0.25	0.35	0.00	0.00	0.00	0.00	0.00	4.93
SE	93.60	4.81	0.00	-0.09	-0.09	0.00	0.00	0.00	0.00	4.37
SK	96.26	9.84	0.00	-0.01	0.01	0.00	-1.27	0.00	0.00	9.80
SL	89.26	1.87	0.37	1.14	0.00	0.00	-1.26	0.00	0.00	8.57
UK	93.45	2.75	0.00	-0.01	0.01	0.00	0.00	-1.51	0.00	0.24
Ø	90.88	4.40	0.14	0.06	-0.02	-0.08	-0.67	-0.43	0.00	5.86

Table 67 displays the future value of the tax base before and after the introduction of a CCTB when rule changes enacted in France, Germany, Italy, the Netherlands and Spain up to the end of 2008 are taken into account.

The status quo in 2006 is applied for all other EU-27 member states. With these changes, the average future value of the tax base for the EU-27 large corporation increases from €89.91 million to €90.88 million. The average deviation in the future value of the tax base decreases slightly from 6.20% to 5.86%.

Table 68: Tax burden (in € millions) for the EU-27 large company under national GAAP and deviation (in %) to CCTB when recent tax reforms are considered in France, Germany, Italy, the Netherlands and Spain

Country	National GAAP	A	B	C	D	E	F	G	H	I
AT	33.05	1.94	0.22	0.77	0.00	-0.59	0.00	0.00	0.00	3.65
BE	31.43	0.19	0.06	0.08	0.00	0.00	0.00	0.00	0.00	2.58
BG	14.52	4.91	0.24	1.23	0.01	0.00	-1.33	0.00	0.00	10.70
CY	18.35	0.40	0.00	-4.22	-0.27	0.00	-2.36	0.00	0.00	-3.82
CZ	23.38	9.83	0.00	-0.01	0.01	0.00	-1.17	0.00	0.00	7.66
DE	**31.38**	**2.51**	**0.25**	**0.91**	**0.00**	**-0.70**	**0.00**	**0.00**	**0.00**	**5.86**
DK	29.40	1.24	-0.02	1.01	0.01	0.00	0.00	0.00	0.00	3.28
EE	15.63	0.00	0.00	0.00	0.00	0.00	0.00	0.00	0.00	0.00
ES	**33.87**	**5.02**	**0.00**	**-0.09**	**-0.08**	**0.00**	**0.00**	**0.00**	**0.00**	**3.88**
FI	26.23	1.50	-0.02	1.09	0.01	0.00	-1.10	0.00	0.00	6.78
FR	**54.85**	**3.81**	**0.00**	**-0.01**	**0.01**	**0.00**	**0.00**	**0.00**	**0.00**	**3.77**
GR	27.77	4.49	0.00	0.60	0.01	0.00	-1.11	0.00	0.00	9.49
HU	38.09	2.19	0.00	0.04	0.00	0.00	0.00	0.00	0.00	2.23
IE	13.86	0.91	0.00	-0.01	0.01	0.00	0.00	0.00	0.00	0.81
IT	**34.18**	**1.39**	**1.64**	**-0.29**	**0.22**	**0.00**	**-2.54**	**0.00**	**0.00**	**1.04**
LT	20.44	10.33	-0.02	-0.01	0.01	0.00	-1.13	0.00	0.00	8.50
LU	29.11	2.52	0.36	-0.40	-0.09	0.00	0.00	0.00	0.00	3.55
LV	16.36	13.06	0.00	0.00	0.00	0.00	0.00	0.00	0.00	11.15
MT	33.63	1.54	0.00	0.90	-0.09	0.00	-1.00	-0.35	0.00	6.11
NL	**25.12**	**1.67**	**0.42**	**0.00**	**0.00**	**-0.42**	**0.00**	**0.00**	**0.00**	**2.23**
PL	19.75	5.80	0.31	-0.01	0.01	0.00	-1.17	0.00	0.00	7.57
PT	26.72	3.00	0.22	0.41	0.01	0.00	-1.12	0.00	0.00	8.11
RO	15.76	6.65	0.25	1.46	0.00	0.00	0.00	0.00	0.00	8.38
SE	27.19	4.64	0.00	-0.08	-0.08	0.00	0.00	0.00	0.00	4.21
SK	19.26	9.34	0.00	-0.01	0.01	0.00	-1.20	0.00	0.00	7.27
SL	28.85	1.45	0.29	0.88	0.00	0.00	-0.97	0.00	0.00	6.63
UK	31.92	2.62	0.00	-0.02	0.01	0.00	0.00	0.93	0.00	2.51
Ø	26.67	3.81	0.15	0.16	-0.01	-0.06	-0.60	0.02	0.00	4.97

Under national GAAP, the future value of the tax base increases in France, Germany, Italy, the Netherlands and Spain. Changes with regard to local taxes are one reason for this result. The tax reforms in Germany, Italy and France all tend to reduce local taxes. As these taxes lower liquidity (or the corporate tax base if they are deductible), the corporate tax base increases. In addition to local taxes, lower corporate tax rates directly lower the corporate tax due and, therefore, the tax base tends to increase. The strongest increase in the future value of the tax base under national GAAP is found for Germany, where, as of 2008, the tax trade on income is no longer deductible from corporate tax. Impacts increasing the tax base stemming from parts of the tax reform in Germany (switch from declining balance depreciation to straight line depreciation), Italy (reduction of accelerated depreciation) and Spain (switch from a system similar to LIFO to the weighted average method) are thus outbalanced by the simultaneous reduction of tax rates.

Table 69: Future value of the tax base (in € millions) for the EU-27 small and medium company under national GAAP and deviation (in %) to CCTB when recent tax reforms are considered in France, Germany, Italy, the Netherlands and Spain

Country	National GAAP	A	B	C	D	E	F	G	H	I
AT	2.87	2.40	0.33	1.03	0.00	-0.68	0.00	0.00	0.00	4.32
BE	2.94	0.09	0.05	0.01	0.00	0.00	0.00	0.00	0.00	1.52
BG	3.43	4.18	0.25	1.01	0.01	0.00	-1.70	0.00	0.00	11.80
CY	3.74	0.72	0.00	-7.63	-0.28	0.00	-4.80	0.00	0.00	-6.91
CZ	3.45	9.53	0.00	-0.01	0.01	0.00	-1.47	0.00	0.00	9.51
DE	**3.36**	**1.88**	**0.26**	**0.80**	**0.00**	**-0.55**	**0.00**	**0.00**	**0.00**	**2.91**
DK	3.29	1.07	-0.01	0.94	0.01	0.00	0.00	0.00	0.00	2.36
EE	3.60	1.04	0.00	0.78	0.00	-0.04	0.00	0.00	0.00	1.77
ES	**3.10**	**2.80**	**0.00**	**-0.07**	**-0.07**	**0.00**	**0.00**	**0.00**	**0.00**	**2.43**
FI	3.42	4.61	-0.01	1.70	0.01	0.00	-1.45	0.00	0.00	9.21
FR	**2.38**	**5.23**	**0.00**	**-0.01**	**0.01**	**0.00**	**0.00**	**0.00**	**0.00**	**5.20**
GR	3.41	6.58	0.00	0.90	0.01	0.00	-1.41	-0.96	0.00	10.31
HU	1.08	15.71	0.00	-0.27	0.10	0.00	0.00	0.00	0.00	15.43
IE	3.54	0.16	0.00	-0.01	0.01	0.00	0.00	-0.92	0.00	-0.77
IT	**3.52**	**2.27**	**2.74**	**-0.53**	**0.00**	**0.00**	**-2.30**	**0.00**	**0.00**	**1.80**
LT	3.38	10.60	-0.02	-0.01	0.01	0.00	-1.63	0.00	0.00	10.48
LU	3.35	1.98	0.33	-0.30	-0.07	0.00	0.00	0.00	0.00	2.26
LV	3.40	10.42	0.00	0.00	0.00	0.00	0.00	0.00	0.00	10.42
MT	3.46	3.32	0.00	0.72	-0.07	0.00	-1.23	-0.94	0.00	5.37
NL	**3.44**	**1.11**	**0.37**	**0.00**	**0.00**	**-0.28**	**0.00**	**0.00**	**0.00**	**1.34**
PL	3.46	6.30	0.36	-0.01	0.01	0.00	-1.60	-0.95	0.00	8.84
PT	3.41	2.98	0.25	0.29	0.01	0.00	-1.44	0.00	0.00	9.92
RO	3.44	1.73	0.35	0.39	0.00	0.00	0.00	0.00	0.00	2.51
SE	3.36	2.94	0.00	-0.07	-0.07	0.00	0.00	0.00	0.00	2.69
SK	3.46	9.48	0.00	-0.01	0.01	0.00	-1.58	0.00	0.00	9.46
SL	3.17	2.47	0.33	0.92	0.00	0.00	-1.58	0.00	0.00	8.25
UK	3.36	1.61	0.00	-0.01	0.01	0.00	0.00	1.19	0.00	0.67
Ø	3.25	4.19	0.21	0.02	-0.01	-0.06	-0.82	-0.10	0.00	5.30

Focusing now on the effects of the introduction of the proposed CCTB on the deviation in future tax base values between the national GAAP and CCTB regimes before and after tax reforms, the deviation decreases in France, Germany, Italy and Spain but increases in the Netherlands.

- The deviation under Option I decreases in France from 9.80% to 9.65%, in Germany from 4.78% to 4.18%, in Italy from 8.75% to 0.18% and in Spain from 4.63% to 4.45%. In all countries this effect can mainly be explained by a reduction in tax rates, which results in a higher future value of the tax base and, therefore, causes a quite strong base effect as the absolute increase of future value of the tax base of Option I is now related to a much higher tax base. In Italy the decrease in the deviation is greater than for the other countries because the abolishment of accelerated depreciation for tangible assets leads to a considerable broadening of the tax base under national GAAP.

- In the Netherlands, the deviation between the national GAAP and CCTB Option I increases from 2.24% to 2.68%. Here, the decrease of the tax burden due to lower corporate income tax rates is overshadowed by loss carry-forward limitations. Losses under CCTB Option I are therefore devalued at a higher rate, leading to a slightly higher CCTB impact on the future value of the tax base.

To sum up, the future value of the tax base for the EU-27 average large corporation increases from €89.91 million to €90.88 million when recent tax reforms in France, Germany, Italy, the Netherlands and Spain are taken into account.[84]

However, the deviation in the future values of the tax base between the national GAAP and CCTB regimes is influenced heterogeneously by the considered tax changes. It decreases in France, Germany, Italy and Spain, but increases in the Netherlands. In total the tax reforms cause the average deviation to decrease from 6.20% to 5.86%.

Small and Medium-Sized Corporation

The results shown for the EU-27 average large company also hold true for the EU-27 average small and medium company. Table 69 displays the results for the calculation of the future value of the tax base before and after the introduction of a CCTB. The future value of the tax base increases in all countries considered here. As a result, the future value of the tax base increases on average from €3.22 million to €3.25 million.[85] The average deviation in the future value of the tax base between the national GAAP and CCTB regimes decreases slightly from 5.57% to 5.30%.

---

[84] For the change in the effective tax burden see Table 68.

[85] For the change in the effective tax burden see Table 70.

Table 70: Tax burden (in € millions) for the EU-27 large company under national GAAP and deviation (in %) to CCTB when recent tax reforms are considered in France, Germany, Italy, the Netherlands and Spain

Country	National GAAP	A	B	C	D	E	F	G	H	I
AT	1.21	1.44	0.19	0.63	0.00	-0.36	0.00	0.00	0.00	2.63
BE	1.13	0.85	0.20	0.21	0.00	0.00	0.00	0.00	0.00	2.80
BG	0.52	4.10	0.25	0.99	0.01	0.00	-1.66	0.00	0.00	9.38
CY	0.67	0.39	0.00	-4.27	-0.16	0.00	-2.69	0.00	0.00	-3.87
CZ	0.84	9.40	0.00	-0.01	0.01	0.00	-1.52	0.00	0.00	7.12
DE	**1.08**	**1.83**	**0.25**	**0.79**	**0.00**	**-0.47**	**0.00**	**0.00**	**0.00**	**2.70**
DK	1.04	1.00	-0.01	0.85	0.01	0.00	0.00	0.00	0.00	2.16
EE	0.55	0.00	0.00	0.00	0.00	0.00	0.00	0.00	0.00	0.00
ES	**1.16**	**3.09**	**0.00**	**-0.07**	**-0.07**	**0.00**	**0.00**	**0.00**	**0.00**	**2.57**
FI	0.94	4.45	-0.01	1.63	0.01	0.00	-1.44	0.00	0.00	6.60
FR	**1.69**	**2.56**	**0.00**	**0.00**	**0.01**	**0.00**	**0.00**	**0.00**	**0.00**	**2.54**
GR	0.99	6.91	0.00	0.90	0.01	0.00	-1.41	0.00	0.00	9.20
HU	1.52	1.80	0.00	0.05	0.01	0.00	0.00	0.00	0.00	1.85
IE	0.49	0.16	0.00	-0.01	0.01	0.00	0.00	0.00	0.00	0.14
IT	**1.23**	**2.25**	**2.73**	**-0.16**	**0.25**	**0.00**	**-3.09**	**0.00**	**0.00**	**1.65**
LT	0.73	9.89	-0.02	-0.01	0.01	0.00	-1.45	0.00	0.00	8.12
LU	1.03	2.02	0.35	-0.36	-0.08	0.00	0.00	0.00	0.00	2.46
LV	0.58	12.10	0.00	0.00	0.00	0.00	0.00	0.00	0.00	10.06
MT	1.21	3.38	0.00	0.75	-0.07	0.00	-1.31	-0.13	0.00	6.21
NL	**0.83**	**1.56**	**0.39**	**0.00**	**0.00**	**-0.24**	**0.00**	**0.00**	**0.00**	**2.12**
PL	0.71	6.02	0.33	-0.01	0.01	0.00	-1.49	0.00	0.00	7.07
PT	0.96	3.11	0.25	0.29	0.01	0.00	-1.40	0.00	0.00	7.62
RO	0.56	5.92	0.34	0.90	0.00	0.00	0.00	0.00	0.00	6.68
SE	0.97	3.01	0.00	-0.07	-0.07	0.00	0.00	0.00	0.00	2.76
SK	0.69	9.02	0.00	-0.01	0.01	0.00	-1.57	0.00	0.00	6.83
SL	1.06	1.83	0.24	0.71	0.00	0.00	-1.24	0.00	0.00	6.19
UK	0.78	1.91	0.00	-0.01	0.01	0.00	0.00	2.08	0.00	1.80
Ø	0.93	3.70	0.20	0.14	0.00	-0.04	-0.75	0.07	0.00	4.27

3.5 Summary of Conclusions

According to our analysis, the introduction of a CCTB would have a considerable impact on the tax base values in all EU member states. An enlargement of the tax base would be witnessed in all countries aside from Cyprus and Ireland.

The results show considerable variation between companies depending on their size, economic sector and financial characteristics. In this connection, assumptions regarding capital intensity and profitability have the most significant impact on estimates of the tax base changes which would result from a CCTB.

Each individual CCTB option has varying effects on the value of the tax base. CCTB rule modifications concerning depreciation have by far the strongest impact on future tax base values.

The countries which would be affected most by a CCTB are Bulgaria, Hungary, Latvia, Lithuania and Portugal. Sensitivity analyses show that Greece, France and Slovakia would also be significantly impacted.

Appendix

Appendix 1: Estimation of Missing Variables

If the number of employees (costs of employees) is not given for a company *j*, this number n_j (costs c_j) is estimated by the ratio $\hat{n}_j$ and the product $\hat{c}_j$ using costs of employees c_j (number of employees n_j) of this company and the average yearly labour costs per country and industry $\overline{a}^{k,l}$ as follows:

$$\hat{n}_j = \frac{c_j}{\overline{a}^{k,l}} \qquad (1)$$

$$\hat{c}_j = n_j * \overline{a}^{k,l} \qquad (2)$$

with

$\hat{n}_j = \textit{Estimated value for the number of employees of company } j$

$c_j = \textit{Reported costs of employees of company } j$

$\hat{c}_j = \textit{Estimated value for the costs of employees of company } j$

$n_j = \textit{Reported number of employees of company } j$

$\overline{a}^{k,l} = \textit{Average yearly labour costs for country } k \textit{ and industry } l.$

Where possible, the average yearly labour costs are estimated for each country and industry on the basis of the information provided in AMADEUS according to the following formula;[86]

$$\overline{a}^{k,l} = \left(\frac{\sum_{i \in N^{k,l}} c_i}{\sum_{i \in N^{k,l}} n_i} \right) \qquad (3)$$

with

$c_i = \textit{Costs of employees of company } i$

$n_i = \textit{Number of employees of company } i$

---

[86] For this purpose only companies are considered when information on both variables (costs of employees and number of employees) is provided by AMADEUS.

$N^{k,l} = Set\ of\ companies\ in\ our\ sample\ belonging\ to\ country\ k\ and\ industry\ l$
$k = Country\ index, l = Industry\ index$ and
$i, j \in N^{k,l}$.

For Malta, the AMADEUS database only provides information on two sectors: the construction and service/trade industries. For the other industries (manufacturing, commerce and transport), average labour costs have to be derived from the Malta average and the EU averages for the specific industry ($\overline{a}^l$) and all industries ($\overline{a}$). For the determination of $\overline{a}$ we referred only to the EU-12 member states:

$$\overline{a}^l = \frac{\sum_{k \in K} \overline{a}^{k,l}}{q}, \ K = \{1 \ldots q\} \tag{4}$$

$$\overline{a} = \frac{\sum_{l \in L} \left(\overline{a}^l\right)}{p}, \ L = \{1 \ldots p\} \tag{5}$$

$$\overline{a}^{MT} = \left(\frac{\overline{a}^{MT,Construction} + \overline{a}^{MT,\ Service/Trade}}{2} \right) \tag{6}$$

$$\hat{c}^{MT} = \frac{\overline{a}^{MT}}{\overline{a}} * \overline{a}^l \tag{7}$$

with

$\hat{c}^{MT,L} = Estimated\ value\ for\ the\ costs\ of\ employees\ in\ Malta\ for\ the\ industries$ $manufacturing, commerce\ and\ transport$
$\overline{a}^{MT,L} = Average\ yearly\ labour\ costs\ in\ Malta$
$\overline{a}^{MT,Construction} = Average\ yearly\ labour\ costs\ in\ Malta\ for\ construction$
$\overline{a}^{MT,Service/Trade} = Average\ yearly\ labour\ costs\ in\ Malta\ for\ service\ trade$
$\overline{a} = Average\ yearly\ labour\ costs\ determined\ over\ the\ countries\ and\ industries$
$L = Set\ of\ industries$
$K = Set\ of\ countries$.

For Greece, Lithuania, Slovakia and Ireland, values for both variables (costs of employees and number of employees) are not given for any of the companies in the sample. Therefore, we used the EUROSTAT database for country- and industry-specific figures on macroeconomic labour costs, and adjusted these figures based on the average difference ($\overline{d}_l$) between the EUROSTAT values for the other countries and the corresponding values determined on the basis of

AMADEUS.[87] This average relative deviation $\overline{d}_l$ is determined separately for the EU-12 member states and the EU-15 member states.

A1, Table 1: Average yearly labour costs per country and industry in € thousands

Country	Manu-facturing	Construction	Commerce	Service/ Trade	Transport
AT	54.22	48.86	37.45	51.70	57.27
BE	48.15	36.51	42.94	42.45	42.03
CZ	6.00	6.08	5.24	5.51	6.56
DE	58.52	46.62	41.49	64.66	40.23
DK	44.47	42.16	42.26	53.16	43.28
EE	4.78	4.66	4.813	5.86	5.95
ES	24.79	21.85	20.25	20.32	29.04
FI	36.93	32.66	32.17	33.96	33.21
FR	39.42	34.65	32.25	36.17	32.27
GB	40.54	39.97	23.70	40.70	35.93
GR*	14.56	14.61	15.42	23.34	26.70
HU	7.60	8.95	7.71	13.72	6.94
IE	40.54	39.97	23.70	40.70	35.93
IT	31.16	31.25	32.35	32.69	37.61
LT*	4.87	4.91	5.10	5.83	4.79
LU	39.16	32.58	36.04	53.16	36.83
LV	4.90	4.25	6.07	10.56	2.5
MT	13.33	8.25	13.41	20.06	11.70
NL	49.32	45.19	39.35	52.70	41.47
PL	8.67	8.72	8.77	9.93	5.31
PT	18.93	22.06	17.92	16.61	36.05
RO	2.12	2.04	1.67	2.32	2.65
SE	29.48	27.20	27.48	32.26	26.36
SK*	5.27	5.28	6.31	8.50	4.59

The following formulae are applied:

$$d^{k,l} = \left(\frac{\overline{a}^{k,l}}{\overline{e}^{k,l}}\right) - 1 \qquad (8)$$

$$\overline{d}^{l} = \frac{\sum_{k \in K} d^{k,l}}{q}, \; K = \{1 \ldots q\} \qquad (9)$$

$$\overline{a}^{k,l} = \overline{e}^{k,l} * \left(1 + \overline{d}^{l}\right) \qquad (10)$$

with

$\overline{e}^{k,l}$ = *Average yearly labour costs for country k and industry l based on EUROSTAT*

[87] For Ireland average labour costs are not available from EUROSTAT. Therefore, we refer to the corresponding values for Great Britain. This is a plausible assumption; see the keyword Arbeitskosten (labour costs) at www.wko.at/statistik.

$\bar{d}^{l}$ = *Average relative deviation of yearly labour costs between AMADEUS and EUROSTAT for industry l*

$d^{k,l}$ = *Relative deviation of yearly labour costs between AMADEUS and EUROSTAT for country k and industry l.*

Table 1 shows the average yearly labour costs obtained for each country and sector based on AMADEUS data. Figures for countries marked with a star were determined based on EUROSTAT data.

For the other variables (sales s_j /operating revenue rev_j and interest paid ip_j /financial expenses fe_j), estimated values are determined correspondingly. If figures are unavailable for a sector specific variable (e.g. sales), a corresponding variable (e.g. operating revenue) adjusted by the average ratio between the two variables (e.g. $\bar{b}^{k,l}$) is used instead.

$$\hat{s}_j = \frac{rev_j}{\bar{b}^{k,l}} \tag{11}$$

$$\widehat{rev}_j = s_j \times \bar{b}^{k,l} \tag{12}$$

$$\widehat{ip}_j = \frac{fe_j}{\bar{z}^{k,l}} \tag{13}$$

$$\widehat{fe}_j = ip_j \times \bar{z}^{k,l} \tag{14}$$

where

$\hat{s}_j$ = *Estimated value for sales of company j*
rev_j = *Reported operating revenue of company j*
$\widehat{rev}_j$ = *Estimated value for operating revenue of company j*
s_j = *Reported sales of company j*

$\widehat{ip}_j$ = *Estimated value for interest paid of company j*
fe_j = *Reported financial expenses of company j*
$\widehat{fe}_j$ = *Estimated value for financial expenses of company j*
ip_j = *Reported interst paid of company j*
$\bar{b}^{k,l}$ = *Average ratio of total operating revenue to total sales for country k and industry l*
$\bar{z}^{k,l}$ = *Average ratio of total financial expenses to total interest paid for country k and industry l.*

Where possible, the average ratios $\bar{b}^{k,l}$ and $\bar{z}^{k,l}$ are again determined as country- and industry-specific averages on the basis of AMADEUS

$$\bar{b}^{k,l} = \left(\frac{\sum_{i \in N^{k,l}} rev_i}{\sum_{i \in N^{k,l}} s_i} \right) \tag{15}$$

$$\bar{z}^{k,l} = \left(\frac{\sum_{i \in N^{k,l}} fe_i}{\sum_{i \in N^{k,l}} ip_i} \right). \tag{16}$$

In Denmark, Great Britain and Ireland (as regard to sales/operating revenue), and Greece, Lithuania and Cyprus (as regard to interest paid/financial expenses), no company provides information on both variables. Thus, we refer to industry-specific EU average ratios, determined separately for the EU-15 and EU-12 member states.

Appendix 2: Formulae for the Determination of the EU-Average Income Statements

A2, Table 1: Determination of EU-average income statements

EU-Average Income Statement	Abbreviations	Formulae
Sales		$\overline{sales} = \frac{\sum_{k \in K} \overline{sales}^k}{q}$
Costs of goods sold	$\overline{cgs}$	$\overline{cgs} = \frac{\sum_{k \in K} \overline{\left(\frac{cgs}{cgs + oo\exp}\right)}^k}{q} * \left(\overline{sales} + \overline{oorev} - \overline{opl}\right)$
Other operating revenue	$\overline{oorev}$	$\overline{oorev} = \overline{sales} * \frac{\sum_{k \in K} \overline{\left(\frac{oorev}{sales} - 1\right)}^k}{q}$
Other operating expenses	$\overline{oo\exp}$	$\overline{oo\exp} = \frac{\sum_{k \in K} \overline{\left(\frac{oo\exp}{cgs + oo\exp}\right)}^k}{q} * \left(\overline{sales} + \overline{oorev} - \overline{opl}\right)$
Operating profit/loss	$\overline{opl}$	$\overline{opl} = \overline{sales} * \frac{\sum_{k \in K} \overline{\left(\frac{opl}{sales}\right)}^k}{q}$
Financial revenue	$\overline{frev}$	$\overline{frev} = \overline{plbt} - \overline{opl} + \overline{ip} + \overline{of\exp}$
Interest paid	$\overline{ip}$	$\overline{ip} = \overline{sales} * \frac{\sum_{k \in K} \overline{\left(\frac{ip}{sales}\right)}^k}{q}$
Other financial expenses	$\overline{of\exp}$	$\overline{of\exp} = \frac{\sum_{k \in K} \overline{\left(\frac{of\exp}{ip}\right)}^k}{q} * \overline{ip}$
Financial profit/loss	$\overline{fpl}$	$\overline{fpl} = \overline{plbt} - \overline{opl}$

Profit/loss before tax	$\overline{plbt}$	$\overline{plbt} = \overline{sales} * \frac{\sum_{k \epsilon K} \overline{\left(\frac{plbt}{sales}\right)}^k}{q}$
Taxes		$\overline{taxes} = \overline{plbt} - \overline{plat}$
Profit/loss after tax	$\overline{plat}$	$\overline{plat} = \overline{sales} * \frac{\sum_{k \epsilon K} \overline{\left(\frac{plat}{sales}\right)}^k}{q}$
Extraordinary income	$\overline{extr}$	$\overline{extr} = \overline{plp} - \overline{plat}$
Profit and loss for period	$\overline{plp}$	$\overline{plp} = \overline{sales} * \frac{\sum_{k \epsilon K} \overline{\left(\frac{plp}{sales}\right)}^k}{q}$

Legend	
$\overline{x}$	Average of item x across all countries
$\overline{x}^k$	Average of item x across the companies for country k

Appendix 3: Formulae for the Determination of the EU-Average Balance Sheets

A3, Table 1: Determination of EU-average balance sheets

EU-Average Balance Sheets	Abbreviations	Formulae
Total assets	$\overline{toass}$	$\overline{toass} = \frac{\sum_{k \epsilon K} \overline{toass}^k}{q}$
Fixed assets	$\overline{fiass}$	$\overline{fiass} = \overline{toass} * \frac{\sum_{k \epsilon K} \overline{\left(\frac{fiass}{toass}\right)}^k}{q}$
Intangible fixed assets	$\overline{\text{int}}$	$\overline{\text{int}} = \frac{\sum_{k \epsilon K} \overline{\left(\frac{\text{int}}{fiass}\right)}^k}{q} * \overline{fiass}$
Tangible fixed assets	$\overline{\tan}$	$\overline{\tan} = \frac{\sum_{k \epsilon K} \overline{\left(\frac{\tan}{fiass}\right)}^k}{q} * \overline{fiass}$
Other fixed assets	$\overline{ofiass}$	$\overline{ofiass} = \overline{fiass} - \overline{\text{int}} - \overline{\tan}$
Current assets	$\overline{cuass}$	$\overline{cuass} = \overline{toass} * \frac{\sum_{k \epsilon K} \overline{\left(\frac{cuass}{toass}\right)}^k}{q}$
Stocks		$\overline{stocks} = \frac{\sum_{k \epsilon K} \overline{\left(\frac{stocks}{cuass}\right)}^k}{q} * \overline{cuass}$
Debtors	$\overline{deb}$	$\overline{deb} = \frac{\sum_{k \epsilon K} \overline{\left(\frac{deb}{cuass}\right)}^k}{q} * \overline{cuass}$
Other current assets	$\overline{ocuass}$	$\overline{ocuass} = \overline{cuass} - \overline{stocks} - \overline{deb}$

Shareholder funds	$\overline{shf}$	$\overline{shf} = \overline{toass} * \frac{\sum_{k \epsilon K} \overline{\left(\frac{shf}{toass}\right)}^{k}}{q}$
Capital	$\overline{cap}$	$\overline{cap} = \frac{\sum_{k \epsilon K} \overline{\left(\frac{cap}{shf}\right)}^{k}}{q} * \overline{shf}$
Other shareholder funds	$\overline{oshf}$	$\overline{oshf} = \overline{shf} - \overline{cap}$
Non-current liabilities	$\overline{liab}$	$\overline{liab} = \overline{toass} * \frac{\sum_{k \epsilon K} \overline{\left(\frac{liab}{toass}\right)}^{k}}{q}$
Long-term debt	$\overline{ltd}$	$\overline{ltd} = \frac{\sum_{k \epsilon K} \overline{\left(\frac{ltd}{liab}\right)}^{k}}{q} * \overline{liab}$
Other non-current liabilities	$\overline{oliap}$	$\overline{oliab} = \overline{liab} - \overline{ltd}$
Current liabilities	$\overline{culiap}$	$\overline{culiab} = \overline{toass} * \frac{\sum_{k \epsilon K} \overline{\left(\frac{culiab}{toass}\right)}^{k}}{q}$
Loans		$\overline{loans} = \frac{\sum_{k \epsilon K} \overline{\left(\frac{loans}{culiab}\right)}^{k}}{q} * \overline{culiab}$
Creditors	$\overline{cred}$	$\overline{cred} = \frac{\sum_{k \epsilon K} \overline{\left(\frac{cred}{culiab}\right)}^{k}}{q} * \overline{culiab}$
Other current liabilities	$\overline{oculiap}$	$\overline{oculiab} = \overline{culiab} - \overline{loans} - \overline{cred}$

Legend	
$\overline{x}$	Average of item x across all countries
$\overline{x}^k$	Average of item x across the companies for country k

Appendix 4: EU-27, EU-12, EU-15 and Industry-Specific Average Model Companies, Large and SME

Appendix 4.1: EU-27 Average Model Company, Large and SME

EU-27 Income Statement	**Large**	**SME**
Sales (€)	158,895,919.63	7,051,093.62
Costs of goods sold (€)	130,635,765.60	5,463,509.46
Other operating revenue (€)	11,641,729.21	352,991.91
Other operating expenses (€)	32,957,163.46	1,591,987.29
Operating profit/loss (€)	6,944,719.78	348,588.78
Financial revenue (€)	1,969,140.96	43,624.61
Interest paid (€)	2,587,194.61	99,612.15
Other financial expenses (€)	743,559.59	21,836.50
Financial profit/loss (€)	-1,361,613.24	-77,824.05
Profit/loss before tax (€)	5,583,106.54	270,764.73
Taxes (€)	1,413,562.88	78,903.52
Profit/loss after tax (€)	4,169,543.65	191,861.21
Extraordinary income (€)	-24,912.09	2,090.88
Profit and loss for period (€)	4,144,631.57	193,952.09
Balance Sheet		
Total assets (€)	**124,963,873.93**	**4,156,227.98**
Fixed assets (€)	**49,308,661.92**	**1,264,186.01**
Intangible fixed assets (€)	2,916,811.67	75,863.58
Tangible fixed assets (€)	37,419,582.21	1,075,985.30
Other fixed assets (€)	8,972,268.04	112,337.13
Current assets (€)	**75,655,212.01**	**2,892,041.97**
Stocks (€)	22,583,728.19	858,296.04
Debtors (€)	32,722,604.43	1,207,978.32
Other current assets (€)	20,348,879.38	825,767.60
Shareholder funds (€)	**44,362,175.24**	**1,239,941.35**
Capital (€)	16,207,741.76	420,923.54
Other shareholder funds (€)	28,154,433.48	819,017.81
Non-current liabilities (€)	**18,136,927.73**	**534,276.42**
Long-term debt (€)	8,349,159.52	288,874.58
Other non-current liabilities (€)	9,787,768.21	245,401.84
Current liabilities (€)	**62,464,770.95**	**2,382,010.21**
Loans (€)	12,268,474.58	408,487.13
Creditors (€)	25,929,780.53	1,121,983.50
Other current liabilities (€)	24,266,515.84	851,539.58
Profit (loss) for period (€)	4,144,631.57	193,952.09
Total assets (€)	124,963,873.93	4,156,227.98
Sales (€)	158,895,919.63	7,051,093.62
Share of tangible fixed assets (%)	29.94	25.89
Return on sales (%)	2.61	2.75
Return on equity (%)	9.34	15.64
Equity ratio (%)	35.50	29.83
Return on assets (%)	5.39	7.06
Inventories to capital (%)	18.07	20.65
Costs for personnel to turnover (%)	21.03	18.38

Appendix 4.2: EU-12 Average Model Company, Large and SME

EU-12 Income Statement	Large	SME
Sales (€)	42,249,427.46	4,537,409.99
Costs of goods sold (€)	38,690,251.39	4,055,787.09
Other operating revenue (€)	5,042,489.78	316,730.76
Other operating expenses (€)	6,501,056.54	569,942.20
Operating profit/loss (€)	2,100,609.31	228,411.45
Financial revenue (€)	482,108.94	45,010.08
Interest paid (€)	727,396.01	82,391.47
Other financial expenses (€)	262,054.60	23,632.19
Financial profit/loss (€)	-507,341.67	-61,013.57
Profit/loss before tax (€)	1,593,267.64	167,397.87
Taxes (€)	217,318.30	36,361.18
Profit/loss after tax (€)	1,375,949.34	131,036.69
Extraordinary income (€)	-29,565.96	-7,838.70
Profit and loss for period (€)	1,346,383.38	123,198.00
Balance Sheet		
Total assets (€)	**32,306,515.05**	**2,995,276.81**
Fixed assets (€)	**15,219,958.20**	**1,038,362.63**
Intangible fixed assets (€)	421,091.65	26,289.71
Tangible fixed assets (€)	13,505,575.54	943,864.95
Other fixed assets (€)	1,293,291.02	68,207.96
Current assets (€)	**17,086,556.85**	**1,956,914.18**
Stocks (€)	6,172,780.37	664,335.37
Debtors (€)	7,270,713.46	865,945.61
Other current assets (€)	3,643,063.01	426,633.21
Shareholder funds (€)	**13,927,697.60**	**911,895.38**
Capital (€)	6,345,534.06	331,966.87
Other shareholder funds (€)	7,582,163.54	579,928.51
Non-current liabilities (€)	**3,923,517.41**	**323,177.52**
Long-term debt (€)	2,169,566.26	191,563.90
Other non-current liabilities (€)	1,753,951.16	131,613.62
Current liabilities (€)	**14,455,300.03**	**1,760,203.90**
Loans (€)	3,079,604.39	293,971.14
Creditors (€)	7,427,866.13	1,003,839.31
Other current liabilities (€)	3,947,829.52	462,393.46
Profit (loss) for period (€)	1,346,383.38	123,198.00
Total assets (€)	32,306,515.05	2,995,276.81
Sales (€)	42,249,427.46	4,537,409.99
Share of tangible fixed assets (%)	41.80	31.51
Return on sales (%)	3.19	2.72
Return on equity (%)	9.67	13.51
Equity ratio (%)	43.11	30.44
Return on assets (%)	6.42	6.86
Inventories to capital (%)	19.11	22.18
Costs for personnel to turnover (%)	21.01	13.17

Appendix 4.3: EU-15 average model company, Large and SME

EU-15 Income Statement	Large	SME
Sales (€)	228,883,814.93	8,559,303.81
Costs of goods sold (€)	175,345,528.36	5,957,995.50
Other operating revenue (€)	10,440,745.58	338,373.10
Other operating expenses (€)	54,801,201.82	2,521,163.01
Operating profit/loss (€)	9,177,830.33	418,518.39
Financial revenue (€)	2,999,306.65	36,356.33
Interest paid (€)	3,598,440.81	100,217.05
Other financial expenses (€)	889,936.73	18,234.87
Financial profit/loss (€)	-1,489,070.89	-82,095.59
Profit/loss before tax (€)	7,688,759.44	336,422.80
Taxes (€)	2,551,512.23	112,094.52
Profit/loss after tax (€)	5,137,247.21	224,328.28
Extraordinary income (€)	38,687.19	12,933.07
Profit and loss for period (€)	5,175,934.40	237,261.34
Balance Sheet		
Total assets (€)	**180,558,289.26**	**4,852,798.68**
Fixed assets (€)	**62,954,656.85**	**1,352,313.23**
Intangible fixed assets (€)	4,913,383.57	109,300.26
Tangible fixed assets (€)	42,922,457.04	1,104,042.27
Other fixed assets (€)	15,118,816.25	138,970.70
Current assets (€)	**117,603,632.40**	**3,500,485.45**
Stocks (€)	30,677,436.92	949,181.26
Debtors (€)	51,360,213.35	1,410,000.19
Other current assets (€)	35,565,982.13	1,141,304.00
Shareholder funds (€)	**55,852,697.48**	**1,429,958.01**
Capital (€)	17,717,286.65	470,371.14
Other shareholder funds (€)	38,135,410.83	959,586.87
Non-current liabilities (€)	**28,924,518.75**	**684,752.95**
Long-term debt (€)	11,707,655.54	348,842.74
Other non-current liabilities (€)	17,216,863.21	335,910.21
Current liabilities (€)	**95,781,073.03**	**2,738,087.72**
Loans (€)	17,787,609.00	477,433.69
Creditors (€)	33,679,939.94	1,114,963.57
Other current liabilities (€)	44,313,524.09	1,145,690.47
Profit (loss) for period (€)	5,175,934.40	237,261.34
Total assets (€)	180,558,289.26	4,852,798.68
Sales (€)	228,883,814.93	8,559,303.81
Share of tangible fixed assets (%)	23.77	22.75
Return on sales (%)	2.26	2.77
Return on equity (%)	9.27	16.59
Equity ratio (%)	30.93	29.47
Return on assets (%)	4.86	6.95
Inventories to capital (%)	16.99	19.56
Costs for personnel to turnover (%)	21.04	21.51

Appendix 4.4: Industry-Specific Average Model Companies, Large and SME

Industries Income Statement	**Manufacturing (Large)**	**Manufacturing (SME)**	**Construction (Large)**	**Construction (SME)**
Sales (€)	169,077,853	7,445,895	100,573,412	3,840,812
Costs of goods sold (€)	137,280,984	5,870,588	93,819,255	3,109,331
Other operating revenue (€)	6,548,660	258,408	9,255,073	268,986
Other operating expenses (€)	29,503,959	1,485,014	11,851,265	775,642
Operating profit/loss (€)	8,841,570	348,701	4,157,964	224,825
Financial revenue (€)	1,906,597	48,284	824,270	5,851
Interest paid (€)	2,765,126	112,909	1,037,932	39,429
Other financial expenses (€)	941,475	27,304	244,960	7,302
Financial profit/loss (€)	-1,800,004	-91,929	-458,622	-40,880
Profit/loss before tax (€)	7,041,565	256,771	3,699,341	183,944
Taxes (€)	1,484,779	69,286	875,855	45,932
Profit/loss after tax (€)	5,556,785	187,485	2,823,486	138,012
Extraordinary income (€)	-447,215	4,567	-234,806	-296
Profit and loss for period (€)	5,109,570	192,052	2,588,680	137,715
Balance Sheet				
Total assets (€)	**155,533,779**	**4,855,805**	**92,539,902**	**2,565,637**
Fixed assets (€)	**69,246,343**	**1,770,345**	**24,502,956**	**651,448**
Intangible fixed assets (€)	3,118,145	85,421	1,034,755	25,980
Tangible fixed assets (€)	53,849,003	1,555,071	17,433,073	564,727
Other fixed assets (€)	12,279,194	129,853	6,035,126	60,741
Current assets (€)	**86,287,436**	**3,085,460**	**68,036,945**	**1,914,188**
Stocks (€)	30,263,806	975,924	16,491,332	481,366
Debtors (€)	35,533,672	1,323,441	34,252,142	841,292
Other current assets (€)	20,489,957	786,093	17,293,469	591,530
Shareholder funds (€)	**61,672,524**	**1,699,532**	**26,756,102**	**792,001**
Capital (€)	23,872,485	559,998	10,036,813	236,067
Other shareholder funds (€)	37,800,039	1,139,533	16,719,288	555,933

Non-current liabilities (€)	**23,899,968**	**697,993**	**9,412,081**	**269,027**
Long-term debt (€)	11,245,312	391,490	4,376,960	142,798
Other non-current liabilities (€)	12,654,655	306,502	5,035,121	126,229
Current liabilities (€)	**69,961,286**	**2,458,280**	**56,371,718**	**1,504,609**
Loans (€)	16,078,557	441,649	7,175,527	155,094
Creditors (€)	27,942,115	1,164,709	24,032,727	770,375
Other current liabilities (€)	25,940,614	851,921	25,163,463	579,138
Profit (loss) for period (€)	5,109,570	192,052	2,588,680	137,715
Total assets (€)	155,533,779	4,855,805	92,539,902	2,565,637
Sales (€)	169,077,853	7,445,895	100,573,412	3,840,812
Share of tangible fixed assets (%)	34.62	32.02	18.84	22.01
Return on sales (%)	3.02	2.58	2.57	3.59
Return on equity (%)	8.29	11.30	9.68	17.39
Equity ratio (%)	39.65	35.00	28.91	30.87
Return on assets (%)	5.06	6.28	3.92	6.90
Inventories to capital (%)	19.46	20.10	17.82	18.76
Costs for personnel to turnover (%)	20.93	22.00	22.78	23.25

(continued, Commerce and Service)

Industries Income Statement	Commerce (Large)	Commerce (SME)	Service/Trade (Large)	Service/Trade (SME)
Sales (€)	235,388,152	9,498,083	102,664,328	3,371,179
Costs of goods sold (€)	198,698,452	7,540,653	83,034,221	2,286,801
Other operating revenue (€)	13,215,583	247,495	5,197,783	208,514
Other operating expenses (€)	41,475,892	1,672,194	20,796,189	1,105,839
Operating profit/loss (€)	8,429,390	532,731	4,031,701	187,052
Financial revenue (€)	1,283,963	67,181	1,127,885	39,002
Interest paid (€)	2,883,029	182,123	1,543,795	52,769
Other financial expenses (€)	848,498	39,248	422,368	12,030
Financial profit/loss (€)	-2,447,564	-154,190	-838,279	-25,797
Profit/loss before tax (€)	5,981,825	378,540	3,193,421	161,254
Taxes (€)	1,872,391	120,469	1,452,794	50,872
Profit/loss after tax (€)	4,109,433	258,071	1,740,627	110,381
Extraordinary income (€)	-15,975	2,644	814,714	1,653
Profit and loss for period (€)	4,093,457	260,715	2,555,342	112,035
Balance Sheet				
Total assets (€)	106,315,228	4,287,924	102,730,927	3,300,054
Fixed assets (€)	33,440,971	1,075,554	37,653,118	1,164,644
Intangible fixed assets (€)	2,403,483	74,520	4,873,959	100,022
Tangible fixed assets (€)	23,628,289	897,553	25,899,530	939,826
Other fixed assets (€)	7,409,198	103,480	6,879,628	124,795
Current assets (€)	72,874,256	3,212,369	65,077,809	2,135,410
Stocks (€)	28,308,771	1,282,076	6,378,588	254,485
Debtors (€)	28,597,498	1,186,432	36,688,625	1,021,125
Other current assets (€)	15,967,986	743,860	22,010,595	859,799
Shareholder funds (€)	30,106,539	1,157,739	31,846,587	1,051,892
Capital (€)	9,974,728	374,432	10,134,509	381,652
Other shareholder funds (€)	20,131,811	783,306	21,712,078	670,239
Non-current liabilities (€)	13,658,429	489,588	16,089,437	447,908
Long-term debt (€)	6,251,157	260,158	7,473,100	240,038

Other non-current liabilities (€)	7,407,272	229,429	8,616,336	207,869
Current liabilities (€)	62,550,259	2,640,596	54,794,902	1,800,254
Loans (€)	11,253,519	458,121	8,140,251	213,558
Creditors (€)	32,055,677	1,411,177	17,611,496	794,955
Other current liabilities (€)	19,241,062	771,297	29,043,155	791,740
Profit (loss) for period (€)	4,093,457	260,715	2,555,342	112,035
Total assets (€)	106,315,228	4,287,924	102,730,927	3,300,054
Sales (€)	235,388,152	9,498,083	102,664,328	3,371,179
Share of tangible fixed assets (%)	22.22	20.93	25.21	28.48
Return on sales (%)	1.74	2.74	2.49	3.32
Return on equity (%)	13.60	22.52	8.02	10.65
Equity ratio (%)	28.32	27.00	31.00	31.88
Return on assets (%)	6.56	10.33	3.99	4.99
Inventories to capital (%)	26.63	29.90	6.21	7.71
Costs for personnel to turnover (%)	11.76	11.77	43.94	31.91

(continued, Transport and Energy)

Industries Income Statement	**Transport (Large)**	**Transport (SME)**	**Energy (Large)**	**Energy (SME)**
Sales (€)	144,241,260	6,120,966	296,085,099	7,678,829
Costs of goods sold (€)	133,240,005	4,241,391	261,509,471	6,473,458
Other operating revenue (€)	16,354,677	675,380	20,539,563	702,492
Other operating expenses (€)	24,004,260	2,262,509	33,503,427	1,415,951
Operating profit/loss (€)	3,351,672	292,445	21,611,763	491,912
Financial revenue (€)	2,116,042	45,010	15,877,461	100,669
Interest paid (€)	3,162,192	101,476	15,646,193	213,171
Other financial expenses (€)	1,031,332	18,613	3,818,999	45,216
Financial profit/loss (€)	-2,077,483	-75,080	-3,587,731	-157,718
Profit/loss before tax (€)	1,274,189	217,365	18,024,031	334,193
Taxes (€)	713,368	65,620	2,777,228	123,139
Profit/loss after tax (€)	560,820	151,745	15,246,803	211,053
Extraordinary income (€)	414,588	5,317	-871,251	31,721
Profit and loss for period (€)	975,409	157,062	14,375,551	242,774
Balance Sheet				
Total assets (€)	157,955,293	4,150,361	500,339,653	12,464,937
Fixed assets (€)	85,605,980	1,795,031	322,502,755	7,171,563
Intangible fixed assets (€)	7,058,491	88,510	14,209,760	365,949
Tangible fixed assets (€)	66,805,984	1,517,782	265,559,532	6,359,894
Other fixed assets (€)	11,741,504	188,737	42,733,462	445,719
Current assets (€)	72,349,313	2,355,329	177,836,898	5,293,373
Stocks (€)	6,554,368	130,816	26,593,834	501,520
Debtors (€)	35,933,038	1,385,270	80,654,834	2,806,239
Other current assets (€)	29,861,905	839,242	70,588,229	1,985,614
Shareholder funds (€)	53,272,938	1,143,078	212,641,399	4,798,461
Capital (€)	21,258,918	424,845	116,398,181	2,126,866
Other shareholder funds (€)	32,014,020	718,233	96,243,218	2,671,594
Non-current liabilities (€)	33,905,016	680,251	103,091,065	3,051,706
Long-term debt (€)	19,518,470	367,268	52,092,336	1,622,869

Other non-current liabilities (€)	14,386,545	312,983	50,998,729	1,428,837
Current liabilities (€)	70,777,339	2,327,030	184,607,187	4,614,769
Loans (€)	14,030,090	450,425	44,667,379	651,014
Creditors (€)	24,767,134	1,078,075	62,347,026	1,972,147
Other current liabilities (€)	31,980,114	798,530	77592781	1,991,607
Profit (loss) for period (€)	975,409	157,062	14,375,551	242,774
Total assets (€)	157,955,293	4,150,361	500,339,653	12,464,937
Sales (€)	144,241,260	6,120,966	296,085,099	7,678,829
Share of tangible fixed assets (%)	42.29	36.57	53.08	51.02
Return on sales (%)	0.68	2.57	4.86	3.16
Return on equity (%)	1.83	13.74	6.76	5.06
Equity ratio (%)	33.73	27.54	42.50	38.50
Return on assets (%)	2.62	6.23	6.00	3.66
Inventories to capital (%)	4.15	3.15	5.32	4.02
Costs for personnel to turnover (%)	28.32	20.62	11.55	20.09

Appendix 5: Information on Shares

After gathering data on direct shareholdings from AMADEUS, we check to see if any values were flawed or inconsistent. Shareholdings are reported using abbreviations (see Table 1).

A5, Table 1: Adjustments to the shareholding information in the AMADEUS database

Information in AMADEUS		Adjustments at first step
Sign	**Meaning**	
X	X%	none
-	unknown	0.00
<X	less than X%	X-0.01
>X	more than X%	X+0.01
CQP1	50% + 1 share	50.01
G	flaw in the database	100.00
MO	majority shareholding	50.01
+/-X	+/-X	X
NG	less than 1%	0.01
WO	more than 98%	98.00

If shareholdings in excess of 100% are reported, the company is ruled out as a plausible adjustment is not possible. Shareholdings for companies with an unknown share (-), reporting a minimum shareholding (> X) or reporting a majority shareholding (MO) are adjusted according to the formula below. This procedure ensures that the shares do in fact add up to 100%.

$$S_a = S_b + \frac{(100 - TS)}{SH} \qquad (17)$$

with

$S_a = Shareholdings\,(in\ per\ cent)\ after\ adjustment$

$S_b = Shareholdings\,(in\ per\ cent)\ before\ adjustment$

$TS = Reported\ total\ shareholdings\ (in\ per\ cent)$

$SH = Number\ of\ shareholders\ whose\ shares\ can\ vary$.

Appendix 6: Present Value of the Tax Base at the Beginning of Period 1

The present value of the tax base is given by the sum of the discounted tax bases at the beginning of period 1. The following Tables 1 and 2 show the present value of the tax base under national GAAP for the large company and the SME as well as the deviations resulting from the application of each CCTB option (A-I). The deviations in per cent are exactly the same as measured by the future value of the tax base (see Tables 21 and 28), as the future value can easily be transformed to the present value. The relation between the future value of the tax base and the present value of the tax base is given by the following formula (with T for total periods of simulation and i for the interest rate):

$$Present\,Value\,of\;the\,Tax\;Base = Future\,Value\,of\;the\,Tax\;Base\;(1+i)^{(-T)}.$$

A6, Table 1: Present value (in € millions) of the tax base for EU-27 large company (benchmark case) under national tax law and deviation (in %) caused by each particular CCTB option A-H and by a simultaneous application all CCTB options (I)

Country	National GAAP	A	B	C	D	E	F	G	H	I
AT	60.41	3.15	0.35	1.26	0.00	-0.96	0.00	0.00	0.00	5.94
BE	58.45	0.23	0.07	0.10	0.00	0.00	0.00	0.00	0.00	3.03
BG	70.42	5.02	0.24	1.26	0.01	0.00	-1.36	0.00	0.00	13.06
CY	78.11	0.70	0.00	-7.38	-0.46	0.00	-4.13	0.00	0.00	-6.68
CZ	71.41	9.98	0.00	-0.01	0.01	0.00	-1.19	0.00	0.00	9.94
DE	55.10	2.38	0.24	0.90	0.00	-0.71	0.00	0.00	0.00	4.78
DK	67.98	1.42	-0.02	1.16	0.01	0.00	0.00	0.00	0.00	3.77
EE	76.81	1.32	0.00	1.00	0.00	-0.05	0.00	0.00	0.00	2.60
ES	63.28	2.66	0.25	-0.08	-0.08	0.00	0.00	0.00	0.00	4.63
FI	70.73	1.59	-0.02	1.16	0.01	0.00	-1.17	0.00	0.00	9.43
FR	41.25	9.89	0.00	-0.02	0.02	0.00	0.00	0.00	0.00	9.80
GR	71.36	4.48	0.00	0.60	0.01	0.00	-1.11	-2.56	0.00	9.13
HU	31.03	12.47	0.00	-0.13	0.03	0.00	0.00	0.00	0.00	12.29
IE	75.20	0.78	0.00	-0.01	0.01	0.00	0.00	-2.43	0.00	-1.54
IT	70.48	5.19	0.33	-0.66	0.00	0.00	-0.98	0.00	0.00	8.75
LT	69.72	11.36	-0.03	-0.01	0.01	0.00	-1.30	0.00	0.00	11.08
LU	69.51	2.66	0.34	-0.33	-0.09	0.00	0.00	0.00	0.00	3.75
LV	69.83	11.30	0.00	0.00	0.00	0.00	0.00	0.00	0.00	11.30
MT	73.06	1.32	0.00	0.88	-0.08	0.00	-0.98	-2.49	0.00	3.84
NL	71.18	1.58	0.41	0.00	0.00	-0.41	0.00	0.00	0.00	2.24
PL	72.52	5.97	0.33	-0.01	0.01	0.00	-1.25	-2.52	0.00	7.69
PT	70.45	3.08	0.22	0.42	0.01	0.00	-1.14	0.00	0.00	10.56
RO	70.81	2.74	0.25	0.35	0.00	0.00	0.00	0.00	0.00	4.93
SE	69.64	4.81	0.00	-0.09	-0.09	0.00	0.00	0.00	0.00	4.37
SK	71.63	9.84	0.00	-0.01	0.01	0.00	-1.27	0.00	0.00	9.80
SL	66.42	1.87	0.37	1.14	0.00	0.00	-1.26	0.00	0.00	8.57
UK	69.53	2.75	0.00	-0.01	0.01	0.00	0.00	-2.63	0.00	0.24
Ø	66.90	4.47	0.12	0.06	-0.02	-0.08	-0.63	-0.47	0.00	6.20

A6, Table 2: Present value (in € millions) of the tax base for EU-27 SME (benchmark case) under national tax law and deviation (in %) caused by each particular CCTB option A-H and by a simultaneous application all CCTB options (I)

Country	National GAAP	A	B	C	D	E	F	G	H	I
AT	2.13	2.40	0.33	1.03	0.00	-0.68	0.00	0.00	0.00	4.32
BE	2.19	0.09	0.05	0.01	0.00	0.00	0.00	0.00	0.00	1.52
BG	2.55	4.18	0.25	1.01	0.01	0.00	-1.70	0.00	0.00	11.80
CY	2.79	0.72	0.00	-7.63	-0.28	0.00	-4.80	0.00	0.00	-6.91
CZ	2.57	9.53	0.00	-0.01	0.01	0.00	-1.47	0.00	0.00	9.51
DE	2.00	1.75	0.23	0.71	0.00	-0.49	0.00	0.00	0.00	2.92
DK	2.45	1.07	-0.01	0.94	0.01	0.00	0.00	0.00	0.00	2.36
EE	2.68	1.04	0.00	0.78	0.00	-0.04	0.00	0.00	0.00	1.77
ES	2.28	1.90	0.27	-0.06	-0.06	0.00	0.00	0.00	0.00	2.64
FI	2.54	4.61	-0.01	1.70	0.01	0.00	-1.45	0.00	0.00	9.21
FR	1.75	5.33	0.00	-0.01	0.01	0.00	0.00	0.00	0.00	5.29
GR	2.54	6.58	0.00	0.90	0.01	0.00	-1.41	-0.96	0.00	10.31
HU	0.80	15.71	0.00	-0.27	0.10	0.00	0.00	0.00	0.00	15.43
IE	2.64	0.16	0.00	-0.01	0.01	0.00	0.00	-0.92	0.00	-0.77
IT	2.52	5.86	0.27	-0.54	0.00	0.00	-1.21	0.00	0.00	8.82
LT	2.52	10.60	-0.02	-0.01	0.01	0.00	-1.63	0.00	0.00	10.48
LU	2.50	1.98	0.33	-0.30	-0.07	0.00	0.00	0.00	0.00	2.26
LV	2.53	10.42	0.00	0.00	0.00	0.00	0.00	0.00	0.00	10.42
MT	2.58	3.32	0.00	0.72	-0.07	0.00	-1.23	-0.94	0.00	5.37
NL	2.54	1.06	0.36	0.00	0.00	-0.27	0.00	0.00	0.00	1.32
PL	2.57	6.30	0.36	-0.01	0.01	0.00	-1.60	-0.95	0.00	8.84
PT	2.54	2.98	0.25	0.29	0.01	0.00	-1.44	0.00	0.00	9.92
RO	2.56	1.73	0.35	0.39	0.00	0.00	0.00	0.00	0.00	2.51
SE	2.50	2.94	0.00	-0.07	-0.07	0.00	0.00	0.00	0.00	2.69
SK	2.58	9.48	0.00	-0.01	0.01	0.00	-1.58	0.00	0.00	9.46
SL	2.36	2.47	0.33	0.92	0.00	0.00	-1.58	0.00	0.00	8.25
UK	2.50	1.61	0.00	-0.01	0.01	0.00	0.00	-0.98	0.00	0.67
Ø	2.40	4.29	0.12	0.02	-0.01	-0.05	-0.78	-0.18	0.00	5.57

Appendix 7: Supplementary Analysis on the Impact of Common Depreciation Provisions

A7, Table 1: Impact (in %) of common rules regarding depreciation for different categories of assets (large benchmark case)

	Application of common depreciation provisions on			
Country	**Buildings**	**Intangibles**	**Machinery and equipment**	**All depreciable assets (Option A)**
AT	0.06	0.10	2.99	3.15
BE	0.02	0.00	0.21	0.23
BG	0.19	0.00	4.83	5.02
CY	0.57	0.00	0.14	0.70
CZ	0.25	0.00	9.73	9.98
DE	0.05	0.07	2.26	2.38
DK	0.04	0.00	1.39	1.42
EE	-0.07	0.00	1.39	1.32
ES	-0.04	0.00	2.70	2.66
FI	0.36	0.00	1.23	1.59
FR	0.36	0.00	9.53	9.89
GR	0.41	0.00	4.07	4.48
HU	-0.13	0.00	12.60	12.47
IE	-0.02	0.00	0.81	0.78
IT	0.44	0.24	4.51	5.19
LT	3.37	0.51	7.49	11.36
LU	0.12	0.00	2.53	2.66
LV	0.38	0.00	10.92	11.30
MT	0.18	0.00	1.14	1.32
NL	0.30	0.00	1.28	1.58
PL	0.00	0.29	5.68	5.97
PT	0.13	0.00	2.95	3.08
RO	0.00	0.00	2.74	2.74
SE	0.19	0.09	4.53	4.81
SK	1.50	0.00	8.35	9.84
SL	0.29	0.00	1.58	1.87
UK	-0.02	0.00	2.78	2.75
Ø	0.25	0.04	4.17	4.47

A7, Table 2: Impact (in %) of common rules regarding depreciation for different categories of assets (SME)

	Application of common depreciation provisions for			
Country	**Buildings**	**Intangibles**	**Machinery and equipment**	**All depreciable assets (Option A)**
AT	0.06	0.07	2.28	2.40
BE	0.02	0.00	0.07	0.09
BG	0.19	0.00	3.99	4.18
CY	0.51	0.00	0.21	0.72
CZ	0.22	0.00	9.31	9.53
DE	0.04	0.05	1.66	1.75
DK	0.03	0.00	1.04	1.07
EE	-0.06	0.00	1.10	1.04
ES	-0.04	0.00	1.94	1.90
FI	0.54	0.00	4.07	4.61
FR	0.32	0.00	5.00	5.33
GR	0.59	0.00	6.00	6.58
HU	-0.21	0.00	15.92	15.71
IE	-0.02	0.00	0.18	0.16
IT	0.33	0.14	5.39	5.86
LT	3.52	0.42	6.65	10.60
LU	0.11	0.00	1.87	1.98
LV	0.33	0.00	10.08	10.42
MT	0.13	0.00	3.19	3.32
NL	0.22	0.00	0.84	1.06
PL	0.00	0.21	6.09	6.30
PT	0.15	0.00	2.83	2.98
RO	0.00	0.00	1.73	1.73
SE	0.16	0.06	2.72	2.94
SK	1.25	0.00	8.24	9.48
SL	0.43	0.00	2.04	2.47
UK	-0.02	0.00	1.63	1.61
Ø	0.23	0.03	4.03	4.29

Sensitivity Analysis Based on a Depreciation Rate of 25% for Pool Depreciation of Machinery and Equipment

The effects of an alternate pool depreciation rate are evaluated under Option A (proposal for the harmonisation of depreciation rules) and Option I (all CCTB options applied simultaneously). While the pool depreciation rate has no bearing when Options B-H are considered in isolation, when all CCTB options are applied together, adjustments to the pool depreciation rate modify the overall impact of Options B-H.

The sensitivity analysis of the effects of an increase in the pool depreciation rate for manufacturing and office equipment from 20% to 25% reveals four findings:

- As shown in section 3.2.2.1 (large benchmark case) and section 3.3.2.1 (small and medium benchmark case), the impact of common depreciation provisions for machinery and equipment largely dominates the increase in the future value of the tax base observed for Option A. Hence, changes in the definition of the proposed depreciation rules on machinery and equipment considerably influence the increase in the future value of the tax base witnessed when a CCTB is introduced. If the depreciation rate for the mentioned assets is fixed at 25% instead of 20% (as in the benchmark case), the average increase of the future value of the tax base due to the isolated application of common depreciation rules amounts 1.26% for the large corporation and to 1.35% for the SME (A7, Table 4 and Table 6). In both cases, the increase associated with a pool depreciation rate of 25% is thus significantly lower than that associated with a rate of 20%.

- This effect is also witnessed when all CCTB options are applied simultaneously: with a 25% pool depreciation rate under Option I, the EU-average increase in the future value of the tax base and in the effective tax burden is significantly smaller than in the benchmark case considered in sections 3.2.1 and 3.3.1 (see A7, Tables 4 and 6 and A6, Tables 1 and 2 for the large company and for the SME)

A7, Table 3: Tax base increase (in %) under alternate depreciation rates when all CCTB options are applied together (EU-average)

	Future Value of the Tax Base		Effective Tax Burden	
	Large Company	**SME**	**Large Company**	**SME**
20% pool depreciation	6.20	5.57	5.15	4.45
25% pool depreciation	1.09	1.96	1.77	2.06

- In contrast to the base case with 20% pool depreciation, now – with respect to the EU-average – the SME faces a higher increase of all measures considered here (future value of the tax base, effective tax burden and present value of the tax base).
- In contrast to the large company benchmark case (with 20% pool depreciation), two countries (Malta and the UK) experience a decrease as opposed to an increase in the future value of the tax base. In the case of Ireland the variation of the pool depreciation rate leads to a decrease instead of an increase in the effective tax burden. For the SME only the UK shows a decrease instead of an increase in the future value of the tax base and in the present value of the tax base. Again, in the case of Ireland the variation of the pool depreciation rate leads to a decrease instead of an increase in the effective tax burden.

A7, Table 4: Future value of the tax base (in € millions) for EU-27 large company (benchmark case) under national tax law and deviation (in %) caused by each particular CCTB option A-H and by a simultaneous application all CCTB options (I) / CCTB option A: pool depreciation 25%

Country	National GAAP	A	B	C	D	E	F	G	H	I
AT	81.19	1.73	0.35	1.26	0.00	-0.96	0.00	0.00	0.00	2.45
BE	78.55	0.15	0.07	0.10	0.00	0.00	0.00	0.00	0.00	0.34
BG	94.64	3.62	0.24	1.26	0.01	0.00	-1.36	0.00	0.00	5.58
CY	104.98	-4.30	0.00	-7.38	-0.46	0.00	-4.13	0.00	0.00	-11.68
CZ	95.97	2.74	0.00	-0.01	0.01	0.00	-1.19	0.00	0.00	2.70
DE	74.05	1.35	0.24	0.90	0.00	-0.71	0.00	0.00	0.00	1.85
DK	91.36	0.18	-0.02	1.16	0.01	0.00	0.00	0.00	0.00	1.31
EE	103.22	-0.25	0.00	1.00	0.00	-0.05	0.00	0.00	0.00	0.70
ES	85.05	1.67	0.25	-0.08	-0.08	0.00	0.00	0.00	0.00	1.89
FI	95.06	0.36	-0.02	1.16	0.01	0.00	-1.17	0.00	0.00	2.16
FR	55.43	2.00	0.00	-0.02	0.02	0.00	0.00	0.00	0.00	1.98
GR	95.90	3.32	0.00	0.60	0.01	0.00	-1.11	-2.56	0.00	1.96
HU	41.70	0.84	0.00	-0.13	0.03	0.00	0.00	0.00	0.00	0.72
IE	101.06	-1.20	0.00	-0.01	0.01	0.00	0.00	-2.43	0.00	-3.64
IT	94.72	1.11	0.33	-0.66	0.00	0.00	-0.98	0.00	0.00	1.63
LT	93.70	3.86	-0.03	-0.01	0.01	0.00	-1.30	0.00	0.00	3.58
LU	93.42	1.50	0.34	-0.33	-0.09	0.00	0.00	0.00	0.00	1.52
LV	93.84	3.75	0.00	0.00	0.00	0.00	0.00	0.00	0.00	3.75
MT	98.18	0.05	0.00	0.88	-0.08	0.00	-0.98	-2.49	0.00	-1.11
NL	95.66	0.21	0.41	0.00	0.00	-0.41	0.00	0.00	0.00	0.14
PL	97.46	2.11	0.33	-0.01	0.01	0.00	-1.25	-2.52	0.00	0.48
PT	94.67	1.90	0.22	0.42	0.01	0.00	-1.14	0.00	0.00	3.28
RO	95.16	1.43	0.25	0.35	0.00	0.00	0.00	0.00	0.00	2.40
SE	93.60	2.28	0.00	-0.09	-0.09	0.00	0.00	0.00	0.00	2.19
SK	96.26	2.55	0.00	-0.01	0.01	0.00	-1.27	0.00	0.00	2.50
SL	89.26	0.58	0.37	1.14	0.00	0.00	-1.26	0.00	0.00	2.95
UK	93.45	0.43	0.00	-0.01	0.01	0.00	0.00	-2.63	0.00	-2.20
Ø	89.91	1.26	0.12	0.06	-0.02	-0.08	-0.63	-0.47	0.00	1.09

A7, Table 5: Effective tax burden (in €millions) for EU-27 large company (benchmark case) under national tax law and deviation (in %) caused by each particular CCTB option A-H and by a simultaneous application all CCTB options (I) / CCTB option A: pool depreciation 25%

Country	National GAAP	A	B	C	D	E	F	G	H	I
AT	33.05	1.06	0.22	0.77	0.00	-0.59	0.00	0.00	0.00	1.51
BE	31.43	0.13	0.06	0.08	0.00	0.00	0.00	0.00	0.00	0.29
BG	14.52	3.54	0.24	1.23	0.01	0.00	-1.33	0.00	0.00	5.36
CY	18.35	-2.46	0.00	-4.22	-0.27	0.00	-2.36	0.00	0.00	-6.68
CZ	23.38	2.70	0.00	-0.01	0.01	0.00	-1.17	0.00	0.00	2.50
DE	38.79	1.24	0.22	0.82	0.00	-0.65	0.00	0.00	0.00	1.70
DK	29.40	0.16	-0.02	1.01	0.01	0.00	0.00	0.00	0.00	1.14
EE	15.63	0.00	0.00	0.00	0.00	0.00	0.00	0.00	0.00	0.00
ES	37.85	1.62	0.25	-0.07	-0.07	0.00	0.00	0.00	0.00	1.83
FI	26.23	0.34	-0.02	1.09	0.01	0.00	-1.10	0.00	0.00	1.82
FR	55.17	0.88	0.00	-0.01	0.01	0.00	0.00	0.00	0.00	0.88
GR	27.77	3.32	0.00	0.60	0.01	0.00	-1.11	0.00	0.00	4.32
HU	38.09	0.15	0.00	0.04	0.00	0.00	0.00	0.00	0.00	0.20
IE	13.86	-1.10	0.00	-0.01	0.01	0.00	0.00	0.00	0.00	-1.10
IT	38.77	2.25	0.97	-0.53	0.00	0.00	-1.70	0.00	0.00	3.07
LT	20.44	3.42	-0.02	-0.01	0.01	0.00	-1.13	0.00	0.00	3.00
LU	29.11	1.42	0.36	-0.40	-0.09	0.00	0.00	0.00	0.00	1.37
LV	16.36	6.56	0.00	0.00	0.00	0.00	0.00	0.00	0.00	6.40
MT	33.63	0.05	0.00	0.90	-0.09	0.00	-1.00	-0.35	0.00	1.05
NL	28.94	0.20	0.40	0.00	0.00	-0.40	0.00	0.00	0.00	0.13
PL	19.75	1.98	0.31	-0.01	0.01	0.00	-1.17	0.00	0.00	2.65
PT	26.72	1.85	0.22	0.41	0.01	0.00	-1.12	0.00	0.00	2.99
RO	15.76	5.38	0.25	1.46	0.00	0.00	0.00	0.00	0.00	6.31
SE	27.19	2.20	0.00	-0.08	-0.08	0.00	0.00	0.00	0.00	2.11
SK	19.26	2.42	0.00	-0.01	0.01	0.00	-1.20	0.00	0.00	2.23
SL	28.85	0.45	0.29	0.88	0.00	0.00	-0.97	0.00	0.00	2.28
UK	31.92	0.38	0.00	-0.02	0.01	0.00	0.00	-0.01	0.00	0.36
Ø	27.42	1.49	0.14	0.15	-0.02	-0.06	-0.57	-0.01	0.00	1.77

A7, Table 6: Future value of the tax base (in € millions) for EU-27 SME (benchmark case) under national tax law and deviation (in %) caused by each particular CCTB option A-H and by a simultaneous application all CCTB options (I) / CCTB option A: pool depreciation 25%

Country	National GAAP	A	B	C	D	E	F	G	H	I
AT	2.87	1.34	0.33	1.03	0.00	-0.68	0.00	0.00	0.00	2.11
BE	2.94	0.06	0.05	0.01	0.00	0.00	0.00	0.00	0.00	0.13
BG	3.43	2.65	0.25	1.01	0.01	0.00	-1.70	0.00	0.00	6.26
CY	3.74	-3.04	0.00	-7.63	-0.28	0.00	-4.80	0.00	0.00	-10.68
CZ	3.45	4.16	0.00	-0.01	0.01	0.00	-1.47	0.00	0.00	4.13
DE	2.68	1.03	0.23	0.71	0.00	-0.49	0.00	0.00	0.00	1.54
DK	3.29	0.18	-0.01	0.94	0.01	0.00	0.00	0.00	0.00	1.10
EE	3.60	-0.17	0.00	0.78	0.00	-0.04	0.00	0.00	0.00	0.57
ES	3.07	1.20	0.27	-0.06	-0.06	0.00	0.00	0.00	0.00	1.42
FI	3.42	0.32	-0.01	1.70	0.01	0.00	-1.45	0.00	0.00	3.80
FR	2.36	1.41	0.00	-0.01	0.01	0.00	0.00	0.00	0.00	1.40
GR	3.41	2.49	0.00	0.90	0.01	0.00	-1.41	-0.96	0.00	4.94
HU	1.08	3.11	0.00	-0.27	0.10	0.00	0.00	0.00	0.00	2.85
IE	3.54	-0.89	0.00	-0.01	0.01	0.00	0.00	-0.92	0.00	-1.82
IT	3.39	0.92	0.27	-0.54	0.00	0.00	-1.21	0.00	0.00	3.51
LT	3.38	5.05	-0.02	-0.01	0.01	0.00	-1.63	0.00	0.00	4.93
LU	3.35	1.14	0.33	-0.30	-0.07	0.00	0.00	0.00	0.00	1.16
LV	3.40	4.83	0.00	0.00	0.00	0.00	0.00	0.00	0.00	4.83
MT	3.46	0.12	0.00	0.72	-0.07	0.00	-1.23	-0.94	0.00	1.64
NL	3.41	0.24	0.36	0.00	0.00	-0.27	0.00	0.00	0.00	0.29
PL	3.46	1.60	0.36	-0.01	0.01	0.00	-1.60	-0.95	0.00	3.42
PT	3.41	1.38	0.25	0.29	0.01	0.00	-1.44	0.00	0.00	4.53
RO	3.44	0.69	0.35	0.39	0.00	0.00	0.00	0.00	0.00	1.64
SE	3.36	1.69	0.00	-0.07	-0.07	0.00	0.00	0.00	0.00	1.62
SK	3.46	4.06	0.00	-0.01	0.01	0.00	-1.58	0.00	0.00	4.03
SL	3.17	0.50	0.33	0.92	0.00	0.00	-1.58	0.00	0.00	4.04
UK	3.36	0.39	0.00	-0.01	0.01	0.00	0.00	-0.98	0.00	-0.59
Ø	3.22	1.35	0.12	0.02	-0.01	-0.05	-0.78	-0.18	0.00	1.96

A7, Table 7: Tax burden (in € millions) for EU-27 SME (benchmark case) under national tax law and deviation (in %) caused by each particular CCTB option A-H and by a simultaneous application all CCTB options (I) / CCTB option A: pool depreciation 25%

Country	National GAAP	A	B	C	D	E	F	G	H	I
AT	1.21	0.76	0.19	0.63	0.00	-0.36	0.00	0.00	0.00	1.27
BE	1.13	0.74	0.20	0.21	0.00	0.00	0.00	0.00	0.00	0.92
BG	0.52	2.60	0.25	0.99	0.01	0.00	-1.66	0.00	0.00	5.41
CY	0.67	-1.71	0.00	-4.27	-0.16	0.00	-2.69	0.00	0.00	-5.98
CZ	0.84	4.03	0.00	-0.01	0.01	0.00	-1.52	0.00	0.00	3.22
DE	1.37	0.94	0.21	0.69	0.00	-0.43	0.00	0.00	0.00	1.48
DK	1.04	0.13	-0.01	0.85	0.01	0.00	0.00	0.00	0.00	0.97
EE	0.55	0.00	0.00	0.00	0.00	0.00	0.00	0.00	0.00	0.00
ES	1.30	1.38	0.28	-0.06	-0.06	0.00	0.00	0.00	0.00	1.61
FI	0.94	0.31	-0.01	1.63	0.01	0.00	-1.44	0.00	0.00	2.83
FR	1.70	0.69	0.00	0.00	0.01	0.00	0.00	0.00	0.00	0.69
GR	0.99	2.64	0.00	0.90	0.01	0.00	-1.41	0.00	0.00	5.24
HU	1.52	0.33	0.00	0.05	0.01	0.00	0.00	0.00	0.00	0.38
IE	0.49	-0.81	0.00	-0.01	0.01	0.00	0.00	0.00	0.00	-0.81
IT	1.42	1.56	0.70	-0.43	0.00	0.00	-2.17	0.00	0.00	3.34
LT	0.73	4.62	-0.02	-0.01	0.01	0.00	-1.45	0.00	0.00	3.92
LU	1.03	1.14	0.35	-0.36	-0.08	0.00	0.00	0.00	0.00	1.12
LV	0.58	7.20	0.00	0.00	0.00	0.00	0.00	0.00	0.00	6.49
MT	1.21	0.02	0.00	0.75	-0.07	0.00	-1.31	-0.13	0.00	2.38
NL	1.02	0.11	0.35	0.00	0.00	-0.24	0.00	0.00	0.00	0.19
PL	0.71	1.49	0.33	-0.01	0.01	0.00	-1.49	0.00	0.00	3.33
PT	0.96	1.46	0.25	0.29	0.01	0.00	-1.40	0.00	0.00	3.74
RO	0.56	5.52	0.34	0.90	0.00	0.00	0.00	0.00	0.00	5.84
SE	0.97	1.72	0.00	-0.07	-0.07	0.00	0.00	0.00	0.00	1.66
SK	0.69	3.77	0.00	-0.01	0.01	0.00	-1.57	0.00	0.00	3.00
SL	1.06	0.29	0.24	0.71	0.00	0.00	-1.24	0.00	0.00	2.97
UK	0.78	0.32	0.00	-0.01	0.01	0.00	0.00	0.00	0.00	0.32
Ø	0.96	1.53	0.14	0.12	-0.01	-0.04	-0.72	0.00	0.00	2.06

Appendix 8: Sensitivity Analysis on Economic Model Assumptions – Tax Burden

Appendix 8.1: Average EU-27 Large Corporation

A8.1, Table 1: Deviation of effective tax burden (in %) from national GAAP caused by a simultaneous application all CCTB options (I) for different levels of capital intensity

Country	Decrease of share of tangible fixed assets by			Benchmark Case[1]	Increase of share of tangible fixed assets by		
	7.50%	5%	2.50%		2.50%	5%	7.50%
AT	2.97	3.20	3.42	**3.65**	3.88	4.11	4.34
BE	1.74	2.02	2.29	**2.58**	2.87	3.17	3.48
BG	9.32	9.78	10.22	**10.70**	11.18	11.67	12.17
CY	-3.75	-3.77	-3.80	**-3.82**	-3.84	-3.87	-3.89
CZ	6.53	6.90	7.27	**7.66**	8.05	8.45	8.86
DE	2.71	2.95	3.21	**3.49**	3.77	4.06	4.36
DK	2.53	2.78	3.02	**3.28**	3.54	3.80	4.07
EE	0.00	0.00	0.00	**0.00**	0.00	0.00	0.00
ES	3.02	3.35	3.67	**4.02**	4.36	4.72	5.08
FI	5.84	6.15	6.45	**6.78**	7.10	7.43	7.77
FR	3.23	3.41	3.59	**3.77**	3.95	4.15	4.40
GR	8.23	8.65	9.05	**9.49**	9.93	10.38	10.84
HU	1.90	2.01	2.12	**2.23**	2.33	2.44	2.54
IE	0.24	0.43	0.61	**0.81**	1.00	1.20	1.40
IT	7.21	7.56	7.90	**8.27**	8.63	9.00	9.39
LT	7.31	7.70	8.09	**8.50**	8.91	9.32	9.75
LU	2.70	2.98	3.25	**3.55**	3.84	4.14	4.44
LV	9.77	10.23	10.67	**11.15**	11.62	12.09	12.58
MT	5.19	5.49	5.79	**6.11**	6.43	6.76	7.10
NL	1.44	1.69	1.93	**2.20**	2.46	2.72	2.99
PL	6.52	6.87	7.21	**7.57**	7.93	8.29	8.67
PT	7.03	7.39	7.74	**8.11**	8.49	8.87	9.26
RO	4.84	5.84	6.98	**8.38**	9.48	10.47	11.02
SE	3.24	3.56	3.87	**4.21**	4.55	4.89	5.25
SK	6.21	6.56	6.90	**7.27**	7.64	8.01	8.40
SL	5.79	6.07	6.34	**6.63**	6.91	7.20	7.50
UK	1.31	1.33	1.36	**2.51**	2.76	3.01	3.27
Ø	4.19	4.49	4.78	**5.15**	5.47	5.79	6.11

[1] For the benchmark case see Table 24.

A8.1, Table 2: Deviation of effective tax burden (in %) from national GAAP caused by a simultaneous application all CCTB options (I) for different levels of profitability

Country	Decrease of return on sales by			Benchmark Case[1]	Increase of share of return on sales by		
	30%	20%	10%		10%	20%	30%
AT	5.16	4.59	4.11	**3.65**	3.21	2.85	2.50
BE	4.33	3.63	3.09	**2.58**	2.11	1.73	1.37
BG	14.67	13.11	11.86	**10.70**	9.65	8.80	8.00
CY	-4.25	-4.09	-3.96	**-3.82**	-3.69	-3.58	-3.46
CZ	10.78	9.56	8.57	**7.66**	6.83	6.15	5.52
DE	5.59	4.65	4.05	**3.49**	2.98	2.60	2.30
DK	5.18	4.44	3.85	**3.28**	2.76	2.35	1.94
EE	0.00	0.00	0.00	**0.00**	0.00	0.00	0.00
ES	6.59	5.49	4.73	**4.02**	3.37	2.86	2.40
FI	9.55	8.47	7.59	**6.78**	6.03	5.42	4.85
FR	6.20	5.21	4.36	**3.77**	3.33	2.92	2.58
GR	13.10	11.69	10.55	**9.49**	8.54	7.76	7.03
HU	3.10	2.60	2.43	**2.23**	2.02	1.84	1.65
IE	2.12	1.61	1.20	**0.81**	0.44	0.16	0.13
IT	11.46	10.14	9.10	**8.27**	7.50	6.88	6.28
LT	11.71	10.47	9.46	**8.50**	7.62	6.90	6.22
LU	5.69	4.85	4.18	**3.55**	2.97	2.51	2.09
LV	14.67	13.31	12.20	**11.15**	10.18	9.39	8.64
MT	8.85	7.77	6.91	**6.11**	5.39	4.80	4.24
NL	3.99	3.28	2.73	**2.20**	1.71	1.33	1.05
PL	10.46	9.34	8.42	**7.57**	6.78	6.15	5.54
PT	11.33	10.08	9.06	**8.11**	7.26	6.56	5.90
RO	11.61	11.80	10.10	**8.38**	6.83	5.61	4.70
SE	6.52	5.61	4.89	**4.21**	3.59	3.10	2.73
SK	10.18	9.05	8.13	**7.27**	6.49	5.85	5.25
SL	8.96	8.07	7.33	**6.63**	5.98	5.44	4.92
UK	4.19	3.54	3.01	**2.51**	1.33	1.29	1.36
Ø	7.47	6.60	5.85	**5.15**	4.49	3.99	3.54

[1] For the benchmark case see Table 24.

A8.1, Table 3: Deviation of effective tax burden (in %) from national GAAP caused by a simultaneous application all CCTB options (I) for different levels of labour intensity

Country	Decrease of labour intensity by		Benchmark Case[1]	Increase of labour intensity by	
	20%	10%		10%	20%
AT	2.89	2.77	**2.63**	2.50	2.36
BE	2.99	2.91	**2.80**	2.70	2.59
BG	9.56	9.47	**9.38**	9.30	9.22
CY	-3.45	-3.64	**-3.87**	-4.14	-4.38
CZ	7.31	7.22	**7.12**	7.03	6.93
DE	2.75	2.62	**2.48**	2.36	2.24
DK	2.34	2.26	**2.16**	2.06	1.95
EE	0.00	0.00	**0.00**	0.00	0.00
ES	3.01	2.90	**2.77**	2.64	2.51
FI	6.78	6.69	**6.60**	6.51	6.40
FR	2.67	2.61	**2.56**	2.53	2.53
GR	9.37	9.29	**9.20**	9.13	9.04
HU	1.85	1.85	**1.85**	1.82	1.78
IE	0.31	0.23	**0.14**	0.14	0.14
IT	7.42	7.31	**7.18**	7.09	6.98
LT	8.29	8.22	**8.12**	8.02	7.91
LU	2.66	2.57	**2.46**	2.33	2.18
LV	10.22	10.15	**10.06**	10.01	9.96
MT	6.41	6.31	**6.21**	6.12	6.01
NL	1.68	1.55	**1.40**	1.24	1.11
PL	7.21	7.15	**7.07**	7.01	6.94
PT	7.78	7.70	**7.62**	7.54	7.43
RO	6.47	6.56	**6.68**	6.94	7.23
SE	2.93	2.85	**2.76**	2.66	2.59
SK	7.01	6.93	**6.83**	6.74	6.64
SL	6.48	6.34	**6.19**	6.04	5.89
UK	2.20	2.02	**1.80**	1.56	1.30
Ø	4.64	4.55	**4.45**	4.36	4.28

[1] For the benchmark case see Table 24.

A8.1, Table 4: Deviation of effective tax burden (in %) from national GAAP caused by a simultaneous application all CCTB options (I) for different levels of inventory intensity

Country	Decrease of inventories to capital by		Benchmark Case[1]	Increase of inventories to capital by	
	9.20%	4.60%		4.60%	9.50%
AT	3.67	3.66	**3.65**	3.64	3.64
BE	2.74	2.66	**2.58**	2.50	2.42
BG	10.93	10.82	**10.70**	10.60	10.50
CY	-3.87	-3.84	**-3.82**	-3.80	-3.78
CZ	8.01	7.83	**7.66**	7.49	7.33
DE	3.55	3.52	**3.49**	3.47	3.45
DK	3.37	3.33	**3.28**	3.24	3.20
EE	0.00	0.00	**0.00**	0.00	0.00
ES	4.25	4.13	**4.02**	3.91	3.81
FI	6.95	6.86	**6.78**	6.69	6.61
FR	3.83	3.81	**3.77**	3.75	3.73
GR	9.76	9.63	**9.49**	9.37	9.24
HU	2.30	2.27	**2.23**	2.19	2.15
IE	0.95	0.88	**0.81**	0.74	0.68
IT	8.41	8.34	**8.27**	8.21	8.15
LT	8.88	8.69	**8.50**	8.32	8.15
LU	3.75	3.65	**3.55**	3.45	3.37
LV	11.55	11.35	**11.15**	10.95	10.76
MT	6.30	6.21	**6.11**	6.02	5.94
NL	2.31	2.25	**2.20**	2.15	2.10
PL	7.85	7.71	**7.57**	7.44	7.31
PT	8.31	8.21	**8.11**	8.03	7.94
RO	9.87	9.72	**8.38**	7.13	5.96
SE	4.48	4.34	**4.21**	4.09	3.96
SK	7.60	7.43	**7.27**	7.11	6.96
SL	6.71	6.67	**6.63**	6.59	6.55
UK	2.69	2.60	**2.51**	2.42	1.36
Ø	5.38	5.29	**5.15**	5.03	4.87

[1] For the benchmark case see Table 24.

Appendix 8.2: Average EU-27 SME

A8.2, Table 1: Deviation of effective tax burden (in %) from national GAAP caused by a simultaneous application all CCTB options (I) for different levels of capital intensity

Country	Decrease of share of tangible fixed assets by		Benchmark Case[1]	Increase of share of tangible fixed assets by	
	5%	2.50%		2.50%	5%
AT	2.30	2.46	**2.63**	2.80	2.98
BE	2.28	2.54	**2.80**	3.07	3.34
BG	8.69	9.03	**9.38**	9.74	10.12
CY	-3.86	-3.87	**-3.87**	-3.88	-3.90
CZ	6.53	6.82	**7.12**	7.42	7.75
DE	2.17	2.32	**2.48**	2.69	2.92
DK	1.77	1.96	**2.16**	2.35	2.56
EE	0.00	0.00	**0.00**	0.00	0.00
ES	2.27	2.50	**2.77**	3.04	3.33
FI	6.10	6.34	**6.60**	6.85	7.12
FR	2.24	2.40	**2.56**	2.71	2.88
GR	8.53	8.86	**9.20**	9.55	9.92
HU	1.70	1.78	**1.85**	1.90	1.94
IE	0.13	0.14	**0.14**	0.28	0.44
IT	6.68	6.92	**7.18**	7.45	7.74
LT	7.48	7.80	**8.12**	8.44	8.77
LU	2.01	2.21	**2.46**	2.68	2.92
LV	9.35	9.70	**10.06**	10.43	10.83
MT	5.72	5.96	**6.21**	6.47	6.74
NL	1.08	1.18	**1.40**	1.62	1.84
PL	6.55	6.81	**7.07**	7.34	7.62
PT	7.06	7.34	**7.62**	7.89	8.19
RO	4.41	5.04	**6.68**	7.53	8.52
SE	2.41	2.51	**2.76**	3.00	3.26
SK	6.27	6.55	**6.83**	7.12	7.43
SL	5.77	5.98	**6.19**	6.41	6.64
UK	1.73	1.74	**1.80**	1.86	1.93
Ø	3.98	4.19	**4.45**	4.70	4.96

[1] For the benchmark case see Table 47.

A8.2, Table 2: Deviation of effective tax burden (in %) from national GAAP caused by a simultaneous application all CCTB options (I) for different levels of profitability

Country	Decrease of return on sales by			Benchmark Case[1]	Increase of return on sales by		
	30%	20%	10%		10%	20%	30%
AT	4.64	3.79	3.19	**2.63**	2.13	1.74	1.64
BE	5.92	4.51	3.61	**2.80**	2.03	1.35	0.68
BG	14.86	12.67	10.84	**9.38**	8.14	7.14	6.23
CY	-4.53	-4.32	-4.12	**-3.87**	-3.69	-3.55	-3.40
CZ	11.46	9.72	8.32	**7.12**	6.09	5.26	4.49
DE	5.61	4.09	3.18	**2.48**	2.06	1.91	1.78
DK	4.61	3.63	2.85	**2.16**	1.69	1.57	1.45
EE	0.00	0.00	0.00	**0.00**	0.00	0.00	0.00
ES	6.06	4.68	3.68	**2.77**	2.21	2.02	1.86
FI	10.58	8.99	7.70	**6.60**	5.64	4.86	4.12
FR	6.05	4.56	3.41	**2.56**	2.08	1.70	1.32
GR	14.57	12.40	10.66	**9.20**	7.95	6.93	6.01
HU	2.84	2.77	2.02	**1.85**	1.61	1.41	1.19
IE	1.78	1.09	0.64	**0.14**	0.13	0.12	0.11
IT	12.43	10.25	8.40	**7.18**	6.29	5.57	4.89
LT	12.69	10.88	9.41	**8.12**	6.96	6.04	5.19
LU	5.30	4.14	3.25	**2.46**	1.88	1.70	1.56
LV	15.12	13.13	11.46	**10.06**	8.88	7.92	7.03
MT	10.84	8.70	7.32	**6.21**	5.26	4.49	3.79
NL	3.85	2.86	2.10	**1.40**	1.01	0.93	0.86
PL	11.26	9.64	8.26	**7.07**	6.04	5.24	4.51
PT	12.14	10.33	8.87	**7.62**	6.52	5.63	4.82
RO	8.91	6.50	5.30	**6.68**	5.30	4.21	3.27
SE	5.65	4.48	3.57	**2.76**	2.34	2.13	1.96
SK	10.92	9.28	7.97	**6.83**	5.85	5.07	4.34
SL	9.37	8.11	7.09	**6.19**	5.39	4.73	4.11
UK	3.41	2.63	2.00	**1.80**	1.90	2.18	2.12
Ø	7.64	6.28	5.22	**4.45**	3.76	3.27	2.81

[1] For the benchmark case see Table 47.

A8.2, Table 3: Deviation of effective tax burden (in %) from national GAAP caused by a simultaneous application all CCTB options (I) for different levels of labour intensity

Country	Decrease of labour intensity by		Benchmark Case[1]	Increase of labour intensity by	
	20%	10%		10%	20%
AT	2.89	2.77	**2.63**	2.50	2.52
BE	2.99	2.91	**2.80**	2.70	2.68
BG	9.56	9.47	**9.38**	9.30	9.22
CY	-3.45	-3.64	**-3.87**	-4.14	-3.99
CZ	7.31	7.22	**7.12**	7.03	6.97
DE	2.75	2.62	**2.48**	2.36	2.37
DK	2.34	2.26	**2.16**	2.06	2.05
EE	0.00	0.00	**0.00**	0.00	0.00
ES	3.01	2.90	**2.77**	2.64	2.63
FI	6.78	6.69	**6.60**	6.51	6.46
FR	2.67	2.61	**2.56**	2.53	2.48
GR	9.37	9.29	**9.20**	9.13	9.04
HU	1.85	1.85	**1.85**	1.82	1.82
IE	0.31	0.23	**0.14**	0.14	0.14
IT	7.42	7.31	**7.18**	7.09	7.03
LT	8.29	8.22	**8.12**	8.02	7.96
LU	2.66	2.57	**2.46**	2.33	2.33
LV	10.22	10.15	**10.06**	10.01	9.92
MT	6.41	6.31	**6.21**	6.12	6.07
NL	1.68	1.55	**1.40**	1.24	1.26
PL	7.21	7.15	**7.07**	7.01	6.94
PT	7.78	7.70	**7.62**	7.54	7.47
RO	6.47	6.56	**6.68**	6.94	6.66
SE	2.93	2.85	**2.76**	2.66	2.64
SK	7.01	6.93	**6.83**	6.74	6.69
SL	6.48	6.34	**6.19**	6.04	6.04
UK	2.20	2.02	**1.80**	1.56	1.67
Ø	4.64	4.55	**4.45**	4.36	4.34

[1] For the benchmark case see Table 47.

A8.2, Table 4: Deviation of effective tax burden (in %) from national GAAP caused by a simultaneous application all CCTB options (I) for different levels of inventory intensity

Country	Decrease of inventories to capital by		Benchmark Case[1]	Increase of inventories to capital by	
	10.60%	5.30%		5.30%	10.60%
AT	2.62	2.63	**2.63**	2.64	2.64
BE	2.97	2.88	**2.80**	2.70	2.58
BG	9.61	9.49	**9.38**	9.33	9.34
CY	-3.92	-3.89	**-3.87**	-3.92	-3.89
CZ	7.52	7.33	**7.12**	6.92	6.73
DE	2.51	2.49	**2.48**	2.48	2.50
DK	2.18	2.19	**2.16**	2.13	2.10
EE	0.00	0.00	**0.00**	0.00	0.00
ES	2.95	2.86	**2.77**	2.65	2.53
FI	6.73	6.69	**6.60**	6.50	6.41
FR	2.71	2.62	**2.56**	2.55	2.60
GR	9.38	9.29	**9.20**	9.12	9.00
HU	1.87	1.86	**1.85**	1.81	1.77
IE	0.29	0.21	**0.14**	0.11	0.05
IT	7.35	7.27	**7.18**	7.17	7.25
LT	8.52	8.29	**8.12**	7.90	7.69
LU	2.61	2.55	**2.46**	2.35	2.23
LV	10.53	10.29	**10.06**	9.93	9.81
MT	6.43	6.32	**6.21**	6.11	6.01
NL	1.57	1.48	**1.40**	1.33	1.26
PL	7.35	7.18	**7.07**	7.01	6.86
PT	7.69	7.65	**7.62**	7.54	7.45
RO	7.77	7.88	**6.68**	5.47	4.42
SE	2.93	2.83	**2.76**	2.63	2.50
SK	7.25	7.05	**6.83**	6.64	6.46
SL	6.28	6.24	**6.19**	6.15	6.12
UK	1.56	1.47	**1.80**	2.44	2.69
Ø	4.64	4.56	**4.45**	4.36	4.26

[1] For the benchmark case see Table 47.

Appendix 9: Sensitivity Analysis on Specific Sectors – Effective Tax Burden

A9, Table 1: Effective tax burden under national GAAP (in € millions) and deviation caused by CCTB for different sectors (large company)

Country	Benchmark Case[1]		Commerce		Construction		Energy		Manufacturing		Service/Trade		Transport	
	Nat. GAAP	**Deviation (%)**	Nat. GAAP	Deviation (%)	Nat. GAAP	Deviation (%)	Nat. GAAP	Deviation (%)	Nat. GAAP	Deviation (%)	Nat. GAAP	Deviation (%)	Nat. GAAP	Deviation (%)
AT	**33.05**	**3.65**	30.17	2.15	20.46	2.88	84.03	7.37	41.91	4.76	24.79	3.34	18.89	16.71
BE	**31.43**	**2.58**	30.55	0.31	18.51	1.34	89.71	8.83	40.88	4.15	17.07	5.05	9.58	25.16
BG	**14.52**	**10.70**	13.95	7.71	8.87	9.77	38.92	16.23	19.18	11.56	8.09	11.69	3.72	82.38
CY	**18.35**	**-3.82**	16.28	-3.22	11.54	-4.19	42.55	-2.34	22.72	-3.87	15.75	-4.72	14.31	-6.40
CZ	**23.38**	**7.66**	22.49	4.90	14.40	6.27	62.27	12.28	30.94	8.31	12.71	11.01	6.46	60.10
DE	**38.79**	**3.49**	36.20	2.30	24.03	2.71	109.02	7.23	52.38	5.28	21.76	3.80	13.93	27.02
DK	**29.40**	**3.28**	27.38	2.11	17.35	2.29	94.23	5.98	39.35	4.32	16.79	4.82	15.43	2.79
EE	**15.63**	**0.00**	13.45	0.00	9.78	0.00	37.75	0.00	21.87	0.00	8.13	0.00	5.60	0.11
ES	**37.85**	**4.02**	36.06	1.84	23.23	2.78	101.69	9.57	50.19	6.16	20.70	6.38	11.55	37.30
FI	**26.23**	**6.78**	24.79	5.38	15.86	5.84	75.49	9.50	34.82	7.35	14.66	8.65	10.02	28.50
FR	**55.17**	**3.77**	61.89	1.79	34.11	3.03	142.64	6.65	68.14	5.55	35.93	4.11	37.07	3.53
GR	**27.77**	**9.49**	26.68	6.66	16.99	8.51	74.64	14.49	36.74	10.26	15.37	11.20	9.13	40.74
HU	**38.09**	**2.23**	51.85	0.59	22.82	1.62	85.63	3.38	45.74	2.51	21.16	3.73	28.28	1.78
IE	**13.86**	**0.81**	12.85	0.12	8.16	0.10	45.45	2.12	18.55	1.82	7.90	2.79	7.13	4.27
IT	**38.77**	**8.27**	37.47	5.88	23.75	7.40	101.33	11.98	50.26	9.76	23.37	9.57	15.09	37.77
LT	**20.44**	**8.50**	19.31	5.82	12.10	6.76	64.52	13.61	27.27	9.19	11.59	12.45	9.51	33.13
LU	**29.11**	**3.55**	27.51	1.75	17.70	2.50	81.44	8.29	38.80	4.74	15.99	5.70	9.10	40.31
LV	**16.36**	**11.15**	15.50	7.67	9.59	8.69	51.53	23.53	21.81	12.16	9.44	14.68	7.55	48.14
MT	**33.63**	**6.11**	31.96	4.89	20.73	5.18	88.48	9.47	44.56	6.85	18.35	8.36	10.41	34.62
NL	**28.94**	**2.20**	27.34	0.99	17.73	1.16	78.41	7.20	38.38	3.54	15.91	3.65	9.04	29.02
PL	**19.75**	**7.57**	18.76	5.16	11.81	6.63	58.51	12.62	26.26	8.23	11.13	9.96	7.62	40.06
PT	**26.72**	**8.11**	25.50	6.07	16.27	7.57	73.94	10.14	35.35	8.84	14.90	9.00	8.10	50.69
RO	**15.76**	**8.38**	15.48	2.80	9.66	5.85	47.24	10.73	21.06	9.03	8.90	9.57	5.56	41.89
SE	**27.19**	**4.21**	25.92	1.87	16.60	3.03	74.82	9.80	36.07	5.59	14.91	6.51	7.86	48.17
SK	**19.26**	**7.27**	18.38	4.83	11.72	5.78	54.20	12.16	25.55	7.91	10.61	10.63	6.29	50.20
SL	**28.85**	**6.63**	26.86	5.50	18.11	5.82	68.29	10.18	36.90	7.28	19.56	7.06	12.72	26.42
UK	**31.92**	**2.51**	29.85	0.78	18.79	1.36	103.03	5.94	42.69	3.68	18.24	4.44	14.40	21.52
Ø	**27.42**	**5.15**	26.83	3.21	16.69	4.10	75.18	9.15	35.87	6.11	16.06	6.79	11.64	30.59

[1] For the benchmark case see Table 47.

A9, Table 2: Effective tax burden under national tax law (in € millions) and deviation caused by CCTB for different sectors (SME)

Country	Benchmark Case[1]		Commerce		Construction		Energy		Manufacturing		Service/Trade		Transport	
	Nat. GAAP	**Deviation (%)**	Nat. GAAP	Deviation (%)	Nat. GAAP	Deviation (%)	Nat. GAAP	Deviation (%)	Nat. GAAP	Deviation (%)	Nat. GAAP	Deviation (%)	Nat. GAAP	Deviati on (%)
AT	**1.21**	**2.63**	1.57	1.75	0.81	2.36	2.04	18.42	1.36	3.74	0.80	1.20	1.16	8.17
BE	**1.13**	**2.80**	1.72	0.39	0.73	2.99	1.92	22.69	1.18	2.40	0.64	1.47	1.08	9.36
BG	**0.52**	**9.38**	0.78	4.17	0.35	7.90	0.79	39.38	0.56	10.88	0.30	6.28	0.50	15.56
CY	**0.67**	**-3.87**	0.79	-2.53	0.44	-3.79	1.14	1.96	0.78	-4.81	0.45	-4.56	0.67	-3.56
CZ	**0.84**	**7.12**	1.25	2.39	0.56	6.32	1.29	31.98	0.90	7.69	0.47	5.13	0.79	13.78
DE	**1.37**	**2.48**	1.99	1.78	0.91	2.24	2.32	20.25	1.49	4.07	0.76	1.45	1.34	9.26
DK	**1.04**	**2.16**	1.49	1.55	0.68	2.01	2.48	-0.19	1.13	2.55	0.64	1.20	1.03	5.14
EE	**0.55**	**0.00**	0.74	0.00	0.36	0.00	0.89	0.00	0.50	0.00	0.32	0.00	0.72	0.02
ES	**1.30**	**2.77**	2.01	1.29	0.84	3.72	2.14	25.07	1.40	3.87	0.70	2.22	1.20	13.39
FI	**0.94**	**6.60**	1.37	2.73	0.62	5.50	1.74	16.65	1.01	6.83	0.54	4.42	0.93	8.16
FR	**1.70**	**2.56**	2.95	0.83	1.05	3.55	3.48	14.15	2.01	3.60	0.99	2.73	1.71	9.90
GR	**0.99**	**9.20**	1.48	3.84	0.66	7.66	1.60	30.06	1.04	10.81	0.55	6.57	0.92	17.90
HU	**1.52**	**1.85**	2.20	0.49	0.79	1.91	2.16	10.30	1.63	1.79	0.72	1.33	1.33	6.67
IE	**0.49**	**0.14**	0.69	0.13	0.32	0.46	1.06	9.30	0.54	0.03	0.30	0.13	0.48	3.49
IT	**1.42**	**7.18**	2.02	3.35	0.95	6.16	2.30	25.00	1.57	9.14	0.82	5.04	1.35	14.59
LT	**0.73**	**8.12**	1.05	2.89	0.47	7.07	1.41	31.45	0.79	8.55	0.45	6.82	0.70	14.74
LU	**1.03**	**2.46**	1.52	1.21	0.68	2.69	1.77	21.29	1.11	2.83	0.58	1.86	0.97	10.03
LV	**0.58**	**10.06**	0.84	4.31	0.38	8.47	1.18	35.89	0.63	11.70	0.37	11.00	0.56	17.14
MT	**1.21**	**6.21**	1.78	2.52	0.81	5.35	1.88	24.52	1.29	7.12	0.67	3.82	1.16	11.15
NL	**1.02**	**1.40**	1.51	0.79	0.68	1.60	1.68	21.08	1.10	1.50	0.57	1.09	0.98	7.05
PL	**0.71**	**7.07**	1.03	2.55	0.46	6.16	1.34	21.24	0.76	7.70	0.42	4.67	0.68	12.76
PT	**0.96**	**7.62**	1.42	3.14	0.64	6.41	1.60	24.22	1.02	8.49	0.55	3.87	0.92	13.28
RO	**0.56**	**6.68**	0.84	4.20	0.37	6.54	1.01	27.52	0.63	4.18	0.33	5.76	0.53	15.09
SE	**0.97**	**2.76**	1.44	1.27	0.65	2.76	1.63	22.48	1.04	3.56	0.56	2.27	0.91	11.14
SK	**0.69**	**6.83**	1.01	2.35	0.46	6.02	1.17	26.95	0.74	7.33	0.40	5.61	0.66	12.59
SL	**1.06**	**6.19**	1.45	3.03	0.71	5.18	1.58	22.57	1.16	6.84	0.64	4.10	1.02	10.06
UK	**0.78**	**1.80**	1.14	-0.14	0.50	1.58	2.03	0.70	0.94	3.58	0.52	0.79	0.80	8.71
Ø	**0.96**	**4.45**	1.41	1.86	0.63	4.03	1.69	20.18	1.05	5.04	0.56	3.20	0.93	10.21

[1] For the benchmark case see Table 47.

List of Figures

Figure 1: Proportion of EU-27 average overall increase of the value of the tax base for each option XII
Figure 2: Ifo Economic Climate Indicator for the euro area (1990-2008) 19
Figure 3: Comparison of future tax base values according to current taxation practice – Deviation from the EU average in % (large company, corporate level, 10 periods) 31
Figure 4: Comparison of effective tax burdens according to current taxation practice – Deviation from the EU average in % (large company, corporate level, 10 periods) 33
Figure 5: Impact of common rules regarding depreciation on the future value of the tax base in % (large company) 38
Figure 6: Impact of common rules for the simplified valuation of inventory on the future value of the tax base in % (large company) 40
Figure 7: Impact of common rules regarding the determination of production costs on the future value of the tax base in % (large company) 41
Figure 8: Impact of common rules regarding R&D costs as part of production costs on the future value of the tax base in % (large company) 43
Figure 9: Impact of common rules regarding provisions for pensions on the future value of the tax base in % (large company) 44
Figure 10: Impact of common rules regarding provisions for warranty payments on the future value of the tax base in % (large company) 45
Figure 11: Impact of common rules regarding exemption of foreign dividend income on the future value of the tax base in % (large company) ... 46
Figure 12: Comparison of the future values of the tax base according to current taxation practice – Deviation from the EU average in % (SME, corporate level, 10 periods) 77
Figure 13: Comparison of effective tax burdens according to current taxation practice – Deviation from the EU average in % (SME, corporate level, 10 periods) 79
Figure 14: Impact of common rules regarding depreciation on the future value of the tax base in % (SME) 84
Figure 15: Impact of common rules for the simplified valuation of inventory on the future value of the tax base in % (SME) 85
Figure 16: Impact of common rules regarding the determination of production costs on the future value of the tax base in % (SME) 86
Figure 17: Impact of common rules regarding R&D costs as part of production costs on the future value of the tax base in % (SME) 87

Figure 18: Impact of common rules regarding provisions for pensions on the future value of the tax base in % (SME) 88
Figure 19: Impact of common rules regarding provisions for warranty payments on the future value of the tax base in % (SME) 89
Figure 20: Impact of common rules regarding exemption of foreign dividend income on the future value of the tax base in % (SME) 90
Figure 21: Proportion of EU-27 average overall increase of the future value of the tax base for option A to H 92
Figure 22: Proportional impact of each CCTB option (A-H) on the overall increase in the future value of the tax base (EU-15 large company and SME) 111
Figure 23: Proportional impact of each CCTB option (A-H) on the overall increase in the future value of the tax base (EU-12 large company and SME) 116

List of Tables

Table 1: Changes in the value of the tax base in case of a CCTB (large company) X
Table 2: Changes in the value of the tax base in case of a CCTB (SME) XI
Table 3: Value of the tax base under national GAAP and increase in % with the introduction of a CCTB (sector averages) XIII
Table 4: Value of the tax base under national GAAP and deviation in case of a CCTB XIV
Table 5: Considered Taxes 6
Table 6: National GAAP, accelerated depreciation (case without tax; in €) 9
Table 7: CCTB option, straight line depreciation (case without tax; in €) 9
Table 8: National GAAP, accelerated depreciation (case with 25% income tax; in €) 10
Table 9: CCTB option, straight line depreciation (case with 25% income tax; in €) 10
Table 10: Comparison of impact assessed with effective tax burden and impact assessed with future value of the tax base (case with 25% income tax; post-tax) 12
Table 11: National GAAP, accelerated depreciation (case with 25% income tax and 5% real estate tax; post-tax including capital tax; in €) 12
Table 12: CCTB option, straight line depreciation (case with 25% income tax and 5% real estate tax; post-tax including capital tax; in €) 13
Table 13: Comparison of impact assessed with effective tax burden and impact assessed with future value of the tax base (case with 25% income tax and 5% capital tax on real estate; post-tax) 13
Table 14: Balance sheets of the implemented EU-27 model firms (period 6, in €) 15
Table 15: Financial ratios of the implemented EU-27 model firms (period 6) 16
Table 16: Determination of the companies used in the study 17
Table 17: Financial information in the AMADEUS database 18
Table 18: Number of companies for which relevant data is provided by AMADEUS (all industries) 19
Table 19: Classification of industries 20
Table 20: Number of companies in the sample 21
Table 21: Comparison of future tax base values (large company, corporate level, 10 periods) 30
Table 22: Comparison of effective tax burdens (large company, corporate level, 10 periods) 32

Table 23. Impact of particular tax categories on the effective tax burden in % (large company) ... 34
Table 24. Changes in the future value of the tax base under a CCTB (large company) ... 35
Table 25: Changes in the effective tax burden under a CCTB (large company) .. 36
Table 26: Future value (in € millions) of the tax base for large benchmark case (large company, EU-27) under national tax law and deviation (in %) caused by each particular CCTB option A-H and by a simultaneous application all CCTB options (I) ... 48
Table 27: Effective tax burden (in € millions) for large benchmark case (large company, EU-27) under national tax law and deviation (in %) caused by each particular CCTB option A-H and by a simultaneous application all CCTB options (I) ... 49
Table 28: Average future value of the tax base (EU-27 large company) for different levels of capital intensity under national tax law and CCTB Option I in € millions ... 51
Table 29: Deviation in the future value of the tax base (EU-27 large company) from national GAAP caused by a simultaneous application all CCTB options (I) for different levels of capital intensity ... 52
Table 30: Average future value of the tax base (EU-27 large company) for different levels of profitability under national tax law and CCTB Option I in € millions ... 53
Table 31: Deviation in the future value of the tax base (EU-27 large company) from national GAAP caused by a simultaneous application all CCTB options (I) for different levels of profitability ... 54
Table 32: Average future value of the tax base (EU-27 large company) for different levels of labour intensity under national tax law and CCTB Option I in € millions ... 55
Table 33: Deviation (in %) in the future value of the tax base (EU-27 large company) from national GAAP caused by a simultaneous application all CCTB options (I) for different levels of labour intensity ... 56
Table 34: Average future value of the tax base (EU-27 large company) for different levels of inventory intensity under national tax law and CCTB Option I in € millions ... 57
Table 35: Deviation (in %) in the future value of the tax base (EU-27 large company) from national GAAP caused by a simultaneous application all CCTB options (I) for different levels of inventory intensity ... 57
Table 36: Financial ratios of sector-specific companies (period 6) ... 59
Table 37: Future value of the tax base (large company) under national tax law (in € millions) and deviation (in %) caused by CCTB for different sectors ... 60
Table 38: Financial ratios for the benchmark case (EU-27 large company) in comparison to EU-15 and EU-12 large model firms ... 67
Table 39: Future value of the tax base (in € millions) for EU-15 large company under national tax law and deviation (in %) caused by each particular CCTB option A-H and by a simultaneous application all CCTB options (I) . 71

Table 40: Effective tax burden (in € millions) for EU-15 large company under national tax law and deviation (in %) caused by each particular CCTB option A-H and by a simultaneous application all CCTB options (I)..71
Table 41: Future value of the tax base (in € millions) for EU-12 large company under national tax law and deviation (in %) caused by each particular CCTB option A-H and by a simultaneous application all CCTB options (I)..74
Table 42: Effective tax burden (in € millions) for EU-12 large company under national tax law and deviation (in %) caused by each particular CCTB option A-H and by a simultaneous application all CCTB options (I)............75
Table 43: Comparison of future tax base values; national GAAP (SME, corporate level, 10 periods)..76
Table 44: Comparison of effective tax burdens (SME, corporate level, 10 periods)..78
Table 45: Impact of particular tax categories on the effective tax burden in % (SME)..80
Table 46: Changes in the future value of the tax base under a CCTB (SME benchmark case)..81
Table 47: Changes in the effective tax burden under a CCTB (SME benchmark case)..82
Table 48: Future value of tax base (in € millions) for EU-27 SME (benchmark case) under national tax law and deviation (in %) caused by each particular CCTB option A-H and by a simultaneous application all CCTB options (I)..93
Table 49: Tax burden (in € millions) for EU-27 SME (benchmark case) under national tax law and deviation (in %) caused by each particular CCTB option A-H and by a simultaneous application all CCTB options (I)............94
Table 50: Average future value of the tax base (EU-27 SME) for different levels of capital intensity under national tax law and CCTB Option I in € millions.95
Table 51: Deviation (in %) in the future value of the tax base (EU-27 SME) from national GAAP caused by a simultaneous application all CCTB options (I) for different levels of capital intensity..96
Table 52: Average future value of the tax base (EU-27 SME) for different levels of profitability under national tax law and CCTB Option I in € millions.......97
Table 53: Deviation (in %) in the future value of the tax base from national GAAP caused by a simultaneous application all CCTB options (I) for different levels of profitability (SME case)..98
Table 54: Average future value of the tax base (EU-27 SME) for different levels of labour intensity under national tax law and CCTB Option I in € millions.99
Table 55: Deviation (in %) in the future value of the tax base (EU-27 SME) from national GAAP caused by a simultaneous application all CCTB options (I) for different levels of labour intensity..100
Table 56: Average future value of the tax base (EU-27 SME) for different levels of inventory intensity under national tax law and CCTB Option I in € millions..101
Table 57: Deviation (in %) in the future value of the tax base (EU-27 SME) from national GAAP caused by a simultaneous application all CCTB options (I) for different levels of inventory intensity...................................102

Table 58: Financial ratios for different sectors ... 103
Table 59: Future value of the tax base (SME case) under national tax law (in € millions) and deviation (in %) caused by CCTB for different sectors ... 104
Table 60: Financial ratios of the EU-27, EU-15 and EU-12 model SMEs ... 107
Table 61: Future value of the tax base (in € millions) for EU-15 SME under national tax law and deviation (in %) caused by each particular CCTB option A-H and by a simultaneous application all CCTB options (I) ... 108
Table 62: Effective tax burden (in € millions) for the EU-15 SME under national tax law and deviation (in %) caused by each particular CCTB option A-H and by a simultaneous application all CCTB options (I) ... 112
Table 63: Future value of the tax base (in € millions) for EU-12 SME under national tax law and deviation (in %) caused by each particular CCTB option A-H and by a simultaneous application all CCTB options (I) ... 113
Table 64: Effective tax burden (in € millions) for the EU-12 SME under national tax law and deviation (in %) caused by each particular CCTB option A-H and by a simultaneous application all CCTB options (I) ... 116
Table 65: Results of the multiple regression analysis ... 118
Table 66: Overview of major tax changes in France, Germany, Italy, the Netherlands and Spain ... 119
Table 67: Future value of the tax base (in € millions) for the EU-27 large company under national GAAP and deviation (in %) to CCTB when recent tax reforms are considered in France, Germany, Italy, the Netherlands and Spain ... 120
Table 68: Tax burden (in € millions) for the EU-27 large company under national GAAP and deviation (in %) to CCTB when recent tax reforms are considered in France, Germany, Italy, the Netherlands and Spain ... 121
Table 69: Future value of the tax base (in € millions) for the EU-27 small and medium company under national GAAP and deviation (in %) to CCTB when recent tax reforms are considered in France, Germany, Italy, the Netherlands and Spain ... 122
Table 70: Tax burden (in € millions) for the EU-27 large company under national GAAP and deviation (in %) to CCTB when recent tax reforms are considered in France, Germany, Italy, the Netherlands and Spain ... 124

References

European Commission (2001b), *Company Taxation in the Internal Market*, COM (2001) 582, Brussels.

Gutekunst, G. (2005), *Steuerbelastungen und Steuerwirkungen bei nationaler und grenzüberschreitender Geschäftstätigkeit*, Lohmar.

Endres, D., A. Oestreicher, W. Scheffler and C. Spengel (2007), *The Determination of Corporate Taxable Income in the EU Member States*, Alphen van den Rijn.

Hermann, R.A. (2006), *Die Besteuerung von Personengesellschaften in den EU-Mitgliedstaaten und den USA*, Lohmar.

Jacobs, O.H. and C. Spengel (1996), *European Tax Analyzer: EDV-gestützter Vergleich der Steuerbelastung von Kapitalgesellschaften in Deutschland, Frankreich und Großbritannien*, Baden-Baden.

Lammersen, L. (2005), *Steuerbelastungsvergleiche*, Wiesbaden.

Meyer, R. (1996), *Computergestützte Simulation von Steuerbelastungen, ZEW Schriftenreihe*, Vol. 12, Baden-Baden.

Schreiber, U., C. Spengel and L. Lammersen (2002), Measuring the Impact of Taxation on Investment and Financial Decisions, *Schmalenbach Business Review* 54, 2-23.

Spengel, C. (1995), *Europäische Steuerbelastungsvergleiche: Deutschland – Frankreich – Großbritannien*, Düsseldorf.

Stetter, T. (2005), *Computergestützte internationale Steuerbelastungsvergleiche; Bausteinbasiertes Metamodell zur Modellierung von Steuersystemen*, Lohmar.

European Council (1990), Council Directive 90/434/EEC of 23 July 1990 on the Common System of Taxation Applicable to Mergers, Divisions, Transfers of Assets and Exchanges of Shares Concerning Companies of Different Member States, *Official Journal of the European Communities L225/1.*

The manufacturer's authorised representative in the EU is Springer Nature Customer Service Centre GmbH, Europaplatz 3, 69115 Heidelberg, Germany. If you have any concerns regarding our products, please contact ProductSafety@springernature.com

Printed and bound by CPI Group (UK) Ltd, Croydon, CR0 4YY
25/09/2026
02222895-0004